ESL Doxography 101

Dr. Clark von Heller

ISBN 0-7414-3246-3

Published by:

PUBLISHING.COM

1094 New DeHaven Street, Suite 100
West Conshohocken, PA 19428-2713
Info@buybooksontheweb.com
www.buybooksontheweb.com
Toll-free (877) BUY BOOK
Local Phone (610) 941-9999
Fax (610) 941-9959

Printed in the United States of America

Printed on Recycled Paper

Published November 2006

TABLE OF CONTENTS

Θ

ESL DOXOGRAPHY 101
The Glory of Writing with the Joy of Language

This work is lovingly dedicated to teachers of English language. No one works as hard as America's teachers. Each day these educators change their world by impacting millions of students from coast-to-coast. Many of them instinctively use forms of Doxography to meet their objectives. Doxography is a pedagogical philosophy that strives to go beyond mundane lessons and attempts to incorporate affective goals into the curriculum, <u>reaching down into the soul of the learning, indeed the very basic elements of alphabet, words, and history</u>. This teaching paradigm invariably results in a more positive classroom with excellence and equity for everyone. So congratulations to these teachers who are striving to teach the glory of writing with the joy of language!

> *"One who speaks, speaks to one's self. But one who writes, speaks to the world!"(Dr.von Heller's Writing class motto)*

The author relaxes in Los Angeles between training sessions.
Dr. Clark von Heller
Canterbury Ranch
1000 E. Eldorado
San Juan, TX 78589 USA
clarkvonheller@yahoo.co.uk

Θ Chapter 1
INTRODUCTION TO DOXOGRAPHY

"Literature is the logos of the soul, a veritable celebration of the imagination and spirit, and indeed all that is good within humankind."

(Dr. Clark von Heller's motto for lit classes).

Welcome to the world of Doxography! Taken from the Greek, "doxos," (glory) and "graphy," (writing), we have taken the liberty to re-coin this ancient word to stand for and describe **"the glory of writing"** in a modern sense, particularly as it relates to ELL (**English Language Learning**). Furthermore, in a larger sense, the term is even more appropriate in this volume because of the wide variety of theoretical applications that are contained therein as well as practical, easy-to-use worksheets and lesson ideas that are of particular help for new teachers of English language, writing or literature.

In this volume we are attempting to equip America's teachers with valuable teaching tools consisting of many varied and eclectic topics on many levels. Each chapter weaves the concept of affective learning into the narrative with questions at the end of each chapter with lessons, activities, and dozens of PowerPoint masters at the end of the book. **The Language Pre-Test** might be an interesting place to begin your study of Doxography 101, located on page 260. The main objective of this work is to show how affective learning is the most effective method to teach language and literacy, particularly to students of English as a second language, whether children or adults. The author gives this work the feel of a handbook, covering both complex as well as very practical subjects that can be taken right out of the text and used straightway in the classroom. We truly hope that teachers will benefit from this brand new education theory as we weave it through diverse topics, ideas and classroom applications.

WORDS OF SILVER ON PAPER OF PURE GOLD

by

Dr. Clark von Heller, 2003

*To my beloved, tortured students of Writing.

So you're sitting down to write but your thoughts go blank

Tired and unmotivated; low vocabulary in the mind bank.

Lack of inspiration; lots of perspiration; you need to start thinking and start thinking fast

Writing isn't easy but it surely will last.

For one who speaks, speaks only to one's self; but one who writes, speaks to the whole world.

Be bold and beautiful and make your writing heard.

For this is your time! Your hour is now!

Spread your wings and write on! Don't worry about how.

For often we are judged by our speech and our word

But what we write is more important than how we are heard.

So build the art of writing into your own mental mould

As you pen words of silver on paper of pure gold.

As we journey through the end of the first decade of this new 21st century, educators are examining new strategies and approaches to teach English on a global scale never known before. The popularity of English as the "lingua franca" of practically the whole world is truly overwhelming! With the amazing tenacity of English language to intrude and even dominate foreign cultures, many traditional questions are now being raised about the "how" of teaching English effectively to such a massive and diverse audience. Which methodologies are most efficient and quick? Adult ESL learners need the language as quickly as possible whereas children have the wonderful luxury of enjoying fabulous strategies that are fun and entertaining in a long-range format. **We will examine the most current theories in second language acquisition**, take a journey into history, look into some of the political controversy that often surrounds bilingual education, and offer a new idea in second language learning and indeed, for education in general: the concept that a spiritual connection and empowerment can be felt between students and the ability to produce the written word, thereby imitating the Creator and becoming creators as well. This phenomenon is called "Doxography," the glory of writing with the joy of language.

Surprisingly, this concept of **empowerment** and spiritual connection with learning and writing is not new at all. A simple historical search will verify that this important link in human development has contributed to American education, resulting in countless scientific discoveries and inventions, and surprisingly was not thought of as negative until the past few decades. To mention God or spirituality in the modern American classroom is now practically forbidden even though mankind has learned and lived in the context of spirituality throughout our existence on this planet. Some modern day academic humanists have taken it upon themselves to dictate that spirituality is no longer needed nor tolerated in education. This author wholeheartedly disagrees. How education philosophy has changed through the years!

Two important domains exist in education, both cognitive and affective. The cognitive addresses the "what?" and the affective addresses the "how?" in education. One need not be an atheist to be a scientist. To the contrary, some of the most famous scientists happen to be Christians including the renown Michael Faraday, Dr. David Catchpoole, Dr. Walt Brown, Dr. Forrest Mims III, Dr. James Allan, Dr. Steven A. Austin, Dr. Eugene F. Chaffin, just to list a few, (answersingenesis.org). The voices and works of this short list of Christians who hold PhD's are amplified across the world, reflecting the many other PhD's whose lives are dedicated to spirituality and science, without viewing these as conflicting in any way. In fact, many of the most profound voices in science, literature, biology, and pedagogy, have promoted and still promote the linkage between **spirituality and knowledge**, with a particular emphasis upon the notion that learning, particularly writing, is an inherent manner of creation itself, glorifying the Creator or Divine Intelligence that created all that we experience, whether by logos or evolution. One interesting source in this matter is <u>Christian Men of Science</u> by George Mulfinger and Julia Mulfinger Orozco (Ambassador-Emerald Publishers).

In her little hands lies the key to Doxography—a book.

Can writing truly glorify God? Absolutely! Writing can glorify God and also the doxos (glory) can be felt by the students. Doesn't this happen naturally when one reads an inspiring poem or touching story? That wonderful feeling is most likely our affiliation with a higher power, the Divine Writer perhaps. Most call this feeling simply "God." For example, when second graders are given a regular academic assignment, often they tend to invest minimal effort, just enough to comply. After all, classwork is by design, divided into simple routines with large prescription of repetition. But in contrast, when an assignment focuses on something meaningful, for example, designing a Mother's Day card, or developing a sympathy card at the loss of a friend, everything changes.

These tasks have inherent human meaning, <u>clear objectives</u>, and most of all, a spiritual connection that will be validated in real terms that have innate meaning as opposed to a subjective grade on a cold grade sheet. The beautiful concept of Doxography is now imbedded within this process and indeed the entire class feels the difference. Students should feel good about their work, not because of a grade but because of how well they accomplished the assignment. When effort by students is directed and carried out with spiritual meaning, almost certainly more positive, higher quality outcomes will result.

Doxography, and related sciences, can be taught but also are quite natural concepts, commonly used in many aspects of life. So why not in the classroom as well? Positive self-esteem increases quality production. Affective teaching, with sincere caring for the students, will almost assuredly improve classroom dynamics. Can this concept be incorporated into the modern humanistic, nearly atheistic system now being employed in 99% of the 18,000 school districts in the USA? Yes, **Doxography can be incorporated** into any school district with proper training and gentle persuasion by caring education professionals whose best interest lies in achievement, not in personal agendas or anti-religious frenzies caused by those who hate religious faith in any form.

The Doxos Principle: Δοξος Θέος and Δοξος Ανθρωπος

Doxos is Greek for "glory" and is the basic root for Doxography, the "glory of writing." The reason that the subject of writing was chosen is because writing is the most effective vehicle in education that allows for invention and creation. Since creation is something that is associated with a Supreme Being, the author thought writing most appropriate to serve as the vanguard subject for this new pedagogical science, thus blending the concepts of creation and writing together in a spiritual context. Other terms that support Doxography are also very important for one to more fully comprehend this significant paradigm shift in education and language appreciation. These terms include "**Doxos Anthropos**" (the glory of man) and "**Doxos Theos**" (the glory of God). These two positions in philosophy, when juxtaposed together, cause a series of events to take place within students, allowing them to have not only a tremendous freedom for study and improvement, but also for discovery and invention. Did Thomas Edison display for the world a true sense of Doxos Anthropos? Or was his enthusiasm part of Doxos Theos? Upon close examination of this life and work ethic, one can surmise that probably both were involved in his life-changing, avant-garde work in electricity, the light bulb, the phonograph, etc. A few probing questions will help illustrate how to determine the answer to the initial question. Did his work glorify man or God? Does God really need an electric light? Does man?

One could argue for both since as man, Edison simply used his innate cleverness of invention to achieve these mighty works, yet it could be argued that his paradigm-breaking works also glorify the magnificent intellect that God gave to man in the first place. But for most Doxographists, Edison's tremendous work would fall decidedly on the side of **Doxos Anthropos**. Edison glorified mankind by highlighting man's conquest of the physical elements involved in physics and the natural world. He took the world's resources around him, reshaped them, and developed an entirely new experience, industry and science, thus becoming a creator by man and for man. He was a true human genius, a true example of **Doxos Anthropos.**

Now let us examine how the concept of DA (Anthropos) and DTh (Theos) affects American education, particularly language classrooms. The philosophy of Doxography is built upon two domains—cognitive and affective. The cognitive addresses "the what?" aspect while the affective addresses "the how?" These are exemplified in two specific outcomes:

---

1. products drive educational achievement (DA)
2. affective principles can affect achievement (DTh)

Imitating life, a balanced combination of these two concepts will lead to a more productive, higher scoring classroom.

Performance Outcomes.

Too much of either cognitive or affective would be counterproductive while a balance will achieve very positive results. Products, the end results of a day's work (or the end of a class period), are what drives a student to work hard for a teacher. They often cannot visualize employment needs or outcomes perhaps, but they can visualize a small product due at the end of class. That is why Doxography requires a product literally at the end of each class! Something tangible must be produced by the student each time, regardless of how small or short it may be. This is the "what?" of the cognitive domain. A real product brings higher self-esteem, even if it needs to be polished over-and-over until it meets the teacher's standards for a high grade.

The grade awarded in the evaluation phase of the **Lesson Cycle** is a spiritual action within the affective domain. Keep in mind that the affective domain addresses the "how?" If a grade is low, students can believe that their personal self-esteem is low as well. This is normal. Students often work toward a grade instead of working for a product. This is neither healthy nor productive. The key is teaching a student to evaluate their own product prior to submitting it for the teacher's evaluation. A student knows when something is truly "good" or not. Even a preK student's work should not be accepted as perfect on the first try. Evaluation is the pinnacle of education. Teachers must instill within that preK student an appreciation of what is good, better, and best. Simply completing a product has no bearing upon the quality thereof. Completing is one thing; quality is another.

Grades are subjective at best, varying from teacher-to-teacher, depending upon a myriad of elements that cannot be controlled by the student. An "A" in one class may not mean the same as an "A" in another. This is unfortunate but true in our profession and thus, another valid reason for a product-driven evaluation process, explained later in this book as **Alternative Assessment.**

With this in mind, we know that students need to see an immediate product from their work as well. If not, they are left with the feeling of low self-worth with poor performance and possible behavior problems resulting. Children in particular, cannot visualize future goals as clearly as older students. That is why teachers trained in Doxography request students to perform so many hands-on tasks, not at the end of the Lesson Cycle, but at the very beginning design phase such as making their own handouts, their own charts to be filled in, crossword puzzles, vocabulary masters, templates to be filled in. The quality of these products will not be as well-formatted as if made by the teacher but the basic principle of Doxography will be enhanced as the children become **the inventors and executors** of their own work or products from both phases, initial and conclusion, all the way to evaluation. Along with having students provide their own templates for rote work, immediate rewards are needed as well to complete the Lesson Cycle. These include immediate products. (Examples of these are given elsewhere in this book).

The younger the child, the more difficult long-term goals are to visualize. In an age of instant gratification, educators must adjust their grading policies as well. If possible, each day of the 181 school days must be "graded". Students often ask,

"Is this for a grade?" Why would they ask this unless they have figured out the system which they believe is basically designed to keep them busy in a baby-sitting format, at least until the State-mandated tests approaches? I hope this is not the case but unfortunately for those reading this book, they certainly know that this is true. How far have we come in American education from true Doxography!

Student work that is **Doxos Anthropos** is worthy indeed and should be applauded. However, if all work is Anthropos-driven, then the classroom becomes static and dull. A combination of both types of Doxos needs to blend together to form the dynamics of an effective classroom, particularly in language classes. This book offers dozens of suggestions for methods that incorporate both.

Language and Doxos Theos

Humility has been said to be the true mark of a true leader. With this in mind we look at language, the basic connector of all humans. How can language affect humility or vice-versa? Use of effective language will increase the likelihood of a high-paying job. Also, effective language plays a solid role in communication in general. Those who know how to manipulate language for good causes are those who exemplify Doxos Theos. For example, scientists such as Dr. Jonas Salk, humanitarians such as Mother Theresa, surely offer positive role models, each humble leaders in their fields, each displaying Doxos Theos. Are American teachers instilling within our students the joy that comes with displaying **Doxos Theos** to the world? I hope so.

The Bible in Public School Curriculum

Many believe that the Bible and a liberal arts education are incompatible but that is not the case at all. The National Council on Bible Curriculum in Public Schools provides Bible curriculum to 37 states and 312 school districts from

9

Alaska to Florida. Offering the Bible as an elective course is a growing phenomenon drawing the ire of opponents and the praise of evangelical Christians. Students opt to take the course as an elective. The curriculum includes Old Testament history and New Testament life of Christ and the Pauline epistles, just to name two components.

<u>Legality of Bible Courses in Public Schools</u>

Surprisingly, teaching Bible courses in public schools is completely legal as supported by **Wiley v. Franklin** and Crockett v. Sorenson. Furthermore, Supreme Court Justice Lewis Powell states, "Since religion permeates our history, a familiarity with the nature of religious belief is necessary to understanding history as well as contemporary events." In Stone v. Grasham the Court said that the Bible, "May constitutionally be used in an appropriate study of history, civilization, ethics and comparative religion, or the like." Religious courses are standard offerings in many universities as well as public schools, including Louisiana State University which has offered Old Testament, New Testament, Jesus in History and Tradition, with the approval of the U.S. Supreme Court.

Celebrating the joys of Nature creates a sense of Doxography.

<u>The Importance of Writing in Doxography</u>. Writing is fundamental in the education process, beginning with pre-K and never ending throughout life. Writing defines our learning, establishes norms, creates opportunities to express thinking, and best of all, allows students to CREATE! How can writing reflect Doxography? As with most things in our universe, learning how to write is a process and this process needs to be learned in a workable framework involving both cognitive and affective domains. We will demonstrate this framework as we place it within the format of a standard public school continuum. ESL Doxography examines the framework and skills necessary to progress from oral language to full and "featureable" literacy skills while acquiring English language, culminating in the most glorious skill and indeed, liberation of all—writing!

> Who often reads will sometimes wish to write."(Shore, E.)

This framework for reading and writing is a process— one that can be very enjoyable and productive to a child or adult being educated for the first time, or this process can be highly distressing to those with learning disabilities such as dyslexia, (and a myriad of "pseudo disabilities" such as ADD and ADHD, some which remain as yet not fully authenticated scientifically). Nevertheless, students that are diagnosed with any of these, have to face awesome and daunting tasks that are naturally associated with the reading process, the sister science of writing. Our study of Doxography examines and highlights the affective processes involved in reading and writing, particularly for ESL/bilingual education students, children or adults, opening up the innate world of human creativity, one of wonder and amazement, exploration and agenda, invention and arrangement: dimensions of the brain that are untapped by most language learning methodologies. Principles contained in <u>Doxography suggest that affective learning in schoolwide</u>

curriculum can increase the level and scope of literacy skills with empirically measured results that will consistently prove superior to traditional cognitive-based learning.

Noam Chomsky in Syntactic Structures (1957) states, "All humans possess innate capacity of language." The role of psychology is paramount to language success from the very genesis of the process. This marvelous component of the human psyche must be tapped during early stages of reading development. The pre-K teacher can be trained to look beyond the benign value of the ABC's and to treat them with the respect they deserve as harbingers of "the word—the logos" of humanity.

> "In the beginning was the Logos and the Logos was with God and the Logos was God..." John 1:1

The logos is the word, **the power of creation**. Our students possess this very ability! "Logos can mean anything from a divine utterance to the principle of cosmic reason that orders and governs the universe. To John the Apostle, it is the infinite wisdom of God personified" (Harris, The New Testament, 4th Ed, 2002). John amazingly records that the logos is actually God. While this is **an attempt to explain the creative energy of God**, it can not diminish the importance of the creative energy of each human being. We inherently possess abilities to discriminate good from bad, things that are beautiful from those that are not. The power of creation is a suggestion of discernment, which in itself, is a type of creation within one's own likes and dislikes. Writing is not only a skill that takes many years to learn effectively, but is also a divine principle of creation, using that wonderful creative energy of Divine Intelligence, an energy we all gloriously possess but unfortunately are not called upon to utilize, particularly in the public classroom. Oh that this natural creative energy could be harnessed for our 48,000,000 school students! In the book, Spirituality in the Workplace by Pierce, the author contends,

"Teaching needs to carry a spiritual dimension in the material studied or else it has no intrinsic value." What about math? Numerology is only one aspect that proves the essential quality of spirituality in math.

True People of Faith: the Scientists

In fields of science, one could contend that scientists are true people of faith. Who else would accept that all matter contains invisible components called atoms? Or, who else would believe that life on our planet started simply by accident? Yes, these are the true people of faith. The world is indeed ready for a renewed sense of spirituality albeit with a cautious enthusiasm. One way of renewal is by examining our human "logos." We are currently involved in a renewed debate over human creation. **Divine Intelligence vs. Evolution** is the new catchphrase in academic circles. School districts, with the new Republican government in power, are exercising their political conservative muscles by proclaiming the Scopes Trial is invalid and we are back to square one in this never-ending debate. For the past fifty years, no serious debate has developed in the USA regarding Evolution which has been taught as fact or at least as the most feasible theory for creation, for all this time. Recently **Creationists** coined a new term, "Divine Intelligence" to mask the word, "God." How clever!

Many are asking, "Where does Doxography stand in this renewed debate?" The answer is that we clearly stand for common sense and that is with scientific fact. Since Doxography concerns educational philosophy and pedagogy, we stand solidly behind only scientific fact, not invented religious "facts". Isn't this in contrast with the basic foundation of Doxography which attributes the logos with creation and thus with God? Not at all. As proponents of liberal arts education and scientific inquiry, Doxographists clearly have no hidden agenda to bring God into the American classroom any more than what is expected through

13

common sense and natural human spirituality which we indeed believe exists in each of us. In other words, we want spirituality (the affective domain) emphasized in American classrooms, yes, but we also have no qualms with Darwinian Evolution which is still classified as a Theory because the truth of the matter regarding the creation of the universe is simply this and here it is: no one really knows anyway! Not the preacher nor the teacher! So therefore, this is why Doxography refuses to become embroiled in this never-ending saga until some day one of the positions is proven.

Logos in the Finite World of Alphabet

Each child is a creator and each child enjoys the innate ability at creation. This is the logos. A renewed examination of the Logos and something as simple as the alphabet **might revolutionize education** as we know it today. Teachers could empower their students to look INTO the lessons they are receiving so that the value of the alphabet letters forming /cat/ are not merely three inanimate, cold, hard shapes with an adjoining artificial phonic, but indeed three influential "messengers" that when learned properly by shaping them and pronouncing them, become pure education energy! They almost become magical on a scope, albeit small, that transcends space and time and enters into the intimate subjective world of the human psyche that has known what /cat/ is for centuries. But at this very moment in a student's career, in this new reality, the child or adult student is shaping reality around them which is required by the natural physics of one fixed, specific instance of time and space. **This is the beginning of Doxographic learning** for these students, a small but significant step in their experiencing of the unique human ability to take in and process information, thereby creating new senses of meaning within their own cerebral cortex, indeed an inspiring thought!

All humans, through all of human existence, are linked together in some wonderful existential manner. This way of thinking has now pervaded education in very relevant manners, including the words of Jim Wingate, well-known conference speaker and education author. He has written on such topics as "psychic energies in the classroom" including one's personal "force field". His books and training sessions deal with educational issues that surround affective learning on many levels (seal.org.uk).

Each human has contributed to the life of the planet. Interesting to note that this is the only sphere yet found to have life at all! If indeed we are unique in this vast, perhaps limitless universe, which at this point we are, then it behooves thinking people to ask pertinent questions about what "this" is all about? What is our reality? What is the reality that we are imitating in the American classroom? Are we merely copying the physical world in the 21st century as we know it? If so, what happens when the students grow up and their world suddenly changes due to war, famine, destruction, or perhaps of extraterrestrials visiting the planet? Are teachers imitating the real world at our peril or pleasure?

Doxography challenges teachers to look beyond the alphabet letters ABCDEFG and go beyond, showing students not only the "what is?" but the "what could be?" The absolute uniqueness of the human experience should be capitalized upon in each class, each period, each lesson, and in each subject area. Books are quickly becoming archaic relics of the past. Computer learning and computer testing, for example, are taking over American education even as you read this paragraph!

This Ain't Your Mama's World!

The Age of Technology is exciting, especially for education. Teachers are amazed at how computer savvy their students are when they walk into the classroom. Kids love electronics! Edison would be so proud. MicroSoft and Apple Computer companies are soaring on the Stock Market. Never has one commodity hit such records as these. The world is absolutely flush with excitement over this revolution worldwide for information, communication, and power.

Your Mama may not even know how to turn on a computer, but her world, as is yours and mine, is now virtually addicted to the power and convenience that computers bring. Along with computers in the classroom comes a wide array of other sophisticated electronic, micro-chip-driven gadgets such as the IPOD and Blackberry, just to mention a few. Watching TV will change forever for Americans in 2009 when the whole country must switch to digital signals. Can one live in this type of hyper society without feeling extra stress? This stress and anxiety are making their way into the American classroom with alarming results. Failure rates are horrible, math and science scores are down, respect for teachers and old-fashioned schools, even the building designs, are now being rejected by the public as the whole modern world wants change and they want it now! How will education continue to produce leaders that will adjust to this shift in paradigm in American education? Doxography has some very interesting, avant garde ideas that can be very helpful.

The Ancient Logos: A Personal Example from History

Writing is a direct reflection of the "Logos," the word. The Logos should be viewed as the highest goal of education. When one is educated, one is expected to be able to communicate effectively in all four basic language skills: listening, speaking, reading, and writing. Furthermore, an educated person is expected to use both formal and informal language in the right circumstances. In times past, erudite individuals were referred to as "persons of letters." How are the outstanding persons from history remembered? One way is by what they wrote. For example, when a judge is being considered for the Supreme Court, legal analysts pour over their published writings to "get into their head" in order to either endorse them or not. Why don't they go by simply what the judges have said? The written word, logos, has much greater power and permanence. If famous persons left no published works however, then we rely upon the next best thing, the writings of others about them.

One of those **"Persons of Letters"** often overlooked by non-academics, yet is read more and quoted more than most anyone else in the world, is Paul of Tarsus (born a Roman citizen in Tarsus, martyred in Rome under Emperor Nero, c.68AD), first century Jewish teacher and later, devotee of Jesus of Nazareth.

Doxography and St. Paul. Paul was a prolific writer, the most important by far of the New Testament. His colossal corpus of writing alone propels him into the history books and annals of great men of letters. The pathos with which he penned carefully edited poetry such as is contained in his first letter to the Church at Corinth, Greece, "Though I speak with tongues of men and of angels, and have not love, I have become as empty sounding brass or clanging of the cymbals…" (I Corinthians 13) This great writer of the 1st century carefully constructed many of his texts in a manner that only one who is conscientiously trying to apply doxos could. In this famous poem, he creates original language around beloved ideas about love that have brought comfort and hope to millions down through the centuries.

Dr. von Heller is welcomed to Israel in 1999 by fans of Doxography at Ben Gurion Airport, Tel Aviv. This is the land in which St. Paul wrote his famous 13 letters contained in the New Testament.

Paul's writings make up the largest portion of the New Testament, having more text canonized than any other writer. Although clearly some of his epistles are lost, he is credited with authoring at least 13 epistles or letters, with the great possibility that he authored the book of Hebrews as well.

Is Doxography apparent in all of his words and works? No. St. Paul probably had no idea anyone would ever want to spiritualize some of his day-to-day correspondence with his friends around the Mediterranean Roman world of his day, although it is certain that his treatises about Jesus of Nazareth were very intentionally written to be used for instruction. He mentions very personal items in his letters such as "please tell him to bring me a coat next time he visits," and "Demos has forsaken me." These are not meant to be spiritual at all, merely a man showing his humanly needs, likes and dislikes. Of course his contribution to the rules and organization of the Christian church are phenomenal and for this, he is highly prized as an outstanding pioneer of the early Christian experience. So his works continue to impress, bless and even stir a maze of controversy some 20 centuries later, a true disciple of Doxographic principles and a true "man of letters." Oh that our students could be known as "men and women of letters" like Paul!

The Logos and Creation: Both Can Be Yours!

The "logos" can refer to either "the word" or "act of creation." To educators, the philosophy of Doxography asks, "What have you written? What have you created?" Students develop their writing skills from first grade on, but also the educator must become a living example of the logos during the writing process of the students. Teachers should bring to class their college essays, Masters Thesis or Doctoral Dissertation. If they are published, even better! Impressive indeed it is for students to see that their teachers are real examples of the logos, in this case, writers. Writing is probably the most respected form of modern literacy. Students become motivated when they view the work produced by their teacher. And if teachers are not writing on a personal level, they should be encouraged to, not only because of the Doxographic principles involved, but more for the marvelous sensation that the creation of a product brings to the creator/writer. This simple action would not require much of an investment on the part of the teacher to join with the students while they are busy writing a paragraph in class and imagine the impression this would make! <u>Modeling is probably the most well known and most effective teaching tool.</u> Why not use it in a true Doxographic sense? For example, how impressive would it be for the teacher to return on Monday morning to class and begin by saying, "Over the weekend I had the opportunity put together a few paragraphs that I would like to run by you today. This is only a rough draft of course, but with your input, I will revise and edit it with you again in a few days. Your input is important." Wow! Since when has anyone ask for a student's input, especially a teacher! Students would be so impressed that not only is writing taught in order for them to pass State tests, but also that writing can be rewarding in itself or just for the "doxos" of it! Please try this and enjoy the wonderful results, feeling the elation that will be imparted upon the entire group.

<u>Spiritual Significance of Alphabet Letters</u>

HEBREW (in reverse order, reading left to right)

יי ו י ו ו ת ש ר ק צ ף פ ע ס נ ן מ ם ל כ ך י ט ח ז ו ה ד ג ב א

ENGLISH

A B C D E F G H I J K L M N O P Q R S T U V W X Y Z

19

Is it possible that alphabet letters have hidden spiritual values? Although not a common idea in English and most modern languages, nevertheless it is a popular idea amongst some who are involved in the history and impact of global language. Our purpose here is to raise awareness of this concept for scholars and educators. Such formidable thinking regarding the letters of alphabets has been on-going for centuries and is not something new, recently discovered by a few scientific "quacks." This is a very serious component of religious linguistics as it were, both historically and scientifically, affecting not only the composition of the Bible and perhaps other writings, but also subsequent religious and secular documents. For example, the ancient Hebrew language is said to contain spiritual value just by reciting it and in particular, reading aloud from the Torah. Carlo Suares, in The Sepher Yetsira, Shambhala, 1976, states,

"We have repeatedly stated that the letters of the Hebrew alphabet have always been, throughout the centuries, the foundation of the true tradition and the only key to the knowledge of the Hebrew Revelation...Therefore this sacred language is not an ordinary instrument capable of pointing something out, but incapable of conveying its meaning. The words "music" and "color"...do not make music heard, colors visible, etc."

He goes on to claim, "The letters of the Hebrew alphabet are the projections of 22 biologically structured energies, or generalized formative archetypes. These archetypes are semantically-accurate signs or representations that project and embody their own meanings—Cosmic Energy is described in both subjective and objective terms as consciousness. The book of Genesis is written in this language."(IBID)

Although the principles of Doxography will not contend that a specific language holds proven hidden meanings, we certainly assert that all written symbols of language might contain extraordinary qualities that if examined properly, could greatly enhance the writing experience and literacy in general. For example, some modern Hebrew linguists believe that their ancient language holds the key to the existence of God and even hidden messages that are now decipherable to tell of future events! Books have recently flooded the market regarding this very topic. One example is <u>Genesis Factor: The Amazing Mysteries of the Bible Code</u> by Yacov Rambsel, published by Lion's Head Publishing, 2000. Movies are being produced in the area of Bible Codes also. This has become big business in the past five short years! While at first glance this whole concept seems totally unbelievable and way out of sync with Christian orthodoxy, thousands are flocking to movie theatres and snapping up millions of copies of books on this subject. Even evangelical Christians have joined the excitement by endorsing conservative Bible scholars who have published on this topic as well, often appearing as guests on TBN (Trinity Broadcasting Network), the largest religious broadcaster in the world, based in Santa Ana, California.

Furthermore, Decoz Numerology of Pensacola, Florida, is one of dozens of organizations that promote the concept of a spiritual connection between numbers and a universal dynamic. Numerology seems to be an attempt to understand the world from the vantage point of numbers as sort of a universal standard. Since ancient times, mathematicians have theorized this very concept. Could it be true? Just how "far out" are these theories about numerology, Kabbalah, and a spiritual connection with letters of alphabets?

Jerusalem business leaders discuss English language needs in Palestine with Dr. von Heller (wearing glasses). English is the language of international trade and is widely used in the Middle East.

Superstitions abound all around us, even in the Western world. Most know what "666" stands for. And then we have the famous 13th floor that is mysteriously left out of hotels. Who wants to stay on Floor 13? What about Friday the 13th? Superstition, religion, and education have been strange bedfellows for centuries. So should the study of numerology with its connection to writing bring much of a surprise as we begin the third Christian millennium? Have we grown so far from our ancient literary heritage(s)?

GREEK: α β γ δ ε ζ η θ ι κ λ μ ν ξ ο π ρ ς σ τ υ φ χ ψ ω

Writing is one of humanity's most remarkable abilities, however, it is not a natural ability but rather one that must be **nurtured, modeled, and carefully taught** during the first few months and years of one's experience with formal education, whether as an adult entering ESL classes for the first time, or a child entering first grade. Writing involves cognition with all the processes that cognition entails. Thinking to think is a metacognitive activity highly related to language and even more related to writing. We should encourage our students to understand their rich linguistic heritage, culminating in both English and Spanish (for millions of citizens). What a heritage indeed!

Express Yourself!

From the very genesis of human existence, humankind have attempted to express themselves through countless ways: *speaking, crying, yelling, grunting, smirking, gesturing, eyeing, hitting, ignoring, pouting, smiling, laughing, painting, drawing, singing, dancing, snorting, humming, ignoring,* and a million others. **Humans have an inherent need for expression** of needs, beliefs, abilities, suggestions, purposes, and persuasion. Where spoken language leaves off, writing begins and accentuates, reflecting speech as closely as possible but of course never 100% with the exact same nuances. One might ponder, when in pre-historic times, were attempts at mimicking speech via writing symbols first realized to be woefully inadequate? One may write precisely as one speaks, using very meticulous formations, however, humans usually prefer to converse in one manner and write in another. For example, when we attempt to describe something in an email, some attempt to express emotions beyond the words by using a happy or sad face symbol. This illustrates that words, while perfectly correct in imitating speech, may not precisely convey the message intended to the full extent the sender desires. Oh the limitations of writing but oh the joy!

Babies "Write in Their Minds"

Perhaps we "write in our minds" as we speak. Dr. Clark von Heller posits that this is possibly one of the natural processes that occur prior to real writing. Babies rehearse "writing" before they even learn to speak. They accomplish this via **pattern recognition.** Through observation, sound, touch, and of course, listening, they are somehow able to recognize patterns long before they are able to reproduce them. Babies tend to departmentalize cognitive ideas and concepts immediately after opening their eyes at delivery into this world! Their brain immediately sets them up for success in the human family through this incredible ability of pattern recognition. Uncanny though it may be, human babies are naturally gifted to language and from that uncanny gift of language supports the reason behind their amazing ability to departmentalize and categorize all elements of their world long before they attempt speech, much less writing on paper.

Babies are so intelligent at birth that they know better than to try to attempt intelligible speech at all! Instead they are naturally endowed with lungs and vocal cords that together, are quickly learned to be helpful in crying which is undoubtedly a survival mechanism long evolved into their psyche, or perhaps naturally endowed by divine appointment. Once the vocal chords are exercised by crying, babies experiment with further sounds such as babbling and cooing; anything that makes noise. **Noise is entertaining and fun but more importantly, babies learn very quickly that crying will bring a response from Mother who offers relief from whatever the need is at the moment**. Silence is alarming and discomforting to humans. For example, Caleb Gattegno's research elaborated upon the alarming effects of silence.

Little Colton Respess practices his new language skills: laughing, crying, cooing, saying "Mama" and just being a sweet boy.

Babies instinctively rehearse and exercise their physical abilities while mentally rehearsing their other significant linguistic abilities as mentioned before such as categorizing information, sounds, sights, touches, textures, etc. Furthermore, humans learn to tune out certain noises either that they cannot tolerate or simply have no desire for. This ability continues throughout life with some becoming quite adept at hearing only what they want. For example, **a banker and a baker** walked down the street together. Suddenly the banker stopped abruptly, "Wait! I heard a coin drop." Sure enough, after scrambling around on the sidewalk for a while, he indeed found a quarter! "How could you possibly have heard such a small thing with all this clatter of the city?" enquired the puzzled baker. As they continued along, the baker commented on a rich aroma he smelled, "Oh my! Someone is baking cinnamon cookies." The banker looked at him very perplexed, "I don't smell anything," he retorted. Amazingly, around the next corner, a little girl walked out of a small shop with an open basket of freshly baked cookies, and yes, just as the baker said, they were cinnamon!

The point of this story is that one tends to develop heightened senses throughout life, depending on a myriad of physical and mental experiences and impressions. Just as some children take longer to develop their language and speak, so too some babies take longer to develop their mental abilities to categorize, departmentalize, and discern patterns. This often causes us to hear what we want to and tune out the rest! Much of this mental ability depends on exposure to other humans, not experience since theirs is so limited at this point in life. For example, if a baby is born to hearing impaired parents with no speech, then the baby will be very reticent to babble and experiment with speech since no modeling is happening around them. Obvious ways to avoid this syndrome is for deaf parents to allow normal noises that would be common in a hearing home such as computer, TV, radio, telephone, cars passing by, fire engines, ambulances, etc. Some of the ways in which researchers can verify this theory is eye movement, hand-eye coordination, and how babies react to certain stimuli. Research indicates that babies of non-hearing parents learn to babble with their fingers! (This topic is covered elsewhere in this book. Refer to Index).

Adults and Second Language Learning

Adults, on the other hand, learn language quicker and more efficiently than children if given the same amount of time and attention. Their past experiences and stimuli form **a huge reservoir of knowledge** from which to add their new language and new experiences in phonetics, speech, and writing. Most people incorrectly think that children "pick up" foreign languages quicker than adults, evidenced by their amazing near-fluent pronunciation ability in a short time period, if immersed in the culture with other kids. While part of this phenomenon is accurate in that children surely pick up oral language quicker in most cases, a very important law of linguistics Doxography comes into play to explain this. Children are usually thrust into the language via playing, interacting with native kids, with little to no inhibitions about practicing the new language, regardless of failures or mispronunciations. Their goal is simply to be included as fast as possible into the games or whatever activities the other kids are doing. On the other hand, their parents will usually take formal language classes inside a building with near 100% artificial access to the language as is imbedded in the culture. The result? The children will pick up the oral language very quickly but will not ever learn how to read the language until they are formally taught in school. The parents, however, will probably learn proficiency in written language, while probably never truly becoming 100% fluent in the pronunciation of the oral language. What a marvelous paradox of second language acquisition! O the doxos of it all!

In summary, writing is not a natural human ability but rather one that is dependent on a more important natural ability, language. **Pattern recognition** may cause a type of "writing in the mind" for infants. This "writing in the mind" is basically the same for adult education students also, but varies in that adult students have already received years of language stimuli that cause them to correlate more quickly their experience with new knowledge entering the mind. Therefore they should theoretically learn written language quicker and more efficiently than children while the children learn the opposite quicker, oral language.

The Spiritual Connection with Writing

In her book <u>Growth Through Meditation and Journal Writing</u>...(1984), Maria L. Santa-Maria explains the **importance of the spiritual connection** with writing using a Jungian approach based on the work of the philosopher, Karl Jung (1875-1961), well-known Christian psychologist. At the 7th Annual Women's Conference (1998) sponsored by Loyola University in Chicago, one of the objectives of the conference was "to reflect on women's writing and spirituality." PeerSpirit™, one of many professional training and motivation organizations, offers seminars on spirituality and writing. From this new emphasis on spirituality, mediation, and their connection to writing, it would appear that even Wall Street sees a correlation between **writing and spirituality** that educators have inadvertently lost over the past 100 years. Is it time to revive our hegemony over this valuable aspect of education? Many ways exist whereby we can accomplish this, one important way being to place more time and resources into every type of writing activity possible in every single subject area possible as much of the school day as possible. After all, students are not machines governed by the laws of physics only; they are mind and spirit which are governed by eternal, spiritual laws which we refer to in Doxography as simply **"affectives."** These affectives are located in the emotional areas of the cerebral cortex. Affectives allow humans the marvelous freedom of feelings. Through feelings we can see our world as more than just a beautiful planet with lovely hills and beaches, colors and sensations, we can actually "see" into the world of the very essence of the Divine Intelligence by imitating that intelligence through creation. And the most powerful form of creation is perhaps by writing.

Can we actually "see" into the essence of the Divine?

The art of writing has been significantly reduced over the centuries to one of mass production and trite strikings on a computer keyboard, often meaning little except to complete an assignment or a project at work. What a shame! Writing is the very highest compliment to student's abilities and determination to learn language. While oral language is fun and productive, nevertheless oral production cannot contend with the audacity, the irreverence, the provocative nature of writing!

The Kabbalah. In the **Kabbalah of the Jews**, we find a belief system built upon energy produced when reciting Hebrew characters. "The Kabbalah has been passed down to us by Abraham, Moses, and the other patriarchs and matriarchs of the Bible, and by the great kabbalists of history, including Rabbi Shimon Bar Yochai and Rabbi Isaac Luria…today it is Rav Berg who carries on the legacy of Kabbalah…in 1922 the Kabbalah Centre was established in Jerusalem by Rabbi Ashlag"(www.kabbalah.com). Could this be "Hebrew ?" Here is a quote from The Energy-Code of the Hebrew Alphabet: An Introduction To The Language of Structure and Energy (www.psyche.com/psyche/energy-language.html), "…let us state that it is impossible to speak of the unknown in our common tongue (including Hebrew) without changing it arbitrarily into recognizable images. This artificial device is at the bottom of all proofs of the existence of God. It is inevitable that our tongues desecrate all that they discuss, because they have their being only in the measurable, in images, appraisements, comparisons…"(p.1). From this same site on p. 5 it posits, "Aleph, א (the first letter of the Hebrew alphabet), archetype of infinite, timeless, life-death, and the germ of life inside all containers. Aleph is the simplest and most basic representation of the Divine, because it represents what is completely beyond human thought." It might be interesting to note here that the entire Hebrew alphabet was placed in the King James Version of the Bible in 1611 within **Psalms 119**, the longest chapter in the entire Bible. In this Psalm, the letters form an acrostic, each beginning with a consecutive letter of the Hebrew alphabet, beginning in verse 10. For example, (in English) "a" is for "apple," which represents the sweetness of the Lord; "b" is for "birds" who sing God's praises, etc.

What about the other ancient languages of Assyria, Mesopotamia and the Orient? Since Western civilization is historically and linguistically built upon **Greek and Latin**, our study will only look at these along with Hebrew due to the influence of the Hebrew Bible, the most widely read book in the world. This is reasonable with the Church being the largest organization on earth! We have already investigated the awesome historical significance of Hebrew. Now we will look at the Greek language. Many college students remember their sorority or fraternity with the famous Greek letters. This author's fraternity was Pi Gamma Chi. (Π Γ Χ).

29

"Friends, Romans, countrymen, lend me your ears…" cries out Dr. Clark as he takes on the role of Mark Antony in Shakespeare's "Julius Caesar," while teaching at Donna High School on the Mexican border in 1988.

Although not well known, a "Greek Kabala" exists and includes websites such as crcsite.org/GreekKabala1.html, which states, "The Greek alphabet has 24 letters and an internal structure of 5 alchemical letters, 7 **planetary letters and 12 zodiacal letters**. The correlation (with Hebrew Kabbalah) is very close" (page 3 at same website for Greek Kabala). In addition, Pythagoras is credited with attributing numerical values to the Greek alphabet as most languages have in one way or another. The ancient Greeks highly valued their 24 letter alphabet and their culture in general. Alexander the Great felt it his divinely-appointed duty to spread the "holy" Greek language and culture to the conquered areas of his domain which he accomplished with great aplomb and success, culminating in the composition of the New Testament in near 100% Greek. But Alexander accomplished much more than just inculcating Greek language and culture into the Eastern Mediterranean area and all the way to India. With the introduction of Greek language came the introduction of **syllogism** (If A=B, and B=C, then A=C), linear logic, (A must lead to B and B to C, etc.) and the philosophy of Socrates, Plato, and Aristotle, his personal tutor. Mankind was taught the art of rhetoric, a fixed debate formulae for grammar, causing language to rise to the highest position yet in the course of human events. The Greeks looked to the gods on Olympus of course, but as Robert Graves so aptly explains, the Greeks created their gods and not the other way around! They were free thinkers, long before the rest of the ancient world knew how to read and write. What a tremendous legacy of Greek Doxography!

After Alexander died, his empire was divided three ways. The Roman Republic was born soon afterwards and of course, Latin language took over the entire Mediterranean world slowly but surely, except in Greece, Cyprus, Crete and Asia Minor. Although Greek remains to this day the official language of several major Christian Orthodox churches in the Eastern Mediterranean, Latin eclipsed it in the West, particularly after the Great Schism during the Middle Ages. From then on until Vatican II which convened from 1962-1965, **Latin was the only official language of the Roman Catholic Church liturgy**. What a tremendous addition to humanity's vast store of lexical items and expressions Latin presented to us! Latin carried the weight of the mighty Roman Republic and later Roman Empire for more than a thousand years. Horace, Ovid, Virgil and many other great writers, forever ensconced their lovely Latin phraseology into the hearts and tongues of millions, even still today in the 21st century. Latin inscriptions can still be seen inscribed in classical script above entrances and fascia of countless temples, public buildings, universities, and churches throughout Europe, the Middle East, and northern Africa. And as might be expected, many who are great lovers of language carry their devotion to such an extent that the language becomes an infatuation instead of a simple vehicle to impart ideas. Here is a clear example.

> "It is possible to care for Latin too much. Excesses in the pursuit of Latin have manifested itself throughout the ages in many appearances. The phenomenon has even been scrutinized in a learned German dissertation in 1720 the schoolmaster Daniel Friedrich Jahn, published an essay De nimio Latinitatis studio, in which he reviewed a long series of statements and comments by authors, who had accorded so much weight and dignity to the Latin language that they deemed it the sole appropriate vehicle of universal learning, without which all sciences would simply collapse" (infinityfoundation.com/mandala, 2003).

But alas, the **influence of Latin**, although still widely heard and felt daily in many European languages, has fallen prey to the ravages of modern linguistic invention and therefore no longer a viable spoken tongue in the modern world. Could it be revised and reinstated to its former glory? Of course! Ancient Hebrew was revived to become the working language for the State of Israel in 1948 and modern Turkey revised their ancient language to that of a new, modern system that is amazingly simple to learn and is used extensively today. One should keep in mind that Latin texts are still readily available in Western libraries, particularly those of universities such as Oxford and Cambridge.

We have seen the demise of ancient Greek and Latin, along with the renaissance of ancient Hebrew. Could a viable reason exist to explain why their usefulness in the Doxographic sense has diminished so much? Hebrew is still viewed as a holy vernacular by millions of Jews but this reverence for language is not in existence in modern everyday Greek usage or even academics who still use Latin texts in research projects. Of course millions of devout Greek Orthodox adherents come close to regarding their ancient and elegant Koine (the language of the New Testament) Greek liturgy as "holy" to some extent I would imagine. Thousands of hold-outs in the Roman Church long for the days of the all Latin Mass. So one can readily see the power and importance of "holy" languages even up to our modern day.

Therefore, although alphabet letters are graphic symbols giving physical, tangible meaning to oral language, they may have deeper meanings than mere surface qualities of shape, phonics and association concepts. **Letters of the alphabets, both ancient and modern, may contain profound dimensions** which are not presented in typical texts or dictionaries. Is this some new "hocus pocus?" Gratefully no. As we have carefully analyzed earlier, the production of writing might itself be seen as a divine manifestation of grace. Is it any wonder that the ancients revered writing and scripting logographs to such a high extent? Alphabet letters may contain hidden characteristics that could be used to provide an easier, more proficient method of teaching worldwide literacy but are yet undiscovered by archeologists or Doxographists. Even the smallest child or adult learning the alphabet for the first time, can become a true disciple of discovery, not just memorizing 26 English letters that have value in relation to a particular space and time, but even more, one that has meaning for <u>every value of space and time</u> imaginable! Think of the possibilities that would afford!

When students truly become aware of the life-changing potential in learning alphabets and expressing real, heartfelt thoughts, their whole world opens up before them as they begin an earnest quest for literacy, the ultimate application of language. Literacy brings liberty, economic opportunities, self worth, potential to work up the ladder of success, and literacy opens more doors than perhaps any other aspect of education. **And it all begins with a few letters of a humble alphabet**. However, literacy has to exceed our expectations of deciphering messages and transcribing thoughts. Literacy needs to become Doxography, realizing the glory in the letters of the alphabet, realizing the glory in the reading and writing, and lastly, realizing the glory in the learning available in our wonderful world!

<u>Metacognition</u>. "Meta" means "with" or "after" (Merriam-Webster on-line), and "cognition" means "the act or process of knowing." In education, we normally use this term to mean "learning about your own learning." From the ERIC Digest, ED376427, 1994, we find:

"Researchers consistently posit that metacognition plays an important role in reading. Metacognition has been defined as "having knowledge…and having understanding, control over and appropriate use of that knowledge" (Tei & Stewart, 1985). Thus, it involves both the conscious awareness and the conscious control of one's learning.

How can one learn best? By association? Modeling? By connecting patterns? With soft music playing? By paying close attention to a teacher and taking mental notes or by taking written notes? We all have different ways to learn but these ways are not necessarily unique. One of the best ways for students to succeed is to learn how to learn effectively. Some students use certain memorization techniques, relaxation, special breathing exercises, using neural and chemical balance, and even "featureship" in their learning, as means to improving retention of information and application of information. These are just a few techniques to incorporate "doxos" (glory) into the **final product**, whatever that may be.

By learning how to learn, students intuitively become aware of their word and their world (Paulo Freire, 1921-1997, Brazilian, education leader). But without the "doxos" no meaningful learning takes place because it is both a "glorious" thing to be literate and it brings "glory to humanity" to be able to share in this esteemed tradition of letters, sounds, characters, and meaning of the written word, the logos. Did the ancient Greeks and Egyptians, for example, realize new dimensions of the word and their world? How was it possible to create such tremendous literary works, symbolic, practical, and oh so breathtaking? Perhaps this was their Doxography and finest hour. Maybe the **ancients discovered some principles of language and learning that modern educators have not yet discovered.** By utilizing concepts and clues to alphabets unknown to us today, the ancients may have used these concepts to build their incredible civilizations. If so, why and how could they lose these amazing principles of Doxography? These principles have been lost to posterity for we have no clear record of their Doxography, merely modern guesses. The Egyptians started it all perhaps, yet with all the discoveries of their amazingly beautiful world of hieroglyphics, we have yet to discover the rationale they must have felt for their alphabet. Was it from the gods? Is science credited with alphabet development? We are not really sure.

But certainly something unusual and wonderful must have occurred in the ancient world to allow them to secure the landmark place in world history that they did. After all, it would take a mountain of books to show the magnificent achievements in science, philosophy, architecture, language, and democracy that the ancient Greeks alone invented and perfected. One brief look around will quickly authenticate the unprecedented Greek influence. And their achievements are still influencing modern life, especially in Europe and America. Recently a commentator said on TV that only a handful of things are genuinely unique to the modern age: vaccines, space travel and the computer. Most everything else can be credited to the Greeks. And it all starts with Alpha, Beta, Gamma. And that leads us on to English, the most widely used language in history!

The English Language Century

Ours is the 21st century world of English, the most powerful language the world has ever known, even eclipsing the Greek of Alexander and the Latin of Augustus Caesar! Since the whole world is frantically trying to learn English, we welcome new readers, "word explorers," to the new world, the world of our **21st century ESL**. But what have we accomplished with this great power as the purveyors of knowledge and science? Unfortunately very little. While advances in sciences are phenomenal and respected throughout the galaxy thanks to **NASA**, have we really kept up with the inner advances of the spirit of English language? Have we taken the time to examine the vast world of nuance, perception, resonance, attitude and effects of English language? The time has come for just that! Along with this magnificent wealth and world power that the "English nations" have amassed, comes the inherent responsibility to insure future generations of English speaking people that our language will be known as a language worthy of the term, "Classical English" in some future generations yet to be born, once it fades into history as so our ancient linguistic antecedents: Hebrew, Greek and Latin. This is indeed, "The English language century!"

Teachers of English are in such great demand, along with Internet classes, textbooks, etc., that the quality of the language has experienced a major downturn since World War II. British English was the dominant root of English language until about 1963. The reasons for this watershed date are Vatican II, JFK, and Britain's imminent decline as a world power. Fortunately Britain reinvented itself via the British Council which sets up English classes and promotes British culture on a global scale. Tony Blair came along in the 90's with "Cool Britannia," a powerful slogan, widely embraced by the British people, to symbolize the new, sleeker, modern nation.

However, this phenomenon could not eclipse the unimaginable power and influence of American pop culture upon the world of satellite TV, movies, radio, and magazines. At any moment of the day or night, people from perhaps every culture on the globe are imitating American culture in some way, whether it is by wearing jeans, singing American rock, or by enjoying a Coke! Even our enemies, who may hate us for political reasons, still seldom stop their massive orders of American movies and manufactured goods so much in demand, whether in times of war or peace. This is perhaps a phenomenon on a scale that has never been seen before in world history! Surely this was seen in the Roman Empire and even British Empire of more recent times, but none of these can compare to the popularity of American culture at this present time.

With this tremendous opportunity to expand American influence and power via language comes a great responsibility to examine our use of English language so that students can have pride in their vocabulary, phonics, style and structures available in this magnificent practical American English. Most who speak English probably have never thought of it as a beautiful medium but we should. Students should be taught to value the language, not just learn the language. Have we lost the glory of English? Is the history of the language really admired? Are lovely intonations really admired in English oral presentations, homilies and speeches that edify the American ear? Sadly, few and far between. Doxography maintains that all languages contain glory and ours is no exception. Let us strive to look for and discover the "glory" that yet is attainable in our rather divided, demoralized and deprived use of American English.

Scientific Technologies Can Advance Literacy

Children learn language naturally. The set of circumstances differs with each experience but nevertheless, language is learned only one way and that is naturally. What takes place between babbling and speaking intelligible utterances?

> "Conventional wisdom teaches that babies' babbling is just the happy accident of babies opening and closing their mouths and jaws, learning how to use their lips and tongues. The latest research suggests instead that babies are enthusiastic code breakers pursuing a high level mission: decoding the secret code by which their parents communicate. They do this the way professionals do, breaking down the code into small chunks" (Alan Greene, MD, DrGreene.com, copyright, 2003).

A study published in the September 6, 2001 issue of *Nature* provides fascinating evidence of this. Dr. Laura-Ann Petitto studied children with normal hearing who were born to deaf parents who communicated primarily with sign language. These babies with normal hearing babbled -- with their hands! This is the magic of human cognition, a branch of language acquisition that has largely eluded science until most recent discoveries about left lobe functions. The brain operates via <u>chemical and electrical</u> impulses and sensations. Language must therefore, ride upon these minute, intricate impulses until patterns are formed and the neurons relate in such a way that the entire anatomy along with a more complete Doxography come into sync so that humble attempts at language result. When will science be able to harness the intricate workings of the inner mind, the cognition that makes speech and understanding possible? We are poised on the threshold of incredible discoveries in this field and indeed, in this new century undoubtedly a discovery at some point will take place as to how to manipulate both language and literacy learning from within the brain itself, before problems with execution take place such as stuttering, dyslexia, etc.

Hence, all persons with normal mental acumen could theoretically be given the power of literacy, but would the powers that be allow it? What if 100% of humanity were literate? Is this an exhilarating thought or a sober warning to would be controllers of knowledge and information? Throughout our existence on this planet, ever since literacy became known, it has been divided between the haves and have-nots. Even today, millions of disenfranchised non-literate persons live in squalid poverty with only the bare essentials of life. What a shame on all of us! During the summer of 2005, a world-wide effort was made to reduce African debt in the hope that this would result in more investment and consequently less poverty. We will surely hope and work toward this end. Education may not be the solution to the world's problems but it certainly moves people in the right direction. Language Doxography is a great starting point.

Billions are spent on dynamic areas of very useful research such as nuclear energy, cold fusion, space travel, the cure for AIDS, etc. Why not allocate more public money to fight against illiteracy and learning problems that are often associated with it? We challenge universities to invest research dollars into neural implantation devices or any other scientific breakthrough that could bring literacy to all, once and for all. For instance, basic teaching theory has not advanced much beyond that of ancient times. We still have wall boards, markers, and hours of lecture in the classroom; all for the most part still as ineffective as always. Students memorize information only to place it in short term storage, later to completely forget 99% of it. Although the printing of books and computers are without doubt the two greatest breakthroughs in classroom education, still the basics are the very same as a thousand years ago! What a pity! And to add insult to injury, we still have the elite being educated, i.e. the rich countries, while the poor countries remain trapped in illiteracy and ignorance, never being able to relish the joy of the wonderful world of Doxography. Can we change this?

Education theory should join together with neural science theory to devise a plan that would harness micro elements of literacy skills before they are transmitted through normal channels from the eyes or fingers (if blind) to the brain. Neural messages, like telephone impulses, are sent at lightning speed to highly sensitive receptors to and from the optic nerve, (or fingertips) to the brain. For a student who is visually handicapped or learning disabled in some other way such as dyslexia, these messages will be only as reliable as the receptors that conceive them at the point of origin. Thus, input will equal poor output. So why can't we improve the condition of the original receptor at the point of origin, i.e., the eye or the fingertips? We propose to accomplish this via new neural implantation techniques that will someday be widely available to parents as a viable option for their children. How wonderful would it be to have all students succeed at reading! Is it possible? Absolutely. The technology will soon exist to accomplish this if not already in rudimentary stages of development.

Neural Implantation for Reading: Cybernetics

Neural manipulation could theoretically increase the reliability of neural signals and impulses so that a corrective could be instantly made to clarify and enhance flawed signals to the brain. The input would be correctly relayed and the resulting output would allow accurate deduction and connotation of alphabet letters, words, syntax, spellings, etc., from a written source. The end result would greatly enhance overall reading skills, increasing production as well as self esteem. Increased worldwide productivity would result in many sectors including manufacturing, industry, government, military, and of course, the classroom.

Dr. Clark von Heller models a writing technique in small groups with South Texas College students. (1998)

Chapter 1 Questions

1. What is the modern definition of "Doxography?"
2. How can a "spiritual connection" possibly exist between text and people who write and read it?
3. What is the "Logos?"
4. One method for motivating students to learn to write well is to have teachers bring in their own writings, i.e., Masters Thesis or Doctoral Dissertations. How could this motivate students?
5. Alphabet letters in English consist of 26 arbitrary characters. Does English language claim a spiritual significance to these characters? Why?
6. How was the spiritual connection of alphabet realized by the ancient Hebrews and even some modern Hebrew scholars?
7. See if you can figure out the numerical values from ancient Hebrew and Latin:

   XV_____Aleph_____XXVI_____Dalet_____MMM_____
8. The brain is extremely complex but basically works from two types of impulses. What are these?
9. Why are children faster at mastering oral language than adults?
10. Are "neural implants for reading improvement and/or language acquisition feasible in the future? Explain.
11. EXTRA CREDIT: Make a chart showing how the 26 letters of the English alphabet have changed through history.

Θ Chapter 2
INFORMATION V. INSPIRATION

The four traditional language skills in order of their natural acquisition are: listening, speaking, reading, and writing. This is an accepted sequence in the process leading to language fluency and literacy, but something is inherently wrong in the Doxography involved. Literacy skills are seen as the proof of a good education, the final product of elementary school, the successful conclusion of the basic reading process. Doxography teachers disagree. The reading process, moreover the literacy processes involved in reading, are just at the beginning stage for the total development of literacy. This is just the beginning of the Doxography journey, one that will take the student from the **"Once upon a time,"** all the way to the **"And they lived happily ever after."** For example, when a child presents a paper with colored drawings on it to the teacher, the teacher says, "Good job" and the child turns around and returns to the seat. This is not an example of Doxography. When the child points out that the dog's tail is blue and the sky has big, fluffy clouds, then that is proof that Doxography is taking place.

In other words the child takes ownership, cognitive understanding of what the drawing represents on a personal, spiritual basis, and most of all, "featureship." This is a new term coined by Doxographists to illustrate one of the most poignant characteristic of Doxography. When a child can truly represent something they have produced as real and relevant to their experience, this is considered not just a feature of their educational experience, but a true **"featureship"** of it. What a compliment to the teacher! The child truly learned from the experience and the child had the desire to feature the work to another person. This is pure

Doxography in action in the classroom. Is it happening in your classroom?

In order to understand one's world, one must fully understand the world in which the word exists. With this in mind, when a child or recently educated adult learns the basics of the reading process, they have just begun the exciting journey of Doxography which will greatly expand that reading ability into the ability to read the world around them via instructions, directions, recipes, contracts, bills, invoices, short stories, poems, novels, and the list goes on-and-on. This is a prime example of real world Doxography.

Aristotle believed that a "pre-existent knowledge" must exist as a pre-requisite to learning. Leibniz believed that language was innate, natural. Any mother will agree that they fully expect their infants to speak in due time. We can speed up the time it takes babies to begin to experiment with speech via reading to them and speaking directly to them so they can mimic lips and mouth motions, etc. Babies will experiment with language when they are ready because language is, of course, natural in humans. But reading and the appreciation of words, the logos, are not natural skills. Parents and caregivers of babies have a wonderful opportunity to model reading, allowing babies and toddlers the wonderful privilege to enter into the magical world of reading and literacy from those who love them. Reading curiosity will emerge eventually if modeled in front of children as this is a natural response. Now comes the hard part: teaching a person how to read effectively.

Reading involves a certain structure or framework in order for the student to understand its dynamics. One learns to read by reading, this is, by making sense of what is on the page (Smith, 1994). Writing involves an art which is inherent to human nature. Aristotle alluded to this concept in his teachings. Once the framework for elementary reading is mastered, then the student can incorporate writing skills. While writing also involves an intricate framework with much learned structure, still a vital vein of skills are tapped that cannot be taught. These skills and natural hidden abilities must be brought out of the student from <u>deep within</u>. This involves tapping into the psyche and indeed spirit of the student to allow fullest potential, perhaps the highest mode of teaching and the most fulfilling for the student.

<u>"You want to know what?"A Testimonial:</u>

> After teaching high school English for many years, I was tapped to teach a GED class at night for that same school district. I will never forget as I greeted not strangers, but my former students who had dropped out, now returning to complete their graduation diploma. I was so proud of them! As we trudged away through the GED exercises in grammar and I was turned, writing away on the board, a student asked: "Sir, would you explain prepositional phrases again?"
>
> I could not believe my ears! In all my years of teaching, I had actually never received a really sincere academic question. This was the first. I nearly fainted.
>
> As I suddenly turned to acknowledge the question, this same student's face returned to my mind from three years earlier when he was a goofball in my class, always causing trouble. Now, married and with a baby, he was the most sincere, sweet young adult in the class. Of course I gladly answered the question and modeled them on the board. What a difference maturity makes!

This testimonial represents all that is good within education and the inquisitive nature of students when they have a specific goal or product in mind. Teachers have the skills to help students become successful if the students are willing to allow the teachers to use these skills and training. This is just another reason to use Doxography in America's classes.

<u>The Mystique of Writing.</u>

Writing is perhaps the highest expression of human creativity, true Doxography, because it comes from within the person. Doxographic principles contained in writing are not a set of "fill in the blank" responses which can be guessed, but relate more closely to those functions occurring in the brain at the very moment of **creation of thoughts**. Then the creation becomes a physical manifestation via transcription on paper—writing. Doxography concerns itself with creation in the sense of the creation of the universe in general, and the creation of humankind with its marvelous ability to think, perhaps unique in the galaxy. By writing, one becomes a creator, perhaps the highest gift of humanity. In the book, <u>Writing Systems and Cognition: Perspectives from Psychology, Physiology, Linguistics, and Semiotics,</u> editor W.C. Watt of the University of California, Irvine, (1993), reports, "The systems through which language is realized on the page are compared in nature and complexity with those through which language is realized as sound, and are seen in their true perspective." Dr. Watt takes an interesting look into the art of calligraphy of ancient Egypt as well as **Roman Majuscules and Greek orthography.** What a wonderful resource in the fascinating study of Doxography.

Consequently, one must look at the way that the brain performs memory functions in relation to functions involved in the writing process, <u>before the writing, into the writing, and after the writing</u>: "a brief look at writing's relationship to memory performance…Most of the research suggests that sending and receiving information in more than one way is the best way to increase memory performance, but the single best encoding strategy appears to be writing" (De Hann, et al, 2000, www. faculty.edcc.edu, 2003).

While **copying** is an important first step, it is not an example of Doxographic learning. This is more of a mechanical stimulus, very useful in establishing boundaries and structure. **Using what another has modeled can never be Doxography.** Only that which comes from within is true Doxography. <u>Only that which comes from within is truly unique and sublime, adding to the "whole" of the human race</u>. This is a simple and beautiful process. Principles contained in Doxography have been used worldwide with tremendous results! Students become better writers, thinkers, innovators, discoverers, explorers, and thinkers. They are the best students because they FIND OUT WHAT THEY ARE CAPABLE OF and with a teacher's guidance, unlock their potential, and become pupils, "one under the care of a tutor; scholar." (Webster's Dict.,1933 Edition). <u>Pupils should have a purpose for taking your class</u>, not just fulfilling a legal obligation mandated by society. For example, what is the difference between "education" and "learning?" In addition, "When is "education" transferred into "learning?" The answer is when a conceived purpose is perceived by the student and the student reacts to that perception whether right or wrong. Will most content information given in school provide purpose? Perhaps not, but language and literacy education have to as they are vehicles upon which all other content subjects are understood. This is another reason that Doxography contained within language and literacy should be understood and capitalized upon by teachers and administrators, and of course, the students.

Writing Information vs. Writing Inspiration

Writing formats will usually either **inform or inspire**. Our definition for writing is: "a simple medium of inaudible expression through the use of symbols, usually on paper." As with most anything else, writing is born of purpose. It is not usually a spontaneous act as eating or socializing with friends. Why else would one take the time to put down words on a piece of paper instead of relaxing or watching TV? Can you remember examples of information writing from your school years? **Probably not 1%** of all you learned in twelve long years! But can you recall a poem, song, or other type of inspirational writing? Yes. Why? We will examine this interesting phenomenon. Probably 99.9% of all the writing in school was information writing. Teachers tend to turn away from inspiration writing, particularly when students enter middle school, incorrectly assuming that larger quantities of sophisticated "need to know" facts and figures are in direct correlation to age. This is certainly not the case! In fact, as humans mature cognitively, the need for more inspiration in life becomes apparent as evidenced by an increase in suicide rates in middle school children for instance. "Suicide rates have been increasing for the past four decades; suicide is the third leading cause of death among…youth between the ages of 10-24. More people die by suicide than by homicide in the USA" (Centers for Disease Control, 2003). Children and young adults indeed need inspiration! Are they receiving it in your classroom?

Although school curricula are very effective with instilling information in the liberal arts curriculum, sadly very little or no attempt is made at meeting the affective needs of students whose bodies sometimes outpace their cognitive development and mental maturity. This causes difficulties in relation to handling serious situations such as romantic crises, other relationship crises, etc.

Ninety nine percent of school writing is informational, testing and/or notation of academic facts. Most writing is for practical reasons which we will place under the category of **INFORMATION**. But another important category is **INSPIRATION.** We use this term as defines as "any sense or spirit of love and peace which comes from human emotion or affection." Since our concern is with classroom issues, we shall limit our study to this area. But here lies the problem. America's schools have virtually eliminated all semblance of affective learning from the classroom. This movement began after WWII and now includes all 18,000 school districts across the country. Enduring problems remain in defining spirituality as should be defined in a public school setting, still the vast majority of America's schools have swung the pendulum of education philosophy to an extreme view of secularized, bland system, homogenized "pure" of all religious thought and spirituality. This goes against common sense to anyone who has ever raised a child or been involved with children for a long time.

Children of all ages need to express their spirituality because spirituality or emotional qualities are natural. This is one of the four integral parts of human design: **Physical, Social, Cognitive, and Spiritual**. To starve one part of these four is to cause confusion and harm. Along with these four components of human design, we need to relate them to the four environments in which they naturally occur and who is responsible for them:

Physical-Personal-occurs in all environments

Social-Community-occurs most in school for students/Work for adults

Cognitive-School mostly but of course everywhere some

Spiritual-Home mostly. Church has traditionally played a large role also.

We should capitalize on common sense and human psychology by incorporating common sense standards back into our modern public school system. Doxography is one way to perform that in a very positive, non-threatening manner. We should allow a 4th grade teacher to be able to explain that Abraham Lincoln was a man of great Christian faith and character. Teachers should be able to put the Christ child back in the central role of the holiday that bears his name. This is simple common sense.

While not trying to be forceful or preachy on this subject, this author feels that a return to basic values prior to 1960, coupled with advanced technology and science, would thrust our students to the forefront of the world instead of lagging so far behind even the developing nations! Our decline in many basic areas of academic achievement over the past fifty years is largely due to a secular system that forbids the reinstitution of basic moral codes back into the education system of this country. This includes a return to freedom of religion in the schools, curricula based on freedom of expression, and school boards that realize and affirm

American's God-given rights to pursue affective instruction in the public schools.

Costumed as "Hamlet" along with a literature student from South Texas College, the author brings Shakespeare to life, using key elements of Doxography such as the "spirit of the literature." (2000)

Inspiration Writing Touches the Spirit of the Student

Inspiration writing sets apart the writing experience by going beyond the mere letters on the page and goes into the heart of the writer. But one could argue, "I do not believe in the spirit." We respond, "Call it what you will, but the manifestation of spirituality happens naturally when reading sweet poetry or listening to certain types of music. The Divine spirit apparently resides in humans. What else could it be? For example, who was not touched in the spirit by the powerful message of consolation delivered by President Reagan when he gave a moving rendition of "High Flight" after the space shuttle explosion in January, 1986?

"Oh I have slipped the surly bonds of earth...
Put out my hand and touched the face of God."

(John Gillespie Magee)

The spirit need not be justified nor explained. It is merely that wonderful feeling which accompanies great Doxography whether in oral or written format. Inspiration writing could be a passion-filled letter to the editor about a subject near to the heart, or a Get Well card to a classmate in the hospital. It would be associated with a Sympathy card or an essay on the true meaning of Christmas, Hanukah, or the origins of any bonafide religious holiday. Principles of Doxography can be included in assignments that **engage the spirit as well as the mind**. Often the two can be combined to create a writing product that will stand apart from the usual, mundane assignments that involve information but no inspiration. A balance must be met between information and inspiration. "All work and no play makes Jack a dull boy." We can add to this axiom by saying,

---

All information writing and no inspiration writing makes Jack a dull boy.

Principles of Doxography enable teachers to conscientiously place within their lesson plans a time each class for some type of spiritual (affective) type of learning, whether through writing or other types of activities. Students will be happier, the time will pass by faster, and the entire teaching process will become more productive and gratifying.

What are the purposes for writing?

- ➤ as a medium of inaudible expression, usually on paper
- ➤ putting down ideas in our own words
- ➤ for correspondence

- for computations and annotations
- for learning to organize ideas and schedules and lists of things to do
- to write books, songs, and illicit emotions often as a result
- for communicating ideas without having direct contact
- to take down notes or important information, directions, instructions
- for correspondence
- for computations and annotations
- to promote a cause or product or idea
- to express ideas inaudibly to provide a buffer between direct eye-to-eye confrontation
- to produce peace treaties, contracts, business documents, white papers, specifications
- journals, reflective writing, historical accounts and diaries
- religious books, song lyrics, chants, prayers, verses, commentaries
- poetry, greeting cards

Of this short list, which ones would fall under the information category? Which ones would fall under the inspiration category? Most of these writing activities are information-based. This is normal. The business world and academic world follow the basic same path that robotic-like writing is the norm and anything otherwise will be squelched. We most vehemently disagree! Although we cannot address business world issues, we can examine what takes place with America's 48,000,000 public school students each day. In other words, specific techniques are available which can greatly improve student writing, including the spiritual aspect of our world, while maintaining the curriculum. Here are some ways to accomplish this:

"One who speaks, speaks to one's self; but one who writes, speaks to the world!"

(Motto for Dr. Clark von Heller's writing classes)

The Writing Process. Teachers know that writing is a difficult task. Students often are reticent to attempt writing long assignments due to a variety of reasons stemming from lack of ability, to pre-conceived notions that writing is hard, to simply being lazy because writing involves thinking and that takes work!

If a distinguishable plan or process is developed and consistently maintained, students are more likely to become better writers and even more productive in other areas of **metacognition.** The most widely used model for the Writing Process is as follows: Invention, Arrangement, First Draft, First Revision, Second Draft, Second Revision, and Final Edit. Then Submission for evaluation.

Teachers often inquire as to specific ways in which affective principles can be incorporated into everyday lesson plans. Here are some helpful suggestions:

DOXOGRAPHY STRATEGIES IN
DAILY CLASSROOM ACTIVITIES

1. Incorporate the family into every conceivable aspect of education.

2. Include the four pillars of society into your teaching: *home, school, church, and community.*

3. Clearly let your students see that even teachers are spiritual beings, whether by reading the Bible or other religious books during lunch or breaks, or by including God in your speech patterns, such as "God willing." This demonstrates your reverence for authority and gently displays respect for spiritual values. Some students are surprised that their teachers actually go to church also!

4. Show great respect to the flag and to traditional values. If a veteran, hang a portrait with your uniform for the students to see.

5. Not only say the *Pledge of Allegiance* but also analyze it along with other treasured documents in American history such as the Mayflower Compact, Declaration of Independence and Bill of Rights.

6. Model a sense of tolerance for all religions, races, and beliefs. Bring religious books of other faiths to showcase along with the Bible and always give them equal respect.

7. Invite guest speakers that have written on inspirational subjects: caring for the poor, etc.

8. Allow students to become active in community projects that help others by encouraging student organizations to take up donations, painting posters for sick children, etc. High school students can actually go into the community on Saturdays and Sundays to help in shelters and Salvation Army, Red Cross, etc.

9. Have students concentrate their writing assignments on positive, uplifting subjects.

10. Subscribe to encouraging magazines such as "Guideposts" by Norman Vincent Peale, the "Readers Digest" and the "Chicken Soup" series. Bring them to class for supplemental reading or place them in your Reading Center.

11. Avoid book reports that feature the negative aspects of society. Reward those who are reading and reporting on positive, nurturing persons and heroes from the past and present such as Mother Theresa, Helen Keller, Abraham Lincoln, Albert Schweitzer, and Cesar Chavez, or other persons from their religious traditions such as Mohammed and the Buddha.

12. *Music.* Classical music can be played to enhance learning and a sense of tranquility. But one must be cautioned at this point. <u>Music must be turned off</u> at crucial intervals so that it will not become simple background noise. An observable visible reaction often occurs when the music is stopped after as little as three minutes of play. This can signal that the teacher has something important to say, or that a student is about to take the floor, etc.

> If used properly, music has been shown to improve student performance and memory retention.

"When children exercise cortical neurons by listening to classical music, they are also strengthening circuits used for mathematics. Music...excites inherent brain patterns and enhances their use in complex reasoning tasks" (Your Child's Brain, <u>Newsweek</u>, 19 Feb 1996). Plato said, "Music is a more potent instrument than any other for education." Scientists are closer to understanding why music trains the brain for higher forms of thinking.

In summary, by consistently using these Doxographic strategies in classroom activities, the teacher's work becomes easier as the students naturally imitate what is heard and studied in the curriculum, falling into a very rewarding academic routine where rote learning is not the norm but rather an innate creation of meaningful products.

> *Children don't really care what we know until they know that we care.*

In a caring classroom, everyone wins: the student, the teacher, the school, and surely the entire community.

But how can we promote **affective learning** in the classroom when so much opposition exists? Cognitive learning takes precedence each time that affective learning tries to work itself into the curriculum. The voices of dissent are widely publicized and receive too much attention. For example, in 2002, Michael Newdow, a California atheist, sued to have "under God" taken out of the **Pledge of Allegiance** on the grounds that his daughter was not raised to believe in God and was therefore forced to participate in what is paramount to a religious exercise each day by reciting the Pledge. He won the case although at this point the decision has been appealed. Some readers may be surprised to find out that for many years the correct salute to the American flag was a hand thrust forward. Did this make us a nation of Nazis or communists? Neither would something so benign as reciting the Pledge make us religious robots. Most feel that the Pledge is a necessary, harmless obligation of loyalty to a great nation. It takes perhaps 15 seconds out of the school day to recite.

The mention of God is one of respect also, not necessarily one of obedience or even acknowledgement of existence. The founders of this country were God-fearing individuals who intentionally incorporated Biblical principles into every aspect of the three branches of government, knowing that human nature needs **direction and accountability**. These elements are reflected in a basic respect for God, the Judeo-Christian God, Yahweh as revealed in Jesus. Most of the early leaders of the United States were highly familiar with the Bible, not only incorporating it extensively in speeches and public appearances, but also many of the early leaders were practicing, church-going religious people, proud of their faith and equally proud of the fact that our British forebears were Christians, protesting the establishment of a formal, national religion as was the case in Great Britain. The Church of England was the established church and those who refused to join were considered dissenters or rebels. These British subjects who chose to worship as Baptists, Presbyterians, etc., were persecuted for their beliefs. Finally they decided to come to America where they took a novel stance once and for all that in this "New Jerusalem" the people would enjoy religious freedom with clear democratic ideals based as much as possible on Judeo-Christian philosophy.

Today, the United States is still composed of millions of citizens who have identical beliefs of our forebears and are in the majority. More Americans are descended from the British Isles than all the minorities of Hispanics, African-Americans, and others combined. However, we also have millions in the minority groups who have other beliefs than those of the original British settlers and framers of our institutions. These citizens, along with their religious views, are welcome and protected by every conceivable means in the *Constitution*. But to go back and try to accommodate every belief system, including atheists, and change original founding principles because they may be offended by something so simple and basic as a *Pledge of Allegiance*, remains nothing more than ridiculous.

However, atheists and others are certainly within their rights to raise this matter if they are offended. We only use it here in reference to point out that some in American society have thrown the "baby out with the bath water" in an effort to homogenize and rid all semblance of religion out of the public schools. In the process we have graduated several generations of liberal-minded, disillusioned citizens who often "buy" into negative thinking trends, and worse, act upon negative impulses to the detriment of our society, which is especially sad when one looks around and notices that American society is one of humanity's last best efforts to maintain civilized, peaceful life on this planet. *Our teacher workforce of 4,000,000+ (the largest in the world) if dedicated to Doxographic principles, could systematically remedy this type of negative mindset with a simple return to a more affective approach to instruction and modeling of positive ideals and attitudes.*

Information Reading vs Inspiration Reading

In direct correlation with the development of writing is reading, the sister science in literacy. Researchers have spent lifetimes analyzing the intricate bond between these two branches of literacy. Does reading come first? In a normal academic setting, reading and writing are inseparable and must be considered symbiotically bound with corresponding elements that cannot be extracted without damaging the theoretical dynamics of each. The magic of the Roman alphabet must be appreciated for its beauty and format, even if perhaps difficult for second language learners. It is after all, the most widely used alphabet on earth! Readers of the language become creators of images that the authors superimposed into the text, but unfortunately something can be lost between the intended purpose of the author and the eyes and mind of the students unless Doxographic principles are used to enhance the beginning reading process. These principles must be used to most carefully and accurately teach English reading. These principles include—reading aloud so that the teacher can monitor, use some type of marker to show the teacher where the reader is, and enhance the text with illustrations and music if possible. Pedagogy shows that alphabet letters, formed into meaningful frameworks of words for most, are simply a mass of incomprehensible images to those who cannot capture the concept of "reading" which is technically, "cognitive comprehension of alphabet symbols on paper." I firmly believe that we are often attempting to teach "**depiction**" of symbols which is paramount to "skimming" instead of cognitive comprehension of alphabet symbols.

Deciphering Information vs. Reading Comprehension

A plethora of books and supplies exist for teachers of reading but the most effective method for teaching reading is to isolate the purpose for the reading, regardless of level. Little children should enjoy reading because of the images that reading invokes. More mature readers should enjoy reading because of the information needed that it brings, or perhaps for the innate entertainment value which of course, children enjoy as well. One wonders, who enjoys reading more for entertainment, children or adults? (Keep in mind that the author is a creator of the logos. The reader is the interpreter of the logos).

Roman alphabet letters form the basis for reading of English and Spanish although Spanish requires more of them than English for conveying the same concept. For bilingual students coming from Spanish reading into English reading, certain phonetic and syntactic hurdles must be overcome which are particular to these learners. Some of these include particular error formations such as the short vowels in English which are not in sync with pronunciation of the five Spanish vowels. (More on this is available at the end of this book). Added to this dilemma are the phonetic structures which are even more different than the vowel comparisons. Grammatically, English requires a solid period at the end of a transitive sentence whereas in Spanish this is not always the case. A comma can substitute for a period in many cases in Spanish writing. This author has encountered this rather odd phenomenon many times in Mexico and Peru. How is a teacher to address these issues? One very positive way is to analyze the two languages in question, whether English/Spanish or English/French, and so on. A comparative analysis will reveal some hurdles that could be avoided by isolating and mastering problems before they occur in the reading process. (This is illustrated at the end of this book also).

Most reading in the classroom will likely involve information, especially for older children and adults learning English. This is only natural and quite correct. Nevertheless, the same principles in writing, as mentioned earlier, can be applied in reading as well. Teachers can usually tell when students have reached their capacity to absorb static, cold information gathering and need a break. We all need breaks from academic exercises in the classroom. Information acquisition, i.e., the collection of facts and figures, is objective reality and must be supplemented with regular, healthy doses of music, fun, laughter, and subjective realities in order to develop positive, successful language and literacy.

Supplemental reading should come from positive, uplifting sources such as **Guideposts, Readers Digest, Catherine Marshal's** works, **Irma Bombeck's** books, and the **"Chicken Soup" series**, just to name a few. Cartoons can add fun and excitement to the classroom. The Internet is a treasure chest of inspirational stories and uplifting literature which can be accessed by merely typing "Inspirational stories" into a search engine. Students like to read real-life stories, particularly those that relate to their own experiences and many are widely available. Real life stories and testimonials about real life problems and solutions provide a means of "rehearsing" events that may take place later in a student's life. By rehearsing their attitudes and solutions now, they increase the chances of their surviving and even mastering these potential future problems themselves.

Stories should have some type of a redeeming motive or **moral value** imbedded since we all need positive role models upon which to build and choose our way in life. This is even more relevant for children in their early formative years and with teens who are struggling with popularity and romantic pressures.

Little Melvin always enjoyed Sunday School at Union Chapel Church. We sang, learned Bible verses, listened to exciting stories, and were mesmerized by missionary stories, all the while picking up valuable social skills along the way. (1963)

Reading our World: Where is the Love?

Teachers have under their mantle of responsibility the enormous challenge of selecting literature that is age and level appropriate. But also, this responsibility is a wonderful one in that affectives can so easily be incorporated into our students as they are read stirring literature that meets academic requirements but also meets Doxographic requirements with love being number one. Love? How can love possibly be manifested into American school curriculum? Is it possible to leave out humanity's most powerful emotion while working with over 48,000,000 children each day? For most school systems, apparently so.

"Without love I am nothing," wrote the Apostle Paul. What a tremendous thought! Parents show love for their children. Grandparents show love for these same children. So why can't teachers also show love for their students? Of course they can and do! Besides the parents, teachers spend more time with children than anyone else. Have you ever had a student accidentally refer to you as "Mama or Dad?" No higher compliment could be given! But have you ever thought of telling them that you loved them? <u>Affective learning will outpace objective learning every time</u>! Using love in our teaching would cause increased self-esteem and quality of work. Including the word, "love" in our teacher vocabulary is essential for the best results from our students.

For example, on Fridays teachers often review the week and thank the students for their hard work as well as give gentle prods to those who have slacked off. This would be an ideal time to say noticeably and publicly to them, "Students I want to tell you that **I love you** just like your parents and grandparents love you also. This is why I care so much about your grades in this class." If you really mean it and use the proper tone of voice, students appreciate it and feel good about themselves.

Of course in middle school and high school the proper setting for saying this has to be correct but it can be accomplished. This author used a simple, direct approach to Mexican-American high school students, letting them know that I cared about them all, whether top students or low achievers, including telling them publicly, usually on Fridays. Never once in my entire career have I seen even one that was not thoroughly appreciative of this approach. One may maintain a professional distance while letting constituents know that love is a part of the class just as well as learning the facts for the test. No higher virtue can be found, no greater value, no more outstanding motivational tool than saying, "I love you."

Secondary teachers, in particular, sometimes see the effects of horrible things happening in American high schools— suicides, pre-marital sex, teen pregnancy, gang violence, hazing, just to mention a few. But teachers also enjoy the privilege of observing the loveliness that comes with innocence and the beauty of youth. Hopefully, all students want to be a success at some point in their life. High school teachers have the unique privilege of helping teens before horrible things happen in their young life. Their students are preparing to step out into the world of real problems and real, wonderful challenges, all opportunities for success.

"Make every problem an opportunity"

This was one of the sayings the author had his high school classes to memorize. Mottos are right-brain activities and very easy to recall years later.

High school students are no different from elementary students in their need for love and affection, only the format changes. Sometimes these students express themselves so differently and often harshly that teachers feel repulsed and tend to withdraw away from any close associations. Sadly, this is very necessary sometimes, but if at all possible, affectives should be worked into the curriculum as much as possible, just the same as elementary. I recall **Wayne Miller**, a well respected math teacher from Donna High School (Donna, Texas), who always had a new "Thought for the Day" placed in bold letters across the front board. He awarded extra credit at the end of the week if a student memorized it. The sayings were attractive and very uplifting. Good job! Very powerful example of Doxography.

Guest Speakers: The Power of Real World Learning

In human nature we naturally lose interest in someone that we see and hear each day such as a teacher. Guest speakers offer variety with increased interest in the class on most any topic, whether the speaker is young or old, smart or not. Guest speakers often provide a springboard upon which the teacher can solicit and gather large amounts of fabulous input from student reaction once the guest speaker has gone. The age of field trips has all but disappeared, so guest speakers are a great substitute for them. If classes cannot go out of the building, at least interesting people from the community can still come in the building, right to your students.

This author has invited Jewish rabbis to talk about Jewish culture, missionaries from Africa to report about their life and experiences, and even Arab university students have come into classes to offer their perspectives on controversial topics such as the War in Iraq and the future of oil in Western economies. Their appearances brought instant reactions from students, causing many to ask really thoughtful questions. As a result, writing assignments are given on the same topics with greatly improved interest and enthusiasm.

Once I even invited the grandfather of one of my students who was visiting from Germany. Since we were studying *The Diary of Anne Frank*, this served as a fabulous Doxographic tool. His answers (in German) were blunt and at first a bit disconcerting, but believe me, none of us has ever forgotten his eye-witness testimony of bombing raids on London as a Luftwaffe pilot. Very interesting indeed!

State Assessments and Lack of Linear Writing in Class

While we note a statistical rise in some state scores from 2004 such as North Carolina and Texas, these states are teaching specific test-related formula and not necessarily the complete state mandated curriculum; unless one argues that the state assessment test has now become the curriculum! Unfortunately this is the reality in many schools across the land. Republican control of Congress, beginning in 2000, brought greater accountability and standards from the Department of Education. Some states complained that the standards for passing state tests were simply too high, resulting in changes in formula for some low-scoring states. Whereas the overall goal of excellence in education is noble, the "*No Child Left Behind Act*" of 2002 seems to push for the near impossible. The number of schools that have been caught cheating on state administration of skills tests has skyrocketed since the Act became law. What will result in all this? With more positive results being announced again in 2005, perhaps the tide is turning and the Republicans are correct in demanding higher standards.

Too often teachers simply have not the time and energy to teach all the components of state curriculum and to satisfy the demand for higher test scores upon penalty from administration.

State assessments are **test-specific** and highly **formula driven**. Students are drilled until they learn the formula; hence, they score well in a small spectrum of learning. Sadly, the real facts indicate that America's students spend less time in meaningful writing and overall composition processes than at lunch! Certainly exceptions to this exist in specialized schools such as magnet schools perhaps, but the vast majority of America's students are busy **copying from books**, downloading information from the Internet, copying the teacher's words on the board, or spending their writing time annotating in short, concise abbreviations, which in any sense should not be considered effective production of writing. However, students who spend a consistent number of minutes each day, not every now and then, with a consistent writing program, will doubtlessly improve their production beyond normal expectations or state requirements. Our goal should be to produce **thinking students** who can produce effective writing, not necessarily affective writing. Nonetheless, affective elements should come out naturally in every product that a student makes, especially those involving writing. **Doxography prohibits teaching of specific religious dogma in a public classroom**. However, teachers are definitely encouraged to actively seek spiritual aspects of life that are positive upon which they can build effective lessons since research overwhelmingly confirms that spirituality (the affective) is very much a part of the human experience, particularly in learning. Much in modern society is meant to denigrate, deny or destroy historically-held values. Doxographic methods can improve mental health and stability of both students and teachers. Results will show a marked increase in scores in all areas of the curriculum and especially in reading and writing.

America's Brain Drain

If an enemy wanted to take over a wonderful country, one way would be to allow the students to become products of 12 year of entertainment with ineffective learning as a result. All the while this rich country would simply substitute their own for professionals and scientists from other lands since we can afford them and actually have to pay them far less than our own American graduates anyway. Sound familiar? It should because each year since 1999, math and reading scores for 17 year olds have shown no improvement whatsoever. On the other hand, math and reading scores for 9-13 year olds have steadily improved from 1973-2004 (NAEP, 2005).

The United States has steadily declined in math and science scores while hiring substantially more foreign professionals to manage our aero-defense industry, medicine, NASA, computer chip engineering, and even sensitive jobs such as in the atomic energy field. Although the USA still leads the world in numbers of Nobel prizes in science, yet this alarming trend of hiring professionals to man America's brain trust in industry continues unabated in 2005.

Companies complain that American graduates are lazy and unskilled. Their English language skills are minimal with very little imagination or promise at developing these skills. The result? We look to India to supply us with engineers, Germany and Britain for scientists, and Philippines for teachers and physicians. All the while, one million Mexicans are crossing the southern border each year to man the "nuts and bolts" of America's booming economy (CNN, June, 2005).

What does this scenario tell us about our public schools? While the private schools are still churning out highly skilled and motivated graduates, our public schools are not. Are we simply another Roman Empire which fell from within? Rome was so rich that their sons had no need to fill the labor force; they simply had to manage the vast wealth pouring in from the Empire. In other words, if American public schools, which are in the vast majority, educating 48,000,000, fail to meet the challenge of 21st century economics and changes that are inherently coming in all fields of manufacturing and industry, then we are most surely going to repeat the mistakes of the Romans. Have we become a "managing society" instead of a "thinking society?" *"Et tu brute?"*

Profile of America's Students and Teachers

Almost **20% of this country's population sits** in America's public schools and nearly 50% of American adults are enrolled in some form of adult education/university, with a grand total of all aged students at 80 million. Enrollment of public children stands at <u>48 million students</u> compared with 52 million projected by 2010. The USA has <u>94,000 public schools,</u> and <u>18,000 school districts</u> (NAEP). California enrolls 6,500,000 while Texas is second with 4,300,000. Ohio and Pennsylvania are about tied with 2,200,000 each. The state with the lowest enrollment is Wyoming with 93,000. The US education budget is now about **$275,000,000,000** which reflects about $6,000 spent on each student in public schools, the most per capita of any country in the entire world. Elementary enrollment is growing more rapidly than secondary (US Dept of Education, 2002).

USA taxpayers spend about $6000 on each student per annum, more than any other country.

The number of teachers, currently at 4 million, is growing faster than pupil enrollment. The estimated annual salary of teachers is **$46,000 per annum** (2004), pitifully under the average for all other major professionals.

Learning Styles Challenge

Students learn best when they are challenged both cognitively and selectively according to their own learning styles and learning abilities. Is learning the state capitals purposeful? Yes. Is learning the multiplication tables purposeful? Again, yes. So what is different about teaching with the principles of Doxography? Lots! For example, in a classroom where the teacher is trained in Doxography, the philosophy of the teacher is not the same as that of a regular liberal education philosophy, the one that has operated America's schools for the last 75 years. **Doxographic teachers look beyond the rote facts** and figures and INTO the learning from the vantage point of their learners, not from experts far removed from classroom realities. Teachers become learners with the students instead of TO the students. Life is exciting and so is learning! These are the basic tenets that set apart Doxography trained teachers. Furthermore, the students change in their view of school life in general. No longer is school just a place to eat lunch, socialize, have sports fun and endure the classes; it is completely reversed. Students learn as they attend class, eat lunch, socialize, and share good times with friends through talking, sports, and by just being with other young people.

Twenty first century children are more sophisticated learners than previous generations, not to mention more demanding. "That's so five minutes ago" has come into American jargon amongst teens. It accurately reflects modern thinking regarding time and values. Computers, video games, virtual reality everything practically, instant everything, modems, satellite technology, space tourism, cloning of humans just around the corner and cell phones are the norm for this generation. VCR's and even regular dimension television are quickly becoming archaic memories of this new century.

School philosophy must adapt to this changing, challenging new world of the 21st century. Have you adapted in your teaching?

What changed? The entire order of their thinking about school is reversed in this model. So how is this "magic formula" applied? **Attitude adjustment** is the key to Student Cycle Reversal, both the attitude of the school, including the teacher, and the attitude of the student. One element of the Cycle cannot work without a complete adjustment from all elements. Not all students or teachers will accept this model perhaps. All we need is the majority. It can be accomplished! **99% of all school academics involve psychology.** Motivating humans to perform something not desired is difficult but certainly not impossible. It is accomplished via psychology. Motivation is paramount to success with this model. Grades are only a marginal motivating factor for most students. They need more! A million ways exist to motivate students. Here are a few hints.

STRATEGIES FOR MOTIVATING STUDENTS

✓ Look around and find out what other successful teachers are doing.

✓ Check the Internet for ideas.

✓ Attend workshops and actually APPLY what was learned. Be innovative!

✓ Experiment. Throw out ideas/methods that are not working.

✓ Talk to your own parents. They have great experience motivating children. Since you are a teacher, then you must have turned out alright! Ask for their advice. After all, the basics to successfully raising children are the same for both parents and teachers; only the fancy names are added to school life to give the professional more credibility with the public.

Unfortunately, one reality in American society is that teachers are still viewed as simply glorified baby-sitters. If this sounds unbelievable, look at what happened in Colorado in 2002 when 47 districts went to 4-day weeks. Scores improved, behavior improved, and parents hated it! Why? Because their highly paid baby sitters were not available on Fridays! Parents need to "get with the program" and join in our efforts to improve education in every way possible so that teachers can help create real problem solvers for the future, not dependent "question askers" and the "what I can get out of" state of mind that exists with many students. (See next paragraph for more on 4 day school week.)

✓ Put yourself in the shoes of the students. How are they thinking? Would you consider your approach as "boring" or interesting if you were in their place?

✓ Incorporate all workable strategies of Doxography. (contained elsewhere in this book.)

Young Ashley Lauren Harris experiences the assurance of prayer. Respect for authority begins at an early age and pays significant dividends in the future for our schools and community.

Modern Trends: The Four Day School Week Model:

Let us examine further that model of shortened school weeks. The Boston Globe on December 27, 2002 reported that in Colorado, 47 school districts went to the 4-day school week, and when final performance tallies were in, no substantial difference was noted between 5 and 4-day schools. This is quite significant! That means that the 4-day week students actually had to outperform the 5-dayers since they attend only four days, although with increased hours slightly. End result? Both scored the same. Why? Psychology! Students are psyched to buy into the idea that their help is needed. They are part of the solution, not part of the "problem," so typical in America's general school population.

Perhaps not all students buy into this concept, but those who are reluctant are prodded into it by their peers. Great! Students see an immediate reward for hard work, not just "in the future when you graduate" type of idea. This is only one example of how an entire school system can be turned around by using psychology effectively. Another testimony comes from Midland, Louisiana, where principal Clyde Briley contends that the 4-day week is not always about money. He reports that student morale and behavior have improved as well as the all-important grade point averages have risen. The Custer District in South Dakota echoes nearly the same results from 2002 school year.

The Noise Factor in Effective Teaching

Can learning take place in a quiet classroom? Of course, the answer is yes, but one must ponder, "to what degree?" Since when did *noise = learning*? This is not to be found in any text on pedagogy. Positive noise and interaction are effective components of the productive classroom but we challenge the current thinking that much noise and activities both in and out of the classroom have to take place for cognition and achievement. Somehow learning took a back seat to activities in the form of keeping children busy because **busy = learning** in the minds of many administrators. For example, when one really wants to be heard, whispering is more effective than yelling. When kids are boisterous and will not pay attention, simply start whispering so they cannot quite hear what is being said. The class becomes so intimidated that they have to get quiet in order to hear what is being said. Quiet can be just as effective to true learning as a cacophony of noisy activities. <u>Humans can become so accustomed to noise that lack of it becomes uncomfortable.</u>

One may inquire, "Why the concern over noise and activities?" Noise and activities have a place in modern education, no doubt. But the human brain appears to process information more efficiently when **small bits of data are given**. Then the brain applies it, rests, and then resumes the learning mode to capture more data (lesson) from the teacher or medium of instruction. In other words, *a cycle of learning* exists that needs to be addressed in effective teaching. After all, when teaching effectively, large doses of information are being utilized. If the information is new, it must be processed in a place in the brain that is available. Therefore, gentle techniques must be used to ensure that the information is not only going into the brain via normal receptacles, eyes and ears, but also into the soft lobes of the brain for recovery and/or utilization at some later time, usually as a test.

Tito Diaz, (Santa Claus) and his big brother, Elton, know how to make lots of noise, oh yes. But they also spend their time on quiet activities such as board games, DVDs, and computers. (2004)

So how does noise affect learning? As far as language is concerned, noise is paramount to success if used correctly. **Language must be heard.** Movies, cassettes, CD's, lectures, repetitions, songs, poems, etc., must all be woven into the school day for effective second language acquisition. However, the Doxographic teacher uses other skills related to noise and activities that are more useful and account for near 100% retention. Here is a practical list:

A PRACTICAL LIST OF PHYSICAL CHANGES IN CLASSROOM MANAGEMENT

1. Use a microphone, preferably one that is attached to the shirt so that the volume is very low.

A mechanical device such as a microphone has advantages over the normal voice in that it rounds out the voice, mellows, and of course, amplifies to give clear, audible signals for vocabulary, directions, and general instruction techniques. Of course, some of these features will depend upon the clarity of the signal and the amplifier used. Also, using a slight amplification keeps the voice fresh and vigorous throughout a long, grueling day of ESL in which usually a great deal of speaking has to occur. But perhaps the most exciting use for a microphone in a language class is that the teacher can whisper and still be heard. Think of the possibilities for intonation as well as something as basic as motivation.

2. Activities: While no practical way exists to keep activities from becoming noisy when working with either kids or adults, still we can lower noise levels by using smaller groups of 2 or 3 instead of "all the boys on this side and all the girls on the other." Activities need not be too sophisticated to be fun and effective. Sometimes the fewer props the better, but keep in mind that in the language classes, physical objects or pictures of the same objects, are definitely needed for comprehension and visual stimulation.

3. Internet: Use it often! When discussing the Water Cycle in 3rd grade bilingual class, pull it up on the Internet and flash the pictures on a multi-media projector. This makes the topic much more interesting that merely seeing the pictures on a page in a textbook, plus the teacher has the added advantage of having tons of raw, up-to-date information at their fingertips.

4. Windows: Use of natural sunlight lowers anxiety and fosters better behavior.

5. Color: White walls are a classical mistake, raising anxiety levels, signifying a sterile environment. If the principal will not allow painting, simply bring wall coverings from home or ask your students to bring art work from home. Also, the class can cover portions of the wall in class projects, etc.

6. Lighting: Use incandescent lighting as much as possible. Fluorescent lighting is potentially harmful to the eyes over extended periods and has been proven an additional visual handicap for those with dyslexia. If the school cannot provide them, simply bring them from home, or ask parents to donate lamps and place them in each corner of the room. Anxiety levels are lowered and student behavior calms.

7. The News Anchor Format. TV is a vital part of most kid's life in America. If a Smart Board is available, use it during lessons. While the teacher is talking about something, flash a picture of it up on the board behind you for emphasis. This is the technique used in news broadcasting and is quite effective. This author uses this technique everyday. If teaching syllogisms in Rhetoric, I go over to the computer console at my desk, find Aristotle, and flash his face on the screen. Once while the President was taking office, I switched on CNN and we watched it live on the wide screen. We have the technology. Let's use it.

8. Journals In The Journal Book, Fulwiler (1987), explains "Journals are useful tools for both students and teachers. They help students prepare for class discussion, prepare for exams, understand reading assignments, and to write papers." Many products are available to make the experience of journal writing fun and rewarding. Some are reasonably priced as well such as <u>Dialogue Journal Writing for Non-native English Speakers: a Handbook for Teachers</u>, (1990) edited by Peyton and Reed. Many different types of journals are in vogue from personal diaries, classroom logs, homework logs, professional work log, etc. The basic benefit seen in journal writing is simple: people tend to retain information when it is organized in one's own words and in the style of organization that best fits that person. What better way to realize this than in a journal format. Grumbacher, 1987, found that students who connected their learning with ideas in their journals, were better at problem solving at the college level.

"The value of journal writing...cannot be overemphasized."
Sommer, 1989, 115

So what is this "connection" theory between journal writing and classroom performance? It is quite simple. Writing carries the weight of organization and a certain sense of finality, of authority. For example, in the movie, "The Ten Commandments" with Charlton Heston, when the Pharaoh would say something important, he would demand, **"Let it be written; let it be done!"** Speaking is one thing; writing is quite another. Which one is the most powerful? This is a difficult question but Dr. Clark von Heller would obviously say writing since he penned the phrase, *"One who speaks, speaks to one's self; but one who writes, speaks to the world."*

Writing down thoughts can serve as a splendid tool for remembering things and is significant for learning in particular because this allows the words of the teacher (or source) to be taken down, changed into "personal lingo" and organized on paper to suit the needs of the learner, uniquely and precisely, regardless of form and format. *This facilitates retention and processing of data.* Imagine how it would be if teachers allowed no notes taken during a class? Moreover, the best part of journal or note taking is that this collection of original text is a creation of the logos! Regardless of appearance, it has value to the student as a body of text with meaning, true meaning: ownership, validity, self-esteem, and indeed Doxography!

<u>6,000+ Global Languages!</u> The Summer Institute of Linguistics (SIL) in Dallas, Texas, calculates the number of human languages, with speakers of at least 200 people, at 6,000+ worldwide and more than 150 linguistic groups in the USA (Summer Institute of Linguistics, Dallas, 2003).

Language holds a special place in our world for many reasons, the most important probably being that language is a personal expression of who a person really is and society as a whole. Often we hear, "the Spanish people" in referring to all people from Latin America when actually they are Spanish only in language, (and some by descent), but certainly not Spanish politically or culturally. Another example we hear along the Mexico-Texas border is, "Do you have any English money?" Of course we are talking about US currency, not British Pound Sterling! A spot of tea anyone?

The author "hangs around" during a break while touring English classes at Istanbul University in the summer of 2002.

Spoken vs. Written Language

Two basic formats exist for language—spoken and written. Written language involves symbols but no sound, hence pronunciation difficulties are removed. This tends to make written language more universal than oral language. After all, when sounds are transcribed into symbols, they become standardized, thus more readily memorized and manipulated on the page. This static quality of morphemic structure causes language learners who are literate, much more ease in transferring skills from L1 to L2.

To illustrate this I must turn to an example in my career. Once I was hired to teach an ESL class of international students. We had seven languages and cultures represented. Also, we had four different distinct levels of literacy, including one student who was non-literate! So I relied on Layered Learning to meet the needs of this very multi-leveled class. I will never forget the two Chinese sisters who were diagnosed at the highest level due to their extensive education in English. They were medical doctors. One was an acupuncturist and the other a traditional practitioner. Their written language was superb with equally lovely syntax, but their oral language was abysmal, totally incomprehensible. I used their prowess in written English to serve as a bridge to their oral language production. This underscores the point of the previous paragraph: students may be well versed in the morphemic structure of the language and with that ability, they can more easily segway their first language writing into second language writing.

Before leaving the two Chinese sisters, both of whom were named "Mei" by the way, I would like to share an interesting, true story. At the beginning of each class I would try to come up with some interesting, well-known event so that all levels of students could understand the intent if not the content. So I chose JFK's famous phrases, "Ask not what your country can do for you..." I passed out a copy of the entire speech, not just the phrase, to each student. The following class, as I was beginning a new opening segment, Mei #1's hand flew up. "Hey teacher, do you want homework?" I made out what she was trying to say. Since I never assigned homework, I thought she was mistaken. Realizing that they were adamant about some "homework" I motioned for the two Mei's to come forward. Perfunctorily, each slowly walked to the front of the class, handed me a copy of JFK's speech, and then proceeded to say the ENTIRE SPEECH verbatim in their perfectly appalling English. I barely managed to follow the words on the paper.

What a surprise! I learned a valuable cultural lesson that night. Oriental students are required to memorize large quantities of text each day. I had no idea! To a roaring applause, we heartily congratulated the two Mei sisters as they just as calmly, picked up their copies of the speech from my hand, and returned to their seats with shy grins in obvious appreciation. Oh what Doxography that night!

So which comes first? Oral or written ability? Obviously the **first skill in language is listening**, so oral ability soon follows. The home situation is essential in nurturing the first language. The language of the home is what unifies, clarifies, and organizes who and just what that home is all about.

Rhetoric: The Art of Speaking

Oral language enjoys a freedom and flexibility that cannot be matched by written language. From ancient Greece the art of speaking (rhetoric) grew to have enormous power in the field of public policy and politics, even becoming such an elevated art form that all schoolboys with high aptitude were expected to master the art of rhetoric. This was a result of the influence of another art, the art of drama. Aeschylus, Aristophanes, and of course Sophocles, raised the art of dramatic speaking so highly that it carried over into the fields of politics and science as well. Students still study the oratory of Antiphon and Leocrates, and from Rome the famous speeches of Seneca and Cicero.

The enormous quantity of linguistic devices, inflection patterns and nuances, are simply infinite. The use of puns, double entendres, parallelism, alliteration, repetition, internal rhyme, end rhyme and iambic pentameter are invaluable tools in poetry and drama, not to mention stand-up comics and television shows.

Public speakers learn to modify their voices for stress and to get certain points of view across. Politicians such as **Churchill and Reagan** were highly effective in manipulating language and bravado in the quest for political and public goals. Children strive for no less albeit in a much simpler format. For example, a baby learns quickly that in Mexican culture when Mom says, "No," a sincere form of "ándale, ándale" can usually cause her to change her mind. But it must be said with a very pathetic, whimper. This single term for "please" has changed the minds of many Hispanic moms through the years, no doubt.

Language Changes With Currents of Social Usage

Semantics, regardless of correct syntax, is the real "mover and shaker" of a language. It matters not how correctly language syntax is being taught in a writing class, it only matters what type of language the "boys" or "homies" are saying down at the hangout and local pub. That would be classified as the "real semantics" of the language, regardless of what is being placed in the textbooks. Social use of language determines not only the shape and structure of the language in the long run, but it also determines which words are going to endure longer in the language and which ones are on the way out.

To illustrate, one need only look at the preponderance of past perfect verbs in English. We often hear on TV or on the street, **"He done it** because **I seen him** clear as day," or **"She**

come by here yesterday on her way to work as she **sung** that new song I like." Of course, the underlined verbs are used incorrectly in that they should all be simple past (did, saw, came, sang). These incorrect patterns are being repeated on television and in popular music so much that in a few years, textbooks will have to mirror this trend and consider the past perfect as being "correct," much to the dismay of grammarians.

Email Dictionary and Instant Messaging

2G4U	Too Good For You
AFAIK	As Far As I Know
AKA	Also Known As
ASAP	As soon as possible
BBIAF	Be Back in a Few
BCNU	Be Seein' You
BBL	Be Back Later

Changes in language are unavoidable. Societies must adapt to changes in language and look upon them as wholesome, a natural evolution of human interlocution. In a day when bilingual families are often frustrated about their political and social identity, we should be careful to create a positive linguistic setting where the cultural values of native language as well as the dominant national language, are carefully spelled out to children. All languages are beautiful and have function in their own right. **No language is superior to another**. All convey meaning and culture. Language identifies, clarifies and defines a nation, a group, a society, a community, and a person.

What About That Accent?

"Are you from Geoooorgia, Maaham?"Do you speak with an accent? Everyone does. The whole concept of accent is a complex matter of preference and audible discernment by the listener. In other words, the detection of an accent can identify us by social position, geography and often by national origin. Accent is an intrinsic part of pronunciation. One will speak as spoken to during formative years of language development, usually from birth to two years. Have you ever had someone comment on where you were from by the use of a particular word or expression?

Once this author had a college professor correctly guess that I was from eastern North Carolina because of the way I used one word, "won't." Amazingly enough, I was not aware that we had always used it in the place of "wasn't" as in **"I won't available" which means "I wasn't available."** He was correct and I quickly changed my grammar! East Londoners and New Englanders are well known for the clipped form of the letter /r/--the "ca" for "car" for example. Of course, Cockney speakers from East London are more incipiently known for their amusing and confusing linguistic patterns that amaze and vex outsiders and tourists. They intentionally play with the language, saying, "apples and pears" instead of "stairs" since it rhymes, plus a host of other must-be-learned phrases and pronunciations before venturing into their linguistic playground.

Jennifer Jenkins (2000), in her book, <u>Phonology of English As a Foreign Language</u>, (Oxford University Press), reports that "RP" (Received Pronunciation) accent is declining both in numbers of speakers and BBC correspondents and DJ's, while "Estuary English" is increasing in numbers, including Cockney pronunciation. All languages and accents are useful and beautiful in their own right and interpretation. Language helps to identify, clarify and define a nation, group, society, community, and a person. How does it define you?

Chapter 2 Questions

1. How does "featureship" work?

2. How does information and inspiration offset and compliment each other?

3. When asked to compile a list of what they write the most, usually students tend to list great amounts of information type of writing. How does this list differ from "inspiration" type of writing?

4. What are the "four pillars of society" according to Doxography?

5. Can music influence learning? Why or why not?

6. What percentage of the entire USA population is enrolled in school?

7. How many millions of students are enrolled in public and private K-12 schools?

8. Discuss the trend of shortening the school day, such as the four day school week in Colorado. Is this a positive trend? Why or why not?

9. What is wrong with the popular pedagogical notion that "noise = learning?"

10. List five of the most effective classroom management modifications that are very practical and can result in dramatic changes for student behavior and learning?

11. List three differences between oral and written language.

12. How does accent define a person?

13. How many languages and dialects are spoken on earth?

These teachers, along with Newspapers in Education Coordinator from the Brownsville Herald, Sandy McGehee (first row, last on right), met at the Annual ESL Institute with Dr. Clark and Audrey in 2002.

Θ Chapter 3
MUTILINGUALS USING THE WORD, THE LOGOS

A few examples of bilingual societies are in Uruguay (Spanish/Guaraní), Canada (French/English), Belgium (French/German), and USA Southwest (English/Spanish). Societies and governments have many different ways dealing with multiple cultures within the same geographic location. Israel, in 1948, decided to choose Hebrew, an ancient classical language, to be revived and selected as the official tongue although most educated citizens mostly spoke Yiddish, German, and many Eastern European languages. Greece had a similar linguistic situation when in 1928 they found themselves free of foreign domination for the first time in centuries. **What language should they speak?** The language of the former rulers, the Ottoman Turks? Or, should they try to return to the language of their original national identity, Greek? They chose Greek but had to teach a whole new generation their new (but actually old) language. With slight modifications, it worked and now Greeks are back to speaking the language of Alexander the Great and Socrates just as Israel also returned to their historical heritage language, Hebrew.

Americans: Hables el ingles?

What about Americans? English is still the "lingua franca" of the country but due to the massive influence of Spanish-speakers from Mexico, 27 states have proclaimed by law, the official language of these states is English. Seems a bit absurd since most, especially immigrants, want to learn English, but these states realized that unless placed into the legal code, Hispanics could demand Spanish language on government applications, similar to Canada, and the English speaking majority simply have no desire for their model. On a federal level, however, the US Congress still refuses to get drawn into the "official" language debate, allowing rather each state to exercise their linguistic freedom. The whole argument may seem rather moot anyway since the original Continental Congress indeed decided formally to use English as the nation's official language at the inception of the country although German was extremely popular at the time. In the 1700's, Spanish was unheard of in colonial times for all intents and purposes.

So the problem arises, how can we teach the minorities the dominant language of the country? Mexico has this same dilemma. They have over 200 languages spoken throughout the country but in their schools they only teach one, Spanish, with a slight variation of the tongue of their former colonial masters from Spain. The US has about 150 languages (Summer Institute of Linguistics) but provides bilingual education for minority children in their first language if requested by the parents and the legal qualifications are met as stipulated in the **Bilingual Act of 1988.** Since most foreign legal residents prefer English taught to their children, ESL is the preferred form of Bilingual Education used. Mexican-Americans, on the other hand, are the only true die-hard proponents of Bilingual Education, demanding Spanish as the medium of teaching their children in elementary grades. This demand alone is enough to keep the program well-funded and in the forefront of philosophical pedagogical debate for a long time.

Bilingual Education received its major seal of approval as a result of the court case Lau vs. Nichols in 1974 when Chinese parents in San Francisco sued for the use of Chinese language in public schools. Almost overnight, bilingual education was born and after 31 years and many different methods, fights, and allocations of funds and "programs," we are finally in the most productive time in the history of this new curriculum concept in the USA. (More is covered in chapters 9 and 10).

Teaching second language is a multi-billion dollar business! Professional organizations, TESOL (Teachers of English to Speakers of Other Language, Alexandria, VA) with a membership of over 30,000 members, and IATEFL (International Association of Teachers of English as a Foreign Language), are active in research and innovation in the field of ESL. So why all the fuss about teaching a second language? The reason is because of the vast numbers of second language speakers in the USA, the world's richest country. And if we are truly to teach bilingual students as effectively as possible, practitioners need to examine their philosophy and practices regarding language acquisition in general. That leads us to look at first language acquisition in children.

> No one can truly teach language since it is a natural process
> Von Humbolt, 1973

As it would be totally absurd to teach a baby how to blink an eye, so too it is totally ridiculous to **attempt to teach language**. Language is an innate, natural human ability. It only needs nurturing via modeling and practice. Since we know that language is acquired naturally, therein lays the enormous challenge for the classroom teacher of "English" or "Language Arts" to make the class meaningful to the student. Even to the ESL student who already has a first language (or two), "teaching" of English relegates itself to a meaningless series of tasks unless some thought and attention is given to making the process of second language learning natural and meaningful.

If the student already knows the "WORD" then how can a teacher cause the word to have meaning? They cannot. Years of low scores in English classes are only proving the obvious; we cannot teach students what they already naturally know. Principles of Doxography allow teachers to take a different approach: teachers encourage students to look into the learning, not at the learning. Words are fascinating, even to teens! Magazines and movies are driving forces amongst English-speaking students. <u>Sports and fashion lead the pack with myriads of written and visual texts that teens enjoy.</u> The Internet is young, fast, exciting. Language used is short, concise: a true reflection of English which is itself youthful and fast-paced. These tools can be used to cause teens to "think" about and explore their language. Traditional textbooks are often viewed by students as static, plain, and "so five minutes ago." Popular topics and current events, however, can bring needed excitement into the high school English class. Students can discover how the ads are created. Why are words arranged as they are? Students can imitate and initiate their own. To be able to organize and manipulate the language needed to get the point across is indeed real information power!

Language is the key to a healthy school, regardless of subject areas. Two-thirds of high school students surveyed by a research firm for the National Governor's Association indicated that they would work harder if expectations were higher. They go on to report that high school is boring with mundane and rote tasks designed for low achievers (*New York Times*, Saturday, July 16, 2005). Does this mean that students are capable of much more than high school curricula demand?

Children are language absorbers. They soak up literally every phonetic "image" and visual picture they experience. A filtering process is automatic. Children pick up what they want and let slide what is perceived as peripheral, not wanted, and/or considered unimportant or irrelevant. Perhaps this is the key to it all. That which is considered irrelevant simply will not penetrate the filter that Krashen, 1974, alluded to in his Monitor Hypothesis.

No one knows exactly **how language is acquired** other than by logical observation of a baby mimicking the parents. Perhaps a "natural approach" best anticipates this idea. The four basic language acquisition skills that are generally learned in this order are: listening, speaking, reading, and writing. Reading and writing are not natural skills but are the only skills tested by the state. Listening and speaking are natural.

> Babies learn language by observation, pattern recognition, imitation, and trial and error.

Babies who have strong reinforcement from parents/caregivers, are more likely to learn beginning words earlier and with greater accuracy. Modeling language is the key for babies to learn. Reading to an infant has remarkable rewards towards future literacy. Listening to the voice of mother while being cradled in her arms is simply off the scale for effective learning! The best teacher most of us ever had was our dear old mother.

First Language vs. Second Language Acquisition

One may think that both first and second language must be acquired the same way but that is not the case. First language is acquired naturally while second is "learned" by bits and pieces from several different role models. First language is intuitively acquired from the world around us. Second language is artificially learned within a four walled enclosure called a classroom.

Knowing this, teachers of language need to formulate a careful philosophy in order than the most effective methods, strategies and techniques may be utilized. An entire school district or at least an entire school faculty should decide on this philosophy and carry it out consistently from pre-K through graduation. How first and second language are acquired can be made relatively similar but much thought and practice needs to be invested to make this so. Most districts simply lack the necessary resources for training and compensation to carry out an effective second language program that adequately imitates natural first language acquisition. In other words, Bilingual Education could conceivably "work" if allowed to imitate how we acquire first language which is naturally. Unfortunately, this is not the case in all practical terms with what is being implemented across the country.

The Skills Test Misnomer

According to the New York Times, reading levels for high school students have not progressed statistically since 2000, however, elementary students have progressed substantially for the same period (July 16, 2005). The article makes no mention whether those surveyed were first language learners or second. This makes a huge difference! Second language learners tend to score lower on state tests since they have had less practice in the English language.

Skills that are tested on most standardized tests today are only the two literacy skills, reading and writing, not all four language skills, which are listening, speaking, reading and writing. This is quite unfair. Millions of children are evaluated on language skills that they are developing while simultaneously learning new subject matter in academics such as math and science. This is a monumental task for ESL students. Of course in tests such as TOEFL (Test of English as a Foreign Language), given to hundreds of thousands each year, all four language skills are intensively evaluated which offers a balanced view of language level and skill.

While school districts contend that state assessment tests are "minimum skills" in all areas, not just language tests, the opposite is in fact, true. These tests are more language oriented than anything else. Many math skill items on standardized tests are "word problems." Abilities needed to correctly master word problems are erudite literacy skills coupled with correctly functioning neural and physical receptors, i.e., hand-eye coordination, vision, penmanship (in writing) spelling and grammar rules, just to name a few.

Also, the students must figure out how to survive mental "minefields" such as, "Which of these is <u>not</u> the correct answer?" **Semantic sinkholes** are intentionally placed in the question to test abilities to maneuver through them and often around them, using logic imbedded in the language, which unfortunately, many ESL/LEP (Limited English Proficient) students have not yet developed very well. Processes used in such intense testing situations involve extensive, masterful use of literacy skills, more than any group of academic skills such as math or science. The end result, especially on state mandated tests, is that LEP students consistently fall behind their monolingual peers year-after-year in a traditional Bilingual Education program. A better way to test has to exist somewhere. Are we teaching to take a test? Or, are we teaching information to enable students to succeed in life?

<u>Make Memory the 24 hour Teacher</u>

Foreign students are usually exposed to many hours of tedious memorization back in their home countries. In the USA our traditional pedagogy has frowned upon this as being mindless, non-productive regurgitation of information, too closely associated with formulaic learning. However, in language classes, memorization plays an important role since language requires constant rehearsal for best results. Why not have ESL/EFL students memorize short poems in English and short songs? Although quite a daunting task depending on level of achievement, teachers may be surprised to hear them recounting these later without any prompting at all. Why? The information has been placed into long-term memory via **rhyme and rhythm** and is now an incorporated part of their new language. This is truly a simple yet effective way to get to the heart of language acquisition and is extremely effective. Songs, poems, raps, riddles, all can be incorporated very easily into any weekly lesson plans. (See the lessons at the end of this book for more ideas.)

HAVING FUN WITH ENGLISH RHYME

by Dr. Clark von Heller

If a teacher were a preacher and a preacher were a beed

How would we ever get to heaven or learn how to read?

If a dog were a cat and a cat were a bat

How would we ever get rid of a rat?

If a man were a woman and a woman a piña colada

Who would be there to make a decent enchilada?

If math teachers taught English and English teachers biology

Would we all have to learn to live without ecology?

If boys only wore rings and girls only wore pearls

Would we really know the difference between most boys and girls?

If English is so hard, then why don't we all demand

A language that plays by the rules and finally one we can all understand!

Chapter 3 Questions

1.   List three bilingual societies.

2.   Explain the position of Von Humboldt: "No one can truly teach language."

3.   In your own opinion, what is the difference of "looking into the learning, not at the learning?"

4.   List the four language skills in order of acquisition, according to Krashen:

5.   How does bias find its way into practically all testing instruments for language?

6.   Memory serves as a virtual 24 hour teacher, especially when raps, music, and poems are studied. Give one example from your own learning experience that has stayed in your mind for several years. Why?

7.   How is first language acquired? Second language? Make a chart to distinguish the differences.

8.   Which ethnic group is almost solely responsible for managing and manning the Bilingual debate?

Dr. Clark strikes his classic pose in front of Kensington Palace, the former home of Princess Diana and her sons, William and Harry. (2000)

Θ Chapter 4
GRASPING THE CONCEPT OF LOGOS

The concept of logos begins at birth (or perhaps in the womb) and continues throughout life. Logos is the beginning of language, the essence of logic, the wonderful experience of creation. What could be more perfect for the young, inquiring minds of kids! **Children are natural explorers**, risk-takers, investigators, manipulators—qualities that unfortunately wane with maturity and age. "O time, thou subtle thief of youth" (Shakespeare). Adult second language learners, while usually more motivated than children in learning a second language, are nevertheless more inhibited when it comes to the PRODUCTION OF THE SECOND LANGUAGE. This natural desire to stifle production of oral practice of the new language causes some adult students to hibernate within such safe, controlled methodologies as Audio Lingual or Grammar-Translation. This is unfortunate since the adult learner is proven to learn foreign language quicker and more efficiently than children, although this may came as a surprise to some. For instance, when the word, "democracy" comes up in a lesson, the adult usually will already have the concept, albeit in the first language. The child, on the other hand, will have to grasp both the CONCEPT and the LANGUAGE before the word will have meaning. Essentially this is double-duty. What a wonderful example of how Doxographic teaching principles could be used here to offset this process.

To continue along this vein of thought, with Doxographic techniques, a teacher can plant the seeds of empowerment so that the term, "democracy" would not require a verbal definition as much as a verbal "picture." Pictures and mental images are powerful! They are much more powerful than words alone. The problem is that children know not their "world" and are only now learning their "word" (language). The teacher uses this deficiency to the advantage of the student, not otherwise. Capitalizing on **meaningful learning** or **"featureship"** means relying on more than a textbook but less than memorization of data. This frees the teacher to concentrate on facilitating learning, not dictating it or doling it out in small tidbits. This leads us to global learners.

Speaking is as old and natural as mankind itself.

Global Language Learners

Teachers can give the option of reviewing the entire textbook on the first day of class! While this seems strange, some valuable pedagogical truths are contained in this wild idea. Some students are Global Learners, that is, they need to see the whole picture before they can be comfortable with starting a course of study or perhaps before starting a new unit, etc. American curriculum is intentionally parceled out in small chunks. While the concept may have many positive aspects, it nevertheless can be modified for those that are **Global Learners**. Why is the curriculum chopped into small units of learning? Obviously some historical and literary periods must be studied in terms of periods of time so the unit study idea is certainly justified. But in reality, teaching in small increments is actually for the comfort of the teacher rather than for the benefit of the students. Why are teachers limiting the output and production of language in assignments by mandating, "Students, answer only questions 1-5"?

Why not say, "Only 1-5 are required today but if desired, you are welcome to answer as many as possible." Allow students to GO BEYOND THE LEARNING. Think of the **empowerment** this brings to the Global Learners! Most students are very content with only five questions. However, by always giving a specific number to assignments, inadvertently we sometimes limit students who could accomplish so much more! Think of where this type of academic freedom would take future scientists! Limits are unknown. Challenges are there to be seized upon! One could surmise that many new cures for diseases would be found. Illiteracy would be done away with forever! Just think what could be accomplished! A correlation may actually exist between dividing time slots into small learning units with decreased self-esteem of students. Would the entire book be overwhelming as a first assignment? Of course it would! But those who think in Doxographic terms realize that while it may not be expedient, it might nevertheless be very uplifting and challenging psychologically to the students to let them decide what is too much.

> The teacher should set the minimum but never the maximum that a student can accomplish.

When does intensive language study become too much? Never! In the Doxographic-based language classroom, the students are inundated with language. They are swimming in it when they enter the classroom; they are mesmerized by language when just passing by the door! **Language should be exposed on the walls, the floor, the side of the desks, everywhere.** The LOGOS is that important! Language class is the most important class students will ever have! It goes beyond their "word" and becomes their "world." Once students are comfortable with manipulating reading and writing in their word, they move with agility into their world which in this case is the world of school and schoolwork.

IONAL ESL INSTITUTE

Region One Texas teachers are the best! Several are pictured with Dr. Clark at the ESL Institute on South Padre Island, Texas, in 1998.

Doxography stipulates that the most BASIC responsibility a student has is to learn the WORD and then to apply it to their WORLD. They accomplish this by working hard, entering into a mental contract with themselves, and earning **the best grade (their "paycheck") possible.** The language classroom can serve as the base for all other learning as language shapes logic, sequential thinking, problem-solving and organizing thoughts. Language classes need to prepare students for other academic subjects, offering vocabulary and exercises that the students may encounter in the academic subjects or at least models so that students may become accustomed to the format.

> Social activities, athletic activities, and any other school distractions or additions, are NOT the real reasons to have a school at all. Schools are for learning; everything else must take second place.

Steps to follow when formulating logistics and approaches to use in the language classroom:

A. Assess students orally.

Find out where they are linguistically with the WORD. Devise a simple rating system or use one that is on the market. Have a short interview with each, being careful to vary questions. Be candid, friendly, and then at the end of the interview, indicate on the rating chart their level of oral proficiency. Although literacy skills are important, usually one's ability to use oral language effectively will give a clearer picture of where the student is in overall language development.

B. Grouping.

Four basic groupings that can be very helpful for new language learners are--**ability, age, gender, and interests** (or by vocational interests if high school or adults). The author has tried all of these with ability grouping being the most effective. The key is to be flexible. Change and mix the groups often and adjust lessons to reflect grouping changes. How about classroom arrangement?

Classroom arrangement can help, hinder, or cause unneeded horrors in the language classroom. Often no feasible ways are possible to re-arrange seating due to overcrowding. But if possible, try to be flexible in arranging your groups in changeable, fun shapes so that things are not static. New language learners are willing subjects when it comes to wanting to learn. All you have to provide is the environment, add the fuel and watch what develops. Language has to result. Gattegno's research certainly would show this to be true. (Caleb Gattegno popularized the method known as **"Silent Way."** Colored Cuisenaire rods are used to induce language without much verbal input from the teacher.) Silence brings on apprehension which will eventually bring on oral production of the WORD. Humans are naturally oriented to speak when in the presence of others. A major problem in the ESL classroom is the OVER PRODUCTION BY THE TEACHER. This is when the teacher talks most and the students sit and listen. Have you ever seen a baby talk incessantly for too long? No! Neither should your new language "babies."

If the teacher becomes the FOCUS of the classroom, little language learning will probably result. A rule of thumb is to use 20% teacher talk and **80% student talk**. This phenomenon is referred to as

> "Stage on the Stage or Guide on the Side."

Which one is your style? **The Doxographic teacher is always a Guide**, not a Sage. Whereas the first language learner is dependent on the modeling of the mother, so the second language learner is equally dependent on their coach (teacher). The coach must form a linguistic bond, showing adequate sensitivity to the learner and see the learner through the dilemmas and pitfalls that come with practicing a new language which of course, is a very difficult accomplishment in itself! **A helping hand and a caring heart** will cause a sense of belonging and self-confidence in the learner and only positive growth can result.

Closing the Culture Gap

Being careful to ease into classroom activities will pay rich and rewarding dividends in the future for the second language learner. While working with Mexican learners of English in the Rio Grande Valley of Texas, the author not only learned to appreciate the culture of the people, but also to incorporate their culture into the English classroom. We discussed curanderos, food, clothing styles, the "Chupa cabra" legend along with other more famous ones such as "La Llorona." Sometimes we slipped into Spanish as needed to get a specific idea across. Mexican-Americans have preserved Spanish language significantly as minority language groups are concerned (Aguirre, 1984, 1988).

But what happens when more than one culture are represented in the classroom? The same techniques exposed here work with multi-groupings also. In fact, the multi-cultural classroom is probably a much more effective setting for learning English than a mono-cultural classroom. Why? Because their only means of communicating during the activities is the target language--English.

Students need to feel at ease in the language classroom. They are already at a decided disadvantage, not being on their "home turf." Students may or may not fully understand all the nuances of the activities around them in a Western country. Although your advanced students may be excellent in their production of English, it is a safe bet that they are still somewhat uncomfortable in this English-speaking environment.

The ESL student, by virtue of enrollment, is obviously from a different culture, even if that student is from an English-speaking country. For example, in Wales, Gaelic classes are offered since their ancient native language is still spoken in parts of this English-speaking land. Would this be GSL? In the US, millions learn not English as their first but rather their second language. These people include **Mexican-Americans, Hopis, Navajos, and Puerto Ricans**, among many other Native American language groups. According to the Summer Institute of Linguistics, over 150 languages exist in the USA!

Making Connections and Building Bridges

A distinction can be made between the ESL (English as a Second Language) and EFL (English as a Foreign Language) student; the most obvious being that the ESL student usually has political residence in the country where the ESL class is given. Often however, the local ESL student is nearly as foreign in cultural traits as the EFL student since in the home a "foreign" language is spoken and perhaps they observe rituals and holidays that are native to their heritage but not to the dominant culture of residence. The Pew Hispanic Center reported in July, 2005 that an estimated 11,000,000 illegal Hispanics are currently residing in the USA.

Building bridges to your students can be one of the most important aspects of classroom teaching, especially in a second language class. When becoming acquainted with the cultures of the students, be sure to take into account their home language first. <u>Language is perhaps the second most important identifying aspect of culture other than ethnic origin as identified by obvious physical features</u>. For example, all African Americans are obviously of African descent. Their native languages have long been lost to them because they were acculturated into America by force, but several other minorities continue to maintain some semblance of their native language. The Mexican-Americans are the largest Hispanic group in the USA. Their proximity to Mexico provides a potent link with their culture and language.

While the teacher may not be familiar with each language represented in the classroom, it is quite easy to make an effort to know something about the language and broader culture by involving those students representing the new places. Geography is a great starting place. Where is the language spoken? How many people/countries speak it? Have the students show a written sample of the characters/alphabet. The class will come alive as a new "bridge" is built in Doxographic student success.

This is Exeter College at Oxford University, looking toward the chapel and the front entrance. The author graduated from the English ESL summer program in 2002.

Native Language Connections. Another effective bridge-building activity in the ESL classroom is to ask students to present a poem or song in their native language. Listening to the cadence/rhythm and expressions are enough to fascinate the others and with the applause afterwards, the student is given positive feedback. Also, the language and related culture are validated publicly before the English-speaking teacher. From then on the student will feel more comfortable with the class, if nothing else, because the teacher cared enough to learn something with the student's language, and more importantly, the language of their mother back home. It is all about CONNECTIONS.

Finally, since all cultures are distinct, an overall appreciation of world cultures via anthropology or sociology courses can greatly compliment the ESL curriculum. Success or failure in the ESL classroom could very well rise or fall on this most important component of human society and personal existence—*home language culture.*

The Language Program Must be Goal-Oriented

The term, "challenge" is perhaps overused in education, but in this aspect it needs to be used but with a bit of clarification. Obviously, it is a challenge for the ESL student to be enrolled in the first place. Secondly, the ESL learner is usually overwhelmed from the start with the new language, new culture, new setting, etc. So as far as presenting an academic challenge is concerned, the need in this case, refers to providing a valid curriculum that will make the class interesting, setting the stage for higher order thinking skills, and breaking inefficient teaching paradigms. **ESL/EFL students are distinct** and come with specific needs. They come into the classroom with much more accentuated needs than others. While this in itself poses special challenges, it should not, however, pose insurmountable obstacles to the operation of the classroom. Practitioners need to work from the vantage point of the student, not vice-versa. This is true use of Doxographic teaching principles.

Setting Language Goals in the Classroom

Goals should be:
a. Student-generated by giving options to stimulate responses.
b. Attainable goals within a reasonable time frame.

Caution! Goals and self-directed learning are new concepts for most **foreign students.** They have been taught using the rudimentary tools and with the highest forms of control and rigid repetition. This naturally leads students to think that they cannot make independent decisions nor become independent learners. Ogbu (1978) poses that students whose backgrounds are valued by the school environment and the larger community, will perform at a higher level.

While adults know exactly why they are enrolled in the ESL classroom, younger students are not so sure. For adults, setting goals is not difficult but verbalizing goals may be. The Doxographic-trained educator encourages them to stipulate their goals in first language if possible. If not, a fellow student, perhaps more advanced, with dictionary in hand, can help. Either way, the student must feel in charge of the learning and especially the goal-setting procedure at the beginning of the semester/class. For wealthy students, perhaps their parents are forcing them to learn English in America. For others, enrollment in a language school in London may be used to fine tune English language for future use in the business world, like my friend, Raj, from India. His father sent him to London to improve his English so that he could take eventually run the family hotels in India.

The Cattle Prod

Children know exactly what they want to eat, play, and enjoy, but they have no clue as to what they want to learn. Students certainly have preferences in school as to their favorite teacher or subjects but their right to choose in the academic realm is practically non-existent which is quite natural. **The typical school system has no place in its decision-making structure in which to include them in meaningful ways.** Children are led here, told when to move there, and so on, not only through the school day but through a complete 13 year cycle from preK-12. Ever seen cattle going through the chutes? Ever seen kids changing classes? "Move em up; head em out!"

Doxography encourages that a conscious attempt be made by faculty to encourage goal setting and decision-making from the students themselves. Imagine what an impression this will have on young, previously disenfranchised students! Think of the advancement of the student's real world learning as opposed to making a certain grade which means "memorized today for the grade; forgotten tomorrow."

While goals can be over-rated as simply curriculum or workshop objectives, nevertheless, they are excellent for setting the pace at the beginning of a program; the more individualized, the better. If the individual goals are not too personal, ask the student to **display the goals in the classroom**. While adults can accomplish this easily, kids will have to be given some models of age-appropriate goals. Periodically examine the goals, offer comments, and have students to actually check the goals off when completed. If you wish, put a star or an "A" if appropriate. While the goals must be real and attainable, grades are highly superficial and subjective. Which would a child rather receive? A gold star and a pat on the shoulder with a solid, "Well done, I see great improvement" or for the teacher to walk 20 feet away and place a grade on a cold, plain gradebook?

Language Goals

Children can set goals just as adults. Modeling a few first, the teacher can gently lead them into distinguishing what is appropriate for their grade level. For instance, 3rd graders could choose from: self-improvement, learning how to concentrate better, staying in my seat, obeying the rules, following instruction, etc. At first they may be hesitant, but with consistent up-dating and referring to the goals, even 3rd graders will take ownership of their goals for that year (or other period of time), and the job of the teacher will be easier with everyone winning all round.

Hello Doggie, How are You Today?

Animals communicate; birds and bees communicate. Body language, form and function are the principal means. Scent, certain actions, and maternal instincts, normally are given as dominant factors in this sophisticated web of interlocution within species. Can animals talk? No.

Can different species communicate with each other? It would appear so. A puppy lets its master know when it is happy or sad. Humans recognize these states of emotion because we transfer our own human feelings to those apparently expressed by the animal. Animals often talk in children's literature and even in religious literature! The serpent spoke in the Garden of Eden. In the book of Numbers a **donkey** spoke to Naaham and the prophet was not particularly bothered by it at all. Jesus Christ is recorded as saying, "If the people shout not out to Yahweh in joy, then the stones will!" And in the book of Revelation the "beasts" speak that surround the very throne of God. So in Biblical literature, both animate and inanimate objects were supernaturally capable of speech.

Whether an animal actually suffers from anxiety or a broken heart when a master dies, one can only surmise from the actions displayed. It is however, interesting that a pet can be taught certain commands in different languages. Or, are they simply responding to tone, not the actual words? Many unknowns remain. However, we are certain that language plays an important part in the development of life for the animal kingdom as for **Homo sapiens.** As for the plant kingdom, that is still anyone's guess. Some people talk to their plants with surprising results, so who is to say?

Prehistory? When Was That?

Humans however, are the only specie which possesses the capacity for language with all the functions that are included. Herein lays the enormous evolutionary gap. While it appears that all species have innate, often observable forms of communication, either sounds or actions, the complicated nature of literacy is exclusively human, at least on this planet. Hollywood likes to fantasize about animals having the power of cognition by producing such films as "Planet of the Apes" and Hitchcock's "The Birds." One commercial depicts a man going through a maze when suddenly he is picked up by a gigantic mouse dressed in a white lab coat!

Not only can humans communicate verbally and in writing, but we also have many other methods of communicating, several which are found in other chapters of this book. Interestingly some scientists believe that humans had no ability to speak intelligibly until recently in our evolution. This author finds this notion disturbing and considers that it is based on faulty research or anecdotal evidence at best. Many world-class scientists believe that man has always had fluency in language with literacy developing much later simply because no need for it existed in pre-historical times. Our study here will concentrate on more standard scientific evidence of linguistic evolution through many millions of years. Ever heard the term "prehistory?" Strange term isn't it? How could time in our existence be when we had no history?

Actually "prehistoric times" refers to **"pre-literate" times**—the era in man's existence when no literacy was apparent other than the use of drawings to convey primitive messages via visual images. Logographic images are seen throughout the world in caves and catacombs, the beginnings of writing, long before Sumerian and Egyptian cuneiform writing. So actually one could surmise that art was the mother of literacy. Indeed, a picture indeed is worth a thousand words!

Art: the Mother of Literacy

The contributions made by art are perfectly suited for the philosophy of Doxography, the glory of writing and the joy of language. One can only imagine that ancient mankind must have taken great pride in their primitive attempts at communicating via symbolic representations on cave walls or in carvings on massive petroglyphs. Was it art? Elegant writing and calligraphy are certainly considered art by most. Whether the paintings and carvings of ancient mankind were truly art is certainly a matter of taste, but scientifically speaking, it was language, and if so, then the "art" of language. This can serve as a tremendous boost for modern language students as we ponder the significance of why our ancestors so cautiously and carefully inscribed their names to monuments, often putting their lives at risk. For example, that they dared to sign the **Magna Carta** or the **U.S. Declaration of Independence** placed all the signers at risk. Yet, one can readily see the flair and dignity with which these signatures are placed on these magnificent literary documents of courage and free thought!

So one can see that pre-history actually means "pre-writing." Apparently, humans have always enjoyed some form of the art of writing and thus, the "art of language," whether logographic, petroglyphic, cuneiform, or alphabetic. All these provided visual messages as verbal descriptions and stories, told around countless campfires, painted mental images of distinct events with limitless applications. Thus, art slowly but surely became the "mother of literacy."

By looking back at our linguistic heritage we can take pride in the intellect that our ancestors displayed in their ancient attempts at communicating in writing, the "art of language."

Chapter 4 Questions

1. Compare and contrast the differences between global and non-global learners in a couple of paragraphs.

2. Why should teachers avoid setting a maximum of what students can attempt, i.e., "Students, please answer questions 1-5."

3. How can grouping become an essential component in classroom management and in the delivery of language information?

4. ESL/EFL students naturally feel a bit shy at responding to teacher questions, often due to underlying cultural reasons and assumptions. How can teachers help close the culture gap? Give at least three suggestions.

5. In relation to Doxography, what is the importance of "connections?"

6. Goal setting is important in any classroom and in particular the language classroom. List several simple goals that a 16 year old student from Mexico might set for himself with no prior knowledge of English.

7. What about "prehistory?" What does this actually mean in relation to writing?

8. How can art be considered the "mother of literacy?"

Foreign cultures are becoming increasingly important in the public school classroom. The Arab culture is one of great interest recently. The author dresses the part in a play for college students, with teacher, Helen Hilton, as a typical blonde, blue-eyed "American tourist."

Θ Chapter 5
SCHOOLS OF THOUGHT IN LEARNING LANGUAGE

Bloomfield (1933) and B.F. Skinner (1957) were major contributors to Behaviorism, a system of stimulus/response/reinforcement processes. Is this how language is learned? Many believe so. It is very simple yet enormously complex. Proponents of Behaviorism reject cognition (or thinking) since it cannot be observed. "Monkey see; monkey do" is the old axiom that best describes this type of thinking which dominated first language science for many decades in England and the USA. Noam Chomsky (1965) champion of the movement called Rationalism, however, firmly disagrees with this philosophy and teaches that humankind is uniquely equipped to learn language naturally; so much that he even coined the term, "Language Acquisition Device," an imaginary component in the brain where language acquisition takes place. All humans are capable of language, even highly mentally retarded persons. Any baby, anywhere, can and will speak, **if hearing human speech is possible** with normal hearing. Unfortunately, if a baby cannot hear, fluency will not be possible. This has not been disproved yet. Language comes not by speaking but by LISTENING. That is why a baby will not speak for about a year. Does the baby communicate? Of course! They communicate in very "readable" and comprehensible ways, but can they literally speak their mind? No. McLaughlin (1978) found that children universally learn language in the same order or sequence of manipulating language skills: *listening, speaking, reading, and writing.*

Behaviorists favor texts that emphasize memorization, repetition with immediate and clear rewards, and positive reinforcement for accuracy. It works! Language can be learned very proficiently like this. Teachers can readily be trained in this approach and students will acquire language relatively quickly and efficiently. Although rules are taught, classes are not "rule driven." Students are given mass quantities of language chunks, often in a thematic or functional-notional context, i.e., "At the Post Office" or "At the Bank." Students need to memorize the texts and imitate the teacher or the tape recorder pronunciation. Many excellent benefits result from this approach, unfortunately though, the very bedrock basis for this approach appears to be flawed.

What about language rules? What about the construction of the sentences? "Our enemies are rats." Who are the rats? Literal rats or are they used merely as a symbolic reference to some type of human enemies? One can not know from this construction because, although it is constructed correctly, it still lacks fundamental, clear reason. Therefore, Rationalists contend that Behaviorism lacks in extending far enough in emphasizing rules that are NOT inherent but must be learned. Can they be learned by natural exposure to the language? Yes.

Children will naturally imitate their peers and parents. Furthermore, they will extrapolate beyond the imitation of terms to try to "play" with the language so that new constructions can be formed. These extrapolations go far beyond what they have heard, so how was this accomplished? Chomsky says that this is part of needed proof that language is rule driven and should be taught that way.

Errors and Error Correction

Errors in language acquisition are natural and to be expected. A new language is like a new bike; only by falling a few times can real learning how to ride take place. Teachers should use subtle forms of **reinforcement** to assure new learners that making errors is not a reflection of character, simply of language development, which is a natural, yet intricate process. Neither bad nor good; it is simply a process. Von Humbolt, 1974, says that

Language cannot be taught, only modeled.

How can this be true? Why then does the state spend billions on language education? What impact does this statement have on teachers of ESL? Aren't they paid to teach?

Actually, according to Von Humbolt, <u>teachers should model the language.</u> Their job is to model it correctly while motivating, acting it out, playing with it, forming it, writing it, reading it, reciting it via poetry, singing it, anything else…but never "teaching it!"

Students have no need to learn something that can be naturally acquired anyway! They only need exposure. Have you ever been in a foreign country and someone come up to you just to hear your English? This author has and it is always very complimentary. Keep in mind that the rest of the world wants to speak English. Although some teachers may be reluctant to model the language for reasons of feeling inadequate, this should not be the case at all. Teachers are the only models of English that most ESL students have. Your best or worst rendition of English is the one that the students will imitate the rest of their life. Sobering thought!

<u>Oral language</u> has probably been around since humankind first appeared on the planet. Written language, however, evolved through the centuries as life became more complicated and diverse. Eventually humans decided to depict their existence, their world, into the "word" for the first time. Think of it! What a momentous day that must have been when in one of the thousands of caves in the world, someone picked up a sharp rock or instrument and began to try to depict a form for pictures that could be interpreted as "words" so that pictographs could became hieroglyphics, pictures with meaning that could be read, not just formed as a picture. Eventually the need for alphabets became apparent as societies relied more on commerce between groups. Alphabets gave control over grammatical structures, normalizing the unusual limitlessness of oral language into workable bits that could readily be transcribed on clay tablets and eventually onto papyrus (paper) thanks to the Egyptians.

The Art of Listening

Along with the rise of alphabetic systems, the need for a standard set of grammar rules caused the highly revered schools of the ancient world to turn their attention to the art of writing, rhetoric, mathematics and drama as means for conveying these newly-appreciated sciences that helped explain our wonderful world. One interesting point to consider here is that the art of LISTENING was elevated to new heights, from performances by the ancient dramas of Aeschylus and Sophocles to the Medieval Easter plays. Both illiterate and literate listeners enjoyed and reveled in the "magical" art of language as it unfolded before them on small stages or even on the back of a wagon. Language has always been a magical way to attract attention, whether through singing or acting out life situations called "dramas." Listening was not necessary to be taught or even learned; it simply was extremely needed in order to enjoy the marvelous campfire stories of the old and to revel in the semantics of either sophisticated dramatists as with the ancient Greek theatre, or in crude Medieval settings with traveling shows. The art of listening requires neither preparation nor training. What a wonderful natural gift given to humankind!

How truly amazing it is to see how that the art of listening to the language has somehow been sidetracked in our modern world. For ESL/EFL learners, this art must be revived as a solid pre-requisite to effective language learning, so in summary, should the WORLD be learned before the WORD? Let us examine some possibilities.

The art of listening began to wane in the period leading up to the work of **Shakespeare** (1564-1616) in Elizabethan England for the first time since Classical Greek times. The reason? The newly invented printed press revolutionized how written information could be disseminated quickly and relatively accurately. While the art of listening began to wane, the art of writing began a needed renaissance. A newly literate European citizenry required written scripts as well as listening to satisfy their entertainment, information and curiosity needs. Popular books and scripts needed to be printed in the common vernacular, the "King's English" which only the nobility and upper classes actually read well, not in the classical languages of only a few years before.

Languages Mentioned in the Bible

Historically, references to foreign languages have been documented in ancient holy writings as well as classical secular writings. In the Jewish Tanach (Old Testament) many interesting references to languages are noted. The book of Genesis records that mankind was at one time "all of one speech." In Genesis chapter 11 the writer provides the explanation as to why the earth later had many different languages--as a punishment for building the Tower of Babel. In the book of Numbers a donkey speaks! In the book of Esther a reference is made of many languages in the vast Persian Empire of the day. The Apostle Peter is identified as a follower of Jesus because of **his Galilean accent.** Acts chapter two is perhaps the most powerful reference to language in the Christian New Testament. A "fire" fell upon the followers of Jesus Christ, causing them to speak in **many languages** although they thought they were speaking normally in their own native language! Thus, people who were visiting Jerusalem from all over the Roman Empire were able to understand the message of the followers of Jesus. This occurred on the Feast of Pentecost. Although **Jesus himself, left no writings** of which we are aware at this time, we have one clear instance of him writing in the sand at the impromptu "trial" of the adulterous woman recorded in John chapter 8.

The Rise of Roman Languages.

With the liberalization and democratization of parts of the former Roman Empire, countries such as France, England, Italy, and Spain, began to formulate their own "vulgar" or native language, highly influenced by Latin or course. Individual national languages began to dominate in the place of smaller regional dialects. English, French, Spanish, and Italian slowly began to dominate Europe and then the whole world, all products of ancient Roman Latin. This rise of nationalism caused sweeping political reforms, persecution of minorities, ethnic cleansing, and the forced acceptance of an official state religion, state government and the STATE LANGUAGE. One can observe the clear rise of the importance of language from one of sheer necessity in Stone Age man to one of political advantage in modern history. Yes, the WORLD and the WORD had come of age and the result was not a pleasant one.

Ours is a world of language, a world of constant change and instant global communication going on somewhere on the planet non-stop 24 hours a day, 365 days a year.

Chapter 5 Questions

1. Explain the theoretical position taken by "behaviorists" in language acquisition theory.

2. How does this approach differ from Chomsky's revolutionary ideas?

3. Explain the statement, "Language cannot be taught, only modeled."

4. Why is the art of listening thought to be a lost art in modern society? Give specific examples.

5. Explain the enormous impact that rhetoric played in ancient times both in Greece and Rome. Compare that impact with modern times. Is it as great? Why?

6. EXTRA CREDIT: How was the art of listening utilized in the time of Shakespeare? How would this be contrasted with modern American adults? Draw a chart comparing the art of listening then and now.

Mexican-American youth are very skilled in the listening and speaking components of language. This group of high school students meticulously produced and acted out the play, Julius Caesar. (1986) Donna High School, Donna, Texas

Θ Chapter 6
THE PRODUCT OF LITERACY IS LITERATURE.

"Literature is the logos of the soul; a veritable celebration of the imagination and spirit, and indeed, all that is good in mankind."

(class motto for lit classes, coined by Dr. Clark von Heller, 2001)

Historical Journey Through Literacy and Language

When was literacy accepted as an integral part of human existence? We must look to the Greeks and Romans for the foundation of Western literacy. Nevertheless, due to the tremendous impact of the Bible on modern thought and language, we will also examine the inordinate and massive influence of the Jews and their religion in Western history. Classical Hebrew writers will lead our march through history as the leaders of the ancient world in literacy achievement. The Jewish Bible was written in Hebrew language (the Old Testament), over a period of about 1,000 years. Hebrew people, later known as "Jews," held their religious writings in highest reverence and respect, something virtually unachieved prior to their arrival on the stage of history about 2000 B.C.E. The patriarch Abraham, originally of Ur in Mesopotamia, is the progenitor of Semitic peoples, Arabs and Jews. He led his extended family to Palestine, what is referred to as the "Holy Land."

Eventually the great liberator and receiver of the Law, Moses, codified the law, along with writing or perhaps editing the first five books of the Bible known as the Pentateuch. Without a doubt, never has a book had the influence upon humanity as the Bible. In Jewish worship, throughout the ensuing years, the Bible has been carefully preserved and read in the original Hebrew language, with modern clarifications and additions as needed to keep pace with syntax and semantics. Even today a Jewish boy must publicly read from the Torah in Hebrew language at his **Bar Mitzvah**, often not an easy task.

Are "holy languages" for real? The question itself is perhaps flawed in logic, but a simple answer seems to be, only in the minds of the adherents. Many observant Jews consider Hebrew a holy language. Latin was considered holy for Roman Catholics until the Vatican II Council under Pope John XXIII in the 1960's, when local vernaculars were finally allowed to be used for the liturgy. Some Protestants have gone so far as to claim the KJV version is the closest to a "holy" language for them, but usually these extreme claims are held by only a few small, more conservative groups. As Jews must read the Torah in Hebrew at the services, so Muslims must read the Qur'an only in Arabic, the original language of inscription as given to Mohammed the Prophet. So one can readily see that language has had an enormous impact upon the world of Doxography, the glory of writing, as language developed into literacy and literature down through the relentless march of history.

Egyptians. Even before the ancient Hebrews began compiling their Bible, Egyptian civilization was flourishing and giving the world a plethora of wonders and in its midst, a beautiful, artistic form of language known as cuneiform. With the **Rosetta stone** discovery in 1799, came the key that unlocked the translation of this ancient language with its elegance and dignity. Written in two languages in March, 196 BCE, in the 9th year of Ptolemy V, the stone was inscribed in Greek and Demotic hieroglyphics (www.thebritishmuseum.ac.uk, 2003). Pythagorus and Euclid remain fine examples of amazing mathematical abilities of the Egyptians to this day. Truly the ancient Egyptians allowed the Western world its first glimpse of true "civilization" and perhaps its first true use of Doxography.

Greeks. Along with prolific gains in literature, Greece also blessed the world with improvements on Egyptian concepts of architecture, sculpture, philosophy, and science. The works (dictated or written by them) of, **Plato, Socrates,** and **Aristotle** are widely known in the Western world as the standards for logic, syllogism, philosophy, and scientific inquiry, to this very day. Plato (428-347 BCE) penned The Republic, which is still in print today! The ancient Greeks had a far-reaching love affair with literature. Most Western students are familiar with Homer's Iliad and Odyssey (c.750 BCE) filled with its magical adventures of a man called Odysseus, with his encounters with the gods and their many foils and notorious deeds both for and against citizens of the Greek world. Hesiod (c.700BCE) wrote the Theogony (birth of the gods). The Greeks appreciated literature to a degree that would rival the modern world. They not only produced literature, they refined the art of Rhetoric. Outstanding playwrights include Aeschylus, Aristophanes, Euripides and of course, Sophocles (496-406BCE) who penned Oedipius Rex and Antigone (www.pegasus.cc.ucf.edu). It seems as though the world caught its breath and sighed a welcomed relief at the beautiful literature being produced during the Graeco-Roman period of history.

The Romans. Next came the intrepid Roman poets--Horace, Ovid, and Virgil, each adding to an extensive collection of what we now refer to as "classical Latin literature". Their contributions, along with world-class historians such as Josephus, allowed the emerging body of knowledge of writing to be ensconced into the educated human psyche as never before, and insured that Latin would become the base for many European languages, one of which would virtually rule the academic world, English!

Muslims. With the decline of the Roman Empire came a dearth of learning in Europe while in the Arab world, writing was taking on renewed dimensions and vigor. See the works of Abou-Nacer Mohammed (870-950AD), Al Farabi, and Ibn-Sina (www5.kuniv.edu.kw, 2003) In the Middle or Dark Ages learning became isolated and literacy and literature took a back seat to wars, killing, plagues, and simple existence. The rise of monasticism saved what would otherwise have been the darkest period in the history of literacy and literature. St. Benedict (480-543AD) began the first effective monastic order outside of the British Isles. Although Christian hermits had long before become well known, most having begun as a result of Roman persecution, nevertheless the concept of monasticism was not well established in the Western Church as it was in the Eastern Church.

Why is English so Mixed Up?

Never has a modern language existed which was so popular yet so mixed up in syntax, history, and lexicon. English is a marvelously flexible language in that whether the subject is first or not, still the message is usually understood. For example, "I want with you the mall to go."

A strange construction of course, nevertheless understandable. Amazing! English also contains the largest lexicon, having borrowed thousands of words not only from our historical founding languages: Greek, Latin, Anglo-Saxon and French, but also from just about every popular language around! Students often are puzzled at just how English came to be such a mixed up language. Here is an important clue: the three invasions of mother England.

The Three Invasions of England

Country	Era	Language	Literacy?
ROMANS	1st Century BCE	Latin	Yes
VIKINGS	4th-9th Centuries	Germanic	No
NORMANS	1066	French	Yes

So whilst the Romans possessed literacy in Latin and produced books, etc, the next group, the Germanic speakers from northern Europe, had no literacy neither an alphabet!

Obviously, the Britons agonized, attempting to speak an Anglo-Saxon language while using the Latin alphabet for writing! Bizarre indeed! This would be similar to playing tennis with football rules! Nevertheless, somehow it worked. Then, William of Normandy fought for and won the English throne of King Harold in 1066, resulting in the immediate injection of French-Norman culture and language into England lasting for 300 years. All of sudden, "pig" became "pork," "cow" became "beef, "fowl" became "poultry," and so on. French language contributions to England are immeasurable and permeate English and American speech with enormous regularity every day and in practically every document! Since French is highly based on Latin, then the original Latin alphabet came in handy after all which was left by the Romans, so as Shakespeare says, "All's well that ends well" and this is part of the reason that English is such a mixed up language.

Christianity and the Rise of Doxography and Democracy

St. Benedict wrote the Holy Rule. "It had an even greater importance for western attitudes and values. It stated that the abbot was in complete control of the monastery, but that he had to consult with the entire body of monks on all important matters, take responsibility for his decisions, and observe the regulations set forth in the Rule" (www.ukans.edu, 2003). This is significant because this document set forth rules toward ruling in a democratic institution, something that was not lost upon succeeding generations of French, Britons and Americans who liked the idea of independence and freedom from tyranny. Ah, the power of Doxography marches on!

Although **literacy was limited in the Middle Ages**, toward the end of this era a growing need for written materials was rekindled in Europe due to the influence of massive forces of politics and religion. We will follow this path in our search for Doxography through history. In England, the Venerable Bede (672?-735AD), historian and doctor of the church, published <u>Ecclesiastical History of the English People</u>. "Bede has told us something of his own life and it is practically speaking, all we know. His words, written in 731, near death, not only show a simplicity and piety characteristic of the man, but they throw a light on the composition of the work through which he is best remembered..." (<u>Catholic Encyclopedia</u>, 2003). It took a conqueror of England to give us another notable work in 1086, the <u>Doomsday Book</u>, a nearly perfect account of property, values of good, etc., in the newly conquered realm of **William, Duke of Normandy** (1001-1025AD). Although a strictly scientific work of accounting goods and property, this document (series of documents) have served to show the enormous ability of the written word to be used to wield and keep power in the political world. Doxography not only can reveal pride in one's writing, but it can also wield POWER! For indeed,

> "The pen is mightier than the sword!"
> Nicolaas Beets

The Printing Press Revolution!

The invention of the printing press has been heralded as the most important event in modern history! John Gutenberg (1398-1468) is credited with this amazing accomplishment. The first book ever printed was the Bible. Inexpensive mass printing was now available to a waiting, slowly emerging literate public. Unfortunately, until the Industrial Revolution, European attitude toward education was that it was for only the wealthy and powerful with most power held by the Church and clergy. Thus, the world-changing Industrial Revolution arrived with most of Europe's population unable to read. People who are at a survival level could not afford the luxury of attending the meager church schools. The earth was colder in this period, transportation was unreliable and simply put, education was not a priority. The people of this period may have known their WORLD but they would never know their WORD.

Language and the Influence of the Christian Religion in Europe and America

The Church codified the Creed beginning in the 4th Century and modified slightly thereafter somewhat. This momentous codification of such a central text of language is much more significant than many historians have realized. It impacted literacy in ways that are unimaginable by modern standards, even with all of our means of satellite communications, etc. It was memorized and recited dutifully each Sunday by millions of people, as was much of the Bible. Keep in mind that the vast majority was non-literate. The Creed had to be memorized (as the Catechism). What impact would this have on Europeans who could not read? The initial impact would be **the desire to read.** So is memorization and captivating the interest of children the first step in literacy and language learning? If one were to learn from history, then the answer would have to be, "Yes!" If so, then how can this technique be applied to the ESL/language classroom? Motivating children to learn language is not difficult since we know of course, that language is natural. Teachers can motivate by singing, displaying, storytelling, drawing, and a million other ways! Memorization needs to play an integral role in language learning. After all, memorization is a 24-hour a day teacher. Poems and songs are the best vehicles for imbedding memorization into the minds of language learners, whether children or adults. Memorization need not be taught; it should be gently imbedded. If it is taught, it will be likely forgotten; if it is gently imbedded in the psyche, it will remain for life. "Roses are red, violets are blue…." "To be or not to be, that is the question."

Poetry and songs have a strong right brain* appeal that are unbeatable as tools for language learning. Plus, it is fun to

121

sing. It is fun to recite something by memory. It impresses and immediately demonstrates "education." Now we shall return to the role of religion in literacy and literature. Doxography ascribes to the current **"right brain, left brain"** theories for learning as being well-authenticated by research. Right brain activities last longer in memory and are vital for affective learning as opposed to purely cognitive learning. With this, holistic practices can accent any positive class.

The written Bible was a catalyst for unity of language and mutual preservation of both language and religion. Religion has been the most effective purveyor of language in history without any doubt; government and kings, not even a close second. Since the Roman Catholic Church was headquartered in Rome, following the martyrdom of St. Peter there, it naturally adopted Latin language as the official language for the liturgy. Bishop Jerome was commissioned to translate the Bible from ancient Hebrew and Greek into what was "modern" Latin of the day. The Latin Vulgate was the final product and a masterpiece of literature it has become; the standard by which other translations have been made for centuries!

Religion was not the only entity interested in literacy. Kings and governments to this day know that staying in control often means controlling information. Only the elite were allowed to learn to read in the Middle Ages. A tight control over literacy produced the desired results for the ruling class. The great mass of people could not read and were therefore at the mercy of the literate, for after all, an agreement wasn't fully legal unless signed and witnessed by signatures. Even the humble sign of the cross, the "X" wasn't enough to keep unscrupulous lords from usurping the rights of the humble illiterate.

With the advent of the **Protestant Reformation** in the 1500's the Bible was translated into popular vernaculars of the various regions in Europe, with the German translation by priest-turned Reformer, Martin Luther (1483-1546) and

Oxford professor, John Wycliffe's (1330-1384) English translation, as hallmarks in this explosion of literature! Of course, with the translation of the <u>King James Version</u> in 1611, the world adopted its most popular edition of the Bible in history, in any language! The King James Version of the Holy Bible has been the #1 best selling non-fiction book since its publication in 1611! Religion seems to benefit greatly from literacy and vice-versa.

Fiction vs. Non-fiction

With so many different literary "genres" it seems a bit strange that writing is basically divided into just two large groups: fiction and non-fiction. Modern writers sometimes take a bit of information from each of these groups and form "historical fiction" or "historical science fiction." Confusing? Perhaps, but modern writing has brought a flexibility that was never enjoyed prior to American Independence in 1776. True, book burnings have gone on from time-to-time, but they are exceptions rather than the rule. Poor John Wycliffe, the translator of the Bible first into English, died a decent old age, but alas his bones were later exhumed and burned symbolically by the **Roman Catholic Church**!

Modern times with modern democracies have both teamed to allow a plethora of beautiful, rich, heavily-laden English vernacular and slang that would have been anathema just a few years ago. **Hollywood** added to the tangle of semantic webs and weaving with its intrusion into the world of literature by buying the rights from novelists and/or their heirs such as Hemingway, Faulkner, Melville, and Twain in order to modify their elegant profusion of English words into the big screen version with all the hoopla and color that movies bring. So, we often find ourself asking, "Which was better, the novel or the movie?" In 99% of the cases, the response is usually, "The book, of course." Ah, the charm of the pen is mightier than the color of the screen! Written language wins over spoken language again! So as our march through history comes to a conclusion, let us keep in mind the words of St. Augustine regarding language, the most marvelous gift.

St. Augustine taught that "Grammar reveals rules of language, dialectic shows the logical structure of thought..." (Holmes, <u>Building the Christian Academy</u>, 23). He further argues that facts cannot in themselves, reveal truth but rather they wake up the mind as it strives for an ordered universe and this truth can only be known as the learner relates the truth to God. Order relates to authority and reason. A superior intelligence unites the entire universe. Language is the foundation of all other sciences" (Augustine, <u>On the Teacher</u>).

Chapter 6 Questions

1. Discuss the concept of "holy languages" with several examples.

2. List three literary works or contributions that ancient Greeks made to literature and drama.

3. Who invented the printing press? In what year?

4. What impact does the printing press continue to have?

5. Is the "pen mightier than the sword?" Give a clear example from history.

6. Fiction and non-fiction. Why are these two broad categories still holding strong after millennia of human civilization?

7. Are you in agreement with the statement by St. Augustine, "Language is the foundation of all other sciences?" Support your opinion in a 250 word essay.

Religious leaders provided innovative views of the logos. Interestingly though, some, such as Jesus Christ, never left written records at all. The Buddha, in contrast, wrote vast volumes of philosophy.

Θ Chapter 7
MODERN PERSPECTIVES OF
LANGUAGE ACQUISITION

Study of foreign language in US schools has fluctuated significantly. In 1905, 88% of US students were enrolled in foreign language classes. In 1982 the percentage dropped to 22.6%. In 1992 that number was 38% (Akron Beacon Journal).

Somewhere along the line, foreign language advocates became sidetracked by use of a very structured albeit time-honored traditional approach to teaching language—**Grammar/Translation Approach.** With this approach, second languages are translated on paper in large doses, with much emphasis and detail given to grammatical constructions, much to the omission of practical use of the language. Minimal oral language is used. Students are not expected to be able to carry on a conversation. Thus, classes produce rudimentary readers and writers of the foreign language, but students lack communicative competence. Lessons are highly structured with rigorous analysis of syntax as a key component. Conjugations of verbs take center stage. It is a comfortable approach to language teaching in that expectations are standardized and tests relatively easy to grade. Language is taught to formula and rules. Students memorize either the grammar rules or fail. It is a simple science, one that needs little imagination or attention.

The folly of this approach, however, is that it has no realistic final product which is beneficial. It took the First World War to shake up foreign language education. Soldiers could not communicate with prisoners of war in spite of their years in foreign language education! What had gone wrong? Another approach to teaching languages had to be taken and it had to have these characteristics:

> It had to be quick.
> It had to be easy.
> It had to be effective.

Thus the traditional Grammar/Translation (G/T) method was tossed aside for a dynamic, new method known as Audio/Lingual (A/L). This approach served a valuable purpose in that it quickly captivates students' attention and gives them meaningful, useful vocabulary rapidly. The choral technique involved in the modeling however, interferes with the natural cadence and rhythm of language. Nevertheless, A/L has been the most effective method available during first half of the 20th Century and remained so until about the 1970's when more adherences to **communicative competence** came into vogue and it was expected that students would actually speak the language, not just manipulate its components on paper.

The US Department of Defense and British Council are large providers of English language instruction worldwide. The Americans tend to use A/L more than the British, but both have realized the merits of this approach for quick and effective English language learning. Specialized language schools, missionary schools, and of course, military courses, still heavily rely upon it. Unfortunately, the A/L approach was and is still used almost exclusively under "battlefield" conditions when a language is needed quickly. However, after WWII, high schools drifted back into the lull of **Grammar-Translation,** with students still today, learning how to read the target language but not being able to speak it.

In summary, teaching foreign language today has not progressed very far in technique or philosophy. While computers have added a great new teaching tool, nevertheless, most US schools are still relying on Grammar-

Translation approach with its methodical exercises and easily referenced results. Therefore, a major overhaul of our teaching system for foreign language is recommended. This author highly recommends using principles and techniques from Doxography.

Chapter 7 Questions

1. How many high school students were enrolled in foreign language classes in 1905?

2. Compare this figure with the number enrolled in 1982. Then compare that figure with the number enrolled in 1992. What trend is apparent? Why?

3. What role does the U.S. Department of Defense and the British Council play in the promulgation of English language worldwide?

4. Compare the differences between the Audio-Lingual approach and the Grammar-Translation approach to second language teaching. You may want to use the Internet for additional support for your answers. Be sure to cite sources used.

5. Having analyzed the above two well-known approaches to teaching second language, which one would you favor in your own classroom?

6. EXTRA CREDIT: Devise three curriculum objectives which support Audio-Lingual Approach

Music is a tremendous tool to use in the effective affective classroom. Some researchers are investigating the potential of music to heal the body as well as the mind. Possible?

Θ Chapter 8
WORLDWIDE LITERACY:
THE WORD AND THE WORLD

Why is learning the word (the logos) so important? Let us examine the importance of writing in the modern world and all that writing implies to the emerging writer in the ESL/language classroom.

"To establish an avenue in effectively interacting with society, one must gain the ability to function appropriately in a literate environment which necessarily includes reading, writing, and thinking skills" (Roberts, 1994). Writing is probably the component of emergent literacy that has been the most neglected and misunderstood. Even though it is an integral part of emergent literacy, the emphasis has been put on reading development. Research findings indicate that, in emergent literacy, reading and writing influence each other (Williams & Snipper, 1990). In the process of obtaining literacy, oral language plays a major role. It is only when speech becomes "insufficient to meet the communicative needs of the individual and the society (that) written language development becomes an extension of that process" (Goodman, 1989).

So how does this affect the ESL/language learner? Literacy skills are the ultimate challenge in ESL. Writing to promote language acquisition has gained popularity especially with learners of a second language. According to Marianne Celce-Murcia, oral communication is more readily acquired than written communication (1992). This was proven by Jim Cummins who developed the **BICS** model (Basic Interpersonal Communicative Skills) as opposed to **CALP** (Cognitive Academic Language Proficiency). Cummins posits that BICS takes from 2-3 years to master, i.e. social language used at school. However, academic language takes from 5-7 years as revealed in his acronym CALP.

> BICS (Social Language) 2-3 years
> CALP (Academic Language) 5-7 years

Some bilingual education proponents hold that written communication will develop naturally after a solid foundation is built upon the first language (L1). Such proponents include Chapman, 1996; Roberts, 1994; and Fletcher, 1993. Our research data will not concur with this. While listening and speaking skills may develop naturally, this is not the case with reading and writing, even with a solid basis of first language to back it up. However, this author enthusiastically concurs with research that shows second language <u>learners will develop literacy skills faster</u> (just not "naturally") once a solid basis has been obtained in L1.

Stephen Krashen, renowned ESL researcher, suggests that "conscious knowledge in grammar is available only as a monitor, or editor in writing, but the monitoring should be done only after all the ideas are written down" (1992).

So when does writing begin to emerge in new language learners? In most cases, children will experiment with English (L2) almost immediately upon enrollment in ESL, regardless of age. Yet those who have very limited background in their native language literacy skills, will certainly have a decided disadvantage in acquiring English quickly and effectively, and will have great difficulty in deciphering the Germanic tones and nuances that pervade English. This is particularly apparent when Spanish speakers attempt English for the first time. The gap between the two language systems remains enormous even though they are surely beginning to corrupt each other as their speakers interact more-and-more.

<u>Cognates.</u> English is approximately 60% Latin-derived (Luschnig, 1982, University Press of America). Spanish is about 80% Latin based (Barrett, "Keys to Language and Cultural

Awareness). Teachers are encouraged to use cognates (those terms that have a common root in both systems), as much as possible during the first few weeks of language study. This helps to build a bridge upon which to facilitate the learning of English. Oddly enough, thousands of **cognates exist between Spanish and Arabic**! This helps explain the roots of many Spanish terms. The Arabs conquered Spain and occupied it for many hundreds of years. Then the Spanish conquered America, so thus the connection of Arabic into American Spanish! Interesting indeed.

Historical Lessons in Teaching English in Foreign Lands: The Missionary Enterprise

At the same time that the boom in second language learning was taking place in the English-speaking world, so a lower-keyed battle loomed in the distant reaches of Britain's far-flung empire as well as in the American lands acquired from Native Americans and as a result of the Mexican War of 1846-48 and the Spanish-American War of 1898. How can we teach Western language to an illiterate people? Should we attempt to teach English first, then literacy? Or vice-versa? And what about their own language? Does it have a place in ESL at all?

Rich oral traditions of stories, poetry, songs, and liturgies, were fascinating to foreign missionaries and politicians, but they were nevertheless bewildered as to what methods to reach out to a "readerless" society of so many millions of heathen. It was quite disconcerting for them to explain, "The Bible says…" and realize that the people not only had never seen a Bible, **they had never even seen a book!** Literacy development surfaced in one place after another as the ultimate key to this dilemma. American and British missionaries rushed to these exotic lands, taking the Gospel, the Bible, medicine, education, Western culture, and of course, English!

The one central need recognized by missionary and foreign political groups was the need to standardize foreign languages into alphabetic systems and eventually to build a literature base for each indigenous group—a daunting task at best! To accomplish this, a new science had to be developed: **applied linguistics**, a systematic study of the intricate components of language, morphology, syntax, and phonology.

Native Language Literacy

At first, native language literacy was not seen as important since many argued back in England and America, "Why can't those people just learn to speak English?" The professionals in the faraway reaches knew the answer to this question. **Dr. Eugene Nida** (noted linguist and former president of the American Bible Society), realized that mere translation of materials into English left much to be desired from frequent misquotes and at times, totally incomprehensible transliterations. The native language had to be addressed before any successful attempt at English could be properly made, if needed at all. Western languages are so far removed from the mindset and cultural heritage of many cultures that it is too time-consuming and relatively meaningless to try to translate concepts that are not in existence in other tongues. Native language literacy was the key, but how? It had never been attempted on a large scale but kept to a simple process, easily duplicated. In the 1970's Dr. Mark Walsh, a Roman Catholic missionary to Peru, researched and developed native language materials for the native population. Later in life he became Director of Continuing Education and now serves as Director of International Studies at Texas A&M University in Kingsville, Texas. His work, along with that of Dr. Ray Graham, his close associate from BYU, can be accessed at the Texas A&M Literacy Center for Adult ESL Education.

Dr. Frank C. Laubach (1884-1970), an American missionary to the Philippines, developed a direct, yet simple approach to meet this need. This Princeton graduate developed a series of phonemic pictographs in the native languages. It was extremely effective in that native peoples were given not only literacy, but also, for the first time, an appreciation for their own native language.

In the 20th Century a need was seen for worldwide literacy as never before. The call went out to not only save souls but also to teach the native peoples literacy in their own language. Many thousands of disenfranchised native tribal groups had no alphabetic form. The simplicity of Laubach's philosophy and methods is astounding "If one can speak a language, then that language is worthy of being read." In other words, native peoples of the world deserved literacy as well as everyone else. This may encapsulate Laubach's philosophy quite succinctly. Thus the "Laubach Method" of native language literacy swept the Philippines, much to the contentment of the post war government, and went on to be the major source of education leadership in the linguistic field worldwide, with the eventual establishment of an international headquarters in Syracuse, New York. **The New Readers Press** stands today as a living monument to the work of this brave linguistic pioneer. The Laubach system relied upon applied linguistics to isolate phonemes (smallest unit of human speech) and codify them into an alphabetic system. This same system is used today to teach literacy worldwide. This author has used Spanish Laubach to teach elderly Mexican people to read and write in Spanish with tremendous success. Dr. Laubach provided dignity to native peoples via literacy and an appreciation of language that brings an appreciation of culture, which ultimately contributes to peace.

Alternative Assessment: Eliminating Testing Anxieties

Another dimension of bilingual education, both with children and adults that deserves marked attention, is our current philosophy toward testing and measurement. One of the major barriers for weak students in our education system is test taking. While testing by pen and paper has always been a part of formal education, it has, however, been much over-rated and deemed much more vital to accurate assessment than it probably really is. Pen and paper testing can have lasting negative effects on students and programs in general with some adult students simply not returning to class altogether.

Arbitrary and static testing methods are not even remotely as effective in accurately assessing students as Alternative Assessment. This assessment is based on a system of dynamics happening in real time in the actual classroom that is on-going, up-to-date, and real. Formative evaluations are not productive measurements for some students, nor accurate measures of ability or knowledge for them. Why? Some students are not prepared to handle the anxiety of a testing situation or procedure, especially if they are new language learners and new to not only the language but also to the culture as well. Instead of administering tests for placement and achievement, teachers are now encouraged to look at the benefits of Alternative Assessment. While most tests are measurements of memory, not ability, in Alternative Assessment, the student is measured as they progress from task-to-task with greater difficulty and outcomes for each step in the development process.

Evaluation usually consists of two major components:

1.   **Formative evaluation** which is conducted on a weekly or even daily basis.

2.   **Summative evaluation** is a more final type of measurement of student progress. It can be administered via a final test, but is usually the last and final cumulative

assessment with all the formative tests calculated into it. Alternative Assessment techniques include a day-by-day type of measurement in which the teacher keeps a Portfolio of all final work produced. At periodic intervals the teacher and student sit down together and evaluate the progress contained within the Portfolio. This enables both to more accurately measure what is going on in the language development of the student. The Portfolio should tell a story, a story which has a beginning, middle and end, the end being the end of the semester or course.

The Renaissance Hotel of McAllen, Texas, was the venue for the Annual ESL Institute in 2001 with team-trainers: (l-to-r) Helen Jones, Audrey Eoff, Clark von Heller, and Louise Reagan.

Periodic quizzes may be given at the discretion of the teacher, but with **Portfolio Assessment**, the amazing thing is that tests and quizzes are really not necessary! Daily work or long-term assignments can be evaluated as they are completed. This way the student feels the joy of accomplishment while affording a simpler approach to grading.

The student will be more likely to understand the grading process also because the work is in clear sight of both student and reviewer so no question should ever rise such as, "How am I going to be graded?" We live in a modern world where product manufacturing is paramount to all we see about us. The cars, the roads, the stores, the buildings: all point to a finished product. Are we accustomed to buying half-finished products at the stores? No. So the Portfolio aspect of Alternative Assessment demonstrates clearly a student who has not progressed well, compared to the student whose "products" are completed circumspectly and in order.

Assigning letter grades: A,B,C,D,F is no different than other types of grading. Products are graded according to whatever criteria the teacher and student set up together: appearance, spelling, format, reliability, accuracy, etc. Each can be weighted such as appearance 50%, spelling 25% and so on. Again the benefits and ease of Alternative Assessment can be seen clearly. Students produce a product that is worthy of a grade, not simply completing a product worthy of their time.

We have looked at Portfolio Assessment as an alternative means of evaluating language learners in the classroom. Both children and adult teachers have used this approach for many years with great success. Can this approach take the place of State-mandated assessments? No. But at least in the classroom, Portfolios can successfully be used alongside less frequent standard types of assessment with the end result being a more positive, less stressful classroom. This is another key feature of Doxographic teaching formula.

Multiple Intelligences. Howard Gardner from Harvard is the leading American expert in this field. Doxographists highly endorse the possibilities and outcomes involved with this research and the application to the classroom. Much has been written on this topic and I encourage teachers and administrators to take a serious look at his Project Zero and all it entails (howardgardner.com).

Chapter 8 Questions

1. In earliest chapters we have established that the "word" can be seen as the "logos." Why is learning the "word" so important, especially in relation to the art of writing?

2. Identify BICS and CALP by Jim Cummins.

3. Explain the significance of the pioneer work in linguistics and language acquisition by Eugene Nida and Frank C. Laubach.

4. Explain the difference in Formative and Summative evaluation.

5. How has America's grading system evolved through the years? Investigate this phenomenon on the Internet.

6. How can Portfolio Assessment be used successfully?

7. What are some negative impacts that Portfolio Assessment could have in relation to other, more traditional forms of evaluation?

8. List all multiple intelligences as researched by Howard Gardner.

*EXTRA CREDIT: Look up the work of Mark Walsh from Texas A&M/Kingsville, in the field of adult literacy. Write a paragraph on his contributions toward adult literacy and native language literacy.

Θ Chapter 9
BILINGUAL EDUCATION THEORY
AND APPROACH IN USA

ESL Doxography takes a very negative view of any approach to second language learning or education in general, which segregates groups of students other than adults, for reasons of experimenting with methodologies that are proven to cause confusion and minimal results at best. Some bilingual programs have accomplished just that, albeit most are greatly improved since their inception in the 1980's. Ideally, bilingual education programs should allow English-speaking pupils to be bilingual, but generally they are directed only to non-English speakers.

Six million students filled bilingual classrooms to capacity in 1999. Bilingual education is big business! California was allocated $110 million in 1999 and Texas, the 2nd largest provider of bilingual services, received a whopping $30 million (Digest of Education Statistics, 2000, Ch 2, Elem/Sec Ed). Bilingual Education is also very controversial, not so much because of a fierce on-going debate over methodologies, but rather because it went from the academic realm, to the political arena in the 1980's and now seems to be swinging back to academia. Whereas the United States has a long heritage of multi languages and cultures, even with the establishment of hundreds of German-speaking schools in the 1800's, nevertheless with the massive funding of bilingual education programs one hundred years later, a terrible battle of words and empirical evidence has raged in **California, Arizona and Florida. Texas and New Mexico** have been spared much of the rhetoric and hurtful policies due to different attitudes that have always favored Mexican immigration and Spanish language.

Bilingual education in the USA was born out of cultural animosity which resulted in several significant court cases:

Cisneros v. Corpus Christi Schools, 1970, ruling that it was unconstitutional to segregate students on the basis of language and/or culture. (Texas was separating Mexican and American students.) Then, on a national level, the US Supreme Court ruled in Lau v. Nichols, San Francisco, 1974, that Chinese students had the constitutional right to instruction in their native language. This is the decision that changed everything since it was a national ruling by the US Supreme Court. States scrambled to conform to the new ruling with many regulations coming from Congress to stipulate how bilingual education should be implemented. Several strong political lobbies lined up and have battled it out for decades. But what about students from Mexico who were not US citizens but were attending US schools? Popular loopholes in the school district residency requirement were to have a Texas family pose as the residence of the student, or rent a post office box over on the US side of the border. In many cases the ploy was logical in that many border residents have houses on both sides of the river in which case it was technically legal to have Mexican children educated on the US side at US taxpayer expense. One example comes from my own experience.

A friend of this author from Reynosa, Tamaulipas, Mexico, is a very wealthy businessman. Each one of his children was born in McAllen Texas, automatically making them American citizens, even though they live and thrive quite well in a palatial home with servants and the good life on the Mexican side. Each day their chauffer crosses the international bridge to take the little boys to school in McAllen, Texas, and at 3pm promptly retrieves them from the US and returns them happily back to Mexico to spend the night and repeat the process Monday through Friday. Some students stay with friends or relatives and return to Mexico on the weekends. For teachers of ESL this poses quite a dilemma as students have a more difficult time parting with Spanish language patterns on Monday due to constant weekend reinforcement of Spanish back in Mexico each weekend.

This issue was addressed in **Plyler v. Doe**, 457 US 202, 1982, in which all undocumented students, residing in any part of this country have the same right of access to a public education that is provided under state and federal law to all US citizens and permanent resident aliens. In border areas where students were merely walking across the international bridge each day, this caused quite a stir: on a national level the court was mandating free education to undocumented children, but taxpayers on the local level would have to foot the bill. Brownsville, Laredo, and McAllen, Texas, along with other border cities, were hard hit by this dilemma as their school populations swelled out of control. Not enough buildings were available to handle these burgeoning student populations and the local taxpayers refused to pay for additional facilities for foreign students. The answer was to appeal for additional federal funding.

The question was more one of money and politics than instructional design. Practitioners of ESL were caught up in the hoopla and lined up on opposite sides of the issue. The result was a fragmented effort that differed from state-to-state, each providing bilingual services to foreign students in a wide variety of methods. Debate still rages today in the USA on the "how" but seldom over the "why". It is widely accepted that the US has a moral obligation to provide bilingual services to foreign-born residents; such a massive program could be underwritten with federal taxes.

Most countries look at this type of program as superfluous or even ridiculous! Teaching students in a foreign language, not the dominant language of the country, is seen as absurd to the vast majority of countries of the world. But one must keep in mind that 1) the USA attracts more immigrants that any other country, and, 2) it is so wealthy that such a program is feasible, and finally 3) the American guilt complex. Americans feel guilty over the way that the

Southwest region was acquired. For example, on February 2, 1848, with the signing of the **Treaty of Guadalupe Hidalgo**, Mexico relinquished land that would eventually become Texas, California and most of Arizona and New Mexico for $15 million. 75,000 Mexican citizens who remained after one year from that date, were granted US citizenship. It was not until 1965 that immigration from Mexico was restricted which means that the US and Mexico have shared a long history of mutual migration of residents back and forth.

Title I and Title VII Federal Carrots

Most large school districts along the US-Mexico border receive millions of federal dollars as a result of having near 100% Mexican enrollment and free lunch, categorized as "Title I students." California received $110 million and Texas received $30 million in 1999. Include the migrant students and the economically disadvantaged, and that makes for a VERY wealthy formula for entitlements from Uncle Sam. The latest US Census figures show Starr County, Texas, with over 95% Hispanic, and more than 20 Texas counties with more than 50% Hispanic population (US Census, 2000). With this in mind, why would any school want their children to learn English and opt out of this free-flowing "cash cow"? Therein lays the "catch 22" that administrators and legislators are still working to remedy.

Bias, discrimination, and misunderstandings have all characterized this massive, multi-billion dollar enterprise since 1974. Although the Democrats have traditionally been seen as the main backers of bilingual education, it wasn't until the Republicans pushed "Dual Language Literacy" in the 1990's that non-foreign language speakers were ever considered for bilingual classes. Half of the class is English dominant, usually Anglo children; the other half non-English dominant, usually Spanish-speaking children from Mexico. The idea is to teach each group the other's language. One drawback however, is that in many places where bilingual

143

education is offered, sufficient numbers of non-Spanish-speakers are not available to form half of a class! In these cases some schools have enlisted predominately English speaking Hispanic students to serve as the "English group" and the regular ESL students from Mexico as the Spanish-dominate group. The problem in theory arises in the irony here that both cultures are the same which some would say renders this "band-aid" attempt as being unviable.

Would the Real English Teacher Please Stand Up?

The general public often lumps all teachers of bilingual/ESL as "ESL" teachers. They are never referred to as "English" teachers since this hallowed qualification is held only by mainstream teachers who teach how the language is used but really are not teaching English at all! We have it completely in reverse! The ones that teach English language are the ESL teachers whereas the students who sit in English classes already know it! (Obviously they need reinforcement via literature, grammar practice, and writing to increase their working knowledge of the language).

But often the terms "bilingual teacher" and "ESL teacher" are used interchangeably. I wish I had a nickel for every time someone has come up to me at a conference and looking at my badge, say something like, "Oh, you're an ESL teacher. Wow. I would like to be certified in ESL but I don't know Spanish." The point is, Spanish or the lack thereof, has NOTHING IN COMMON WITH the concept of ESL! This message needs to be made very clearly. In fact, it is better NOT to know Spanish if teaching 16 year olds in an ESL high school class in USA. This way no "cheating" is possible by relying on their first language to get the lesson objective across. It is very tempting for Hispanic ESL teachers to slip back into Spanish for clarification and exposition. This is not good. The student needs to hear as much of the target language as possible. Slipping into Spanish to clarify is definitely a step backwards. For example, how would you like it if, while studying in Spain and enrolled in a very expensive Spanish class, when a problem arose, the professor reverted to English? Although clarification needed would be given, you would not receive the "comprehensible input" that Krashen calls for.

The National ESL Institute sponsored the Annual ESL Institute on South Padre Island in June, 1999 with hundreds of teachers from all over the state of Texas and northern Mexico. Pictured here are: (l-to-r) Carlos Garcia, staff member; two outstanding teachers, and the author, Dr. Clark.

Once when monitoring an EFL teacher in Mexico, the author recalls a classic example of slipping back into first language. She was trained by this author never to revert into Spanish to explain a term or idea in English. Students were expected to find that information via the dictionary or computer. They were paying handsomely for her beautiful English language skills and pronunciation at a prestigious university in Reynosa, Tamaulipas. While the class was very effective, at the end of the class someone inquired about the **Christmas**

party. (The whole question by the student was asked in very correct, intentional English). The teacher became so comfortable with this topic that she inadvertently slipped into total Spanish for the whole discussion about when and who would bring what, etc. to the party. What a missed opportunity for comprehensible input! All the students were familiar with the normal trappings for a traditional Christmas party. What they knew not, but needed to know, is how to say those **items and ideas in English**. This normally very professional Mexican teacher temporarily put aside her training on Comprehensible Input, robbing her students of a golden opportunity for true, meaningful language because who would not be interested in going to a fun Christmas party! As a bilingual education class, this would have been perfect because Spanish language was reinforced, but for an ESL/EFL class, no.

ESL and bilingual classes are very distinct with major differences in curriculum, materials, language used, and approach. In fact, the difference is so distinguished that state certification offices and universities offer teaching degrees in both or either separately. Most elementary teachers in Texas (and other states where appropriate) are encouraged to be "bilingually certified" but not necessarily "ESL certified" since elementary students are taught in Spanish if their parents have enrolled them in the program. If not, students are placed in "ESL" classes, which in some cases are basically the same thing but since the term "English" appears at the beginning, everyone is happy. While this is an oversimplification of a very complicated designation which varies by districts, still it certainly occurs frequently. The **"Bilingual Program"** per se refers to the entire, federally funded, broad curriculum stretching from K-12 as mandated by the 1988 Bilingual Education Act. It changes names automatically to "ESL" at secondary level, if the student is still in need of second language services. Once a student passes the reading portion of a state test they are classified as "non-LEP," or "non-Limited English Proficient" and removed from classrooms taught by ESL endorsed teachers, placing them instead in "regular" academic courses. Students are monitored for two more years to see if their acquisition of English is final and productive enough for them to be successful in the mainstream classes by the **LPAC Committee** (Limited Proficiency Assessment Committee). Regulations for Bilingual Education in the state of Texas are found in Chapter 89 of the Texas Education Code.

Fundamentally, the difference between ESL and Bilingual Education is simply that ESL promotes English language acquisition with little regard, if any, to the native language while the other does. The teacher need only be well versed in English to be certified in ESL. 100% emphasis is placed on quick and effective English language acquisition in the ESL classroom, whether using Maintenance Approach or the more familiar Transitional Approach.

In contrast, Bilingual Education requires not only the teaching of ESL but also requires **teaching content data in first language** at the same time. Obviously the teacher must be bilingual as well. The belief is that a student, particularly a young one, will grasp the second language more efficiently if introduced to a strong foundation in the first language. These skills may include reading and writing, math, understanding the main idea in a passage, being able to manipulate linguistic "devices" etc. When students are thoroughly versed in "native language literacy" they are transitioned into all English classes.

Correlation With Native Language Literacy

Hakuta (1990) found that second language acquisition has a direct correlation to the amount of proficiency acquired in first language prior to enrolling in second language study. Furthermore, the continuation of native language instruction has been shown to be a significant factor in the development of second language proficiency (Saville-Troike, 1984, 214). Some, however, have posed that bilingual strategies might work well with some alphabet systems such as Roman-based to Roman-based, i.e., Spanish to English, but what about other alphabets such as Russian Cyrillic or Chinese characters?

It seems that reading ability transfers from languages other than Roman-based alphabet systems--Chinese to English (Hoover, 1982), from Vietnamese to English (Cummins, Swain, Nakajima, Handscombe, Green, & Tran, 1984), from Japanese to English (Cummins et al), and from Turkish to Dutch (Verhoeven, 1991). It would appear that those who read well in their native language read well in their second or third languages (as long as length of residence in the country is taken into account because of the first language loss that is common). Proponents of bilingual education point to these data to argue their point that reading skills are transferable, it would appear, almost universally amongst human language systems.

Time Frame for Learning a Second Language

Jim Cummins concluded from his research findings in 1981 that from 5-7 years of study were needed for students to achieve norms comparable to native English speakers on standardized achievement reading tests. (See BICS-Basic Interpersonal Communicative Skills and CALP-Cognitive Academic Language Proficiency). Furthermore, his findings noted students with up to two years of formal training in their first language before arrival in Canada, reached the 50th percentile within 5-7 years but those without these two years of study, tended to reach the 50th percentile only after 7-10 years of second language exposure.

Virginia Collier made it clear that the impact of first language study on second language was indeed dramatic. She states, "L1 instruction throughout elementary school years, coupled with gradual introduction of the second language, seems to produce a consistent pattern of greater achievement in the second language at the end of 4-7 years of schooling, even though the total number of hours of instruction in the second language may be dramatically smaller when compared with schooling in the second language only" (Collier, 1989, 522).

What a clear endorsement of bilingual education! It would only seem natural that one can learn something else once something is learned first to serve as a model. Isn't this the model we use in teaching almost everything? Drawing from a pattern or a model gives the brain something to relate to for easier comprehension. When a student learns "democracía" in Spanish, it will be simple to transfer this model to the English term when it comes up as "democracy." Will the teacher have to re-teach the concept? No. The teacher merely needs to expose the student to the new spelling for English, etc. For more theoretical learning such as nuclear physics, for example, it may more difficult to "model" a hypothesis since it is not proven yet, but the professors will certainly give the students some type of correlation (or pattern) from known experience so that students (investigators) can have an idea of the general components and eventual outcomes of the hypothesis. In education, every concept has no clear mandate or need to be proven to be considered a reality. (Einstein, 1879-1955, could not prove his Theory of Relativity until a certain telescope could safely inspect the corona around the sun during a total eclipse in England, 1919).

A number of studies comparing the achievement of students schooled in English only and bilingual education programs found that after 4-5 years of instruction, bilingual program students made dramatic academic gains and the English-only group dropped below their grade level (Lewelling 137). Even well-documented cases showing the opposite, have been heavily disputed by Stephen Krashen, one of the most noted gurus of ESL. He states,

"A common argument against bilingual education is the observation that many people have succeeded without it.

This has certainly happened. In these cases, however, the successful person received plenty of comprehensible input in the second language, and in many cases had a de facto bilingual education program. For example, Rodriguez (1982) and de la Peña (1991) are often cited as counter-evidence to bilingual education" (ERIC document RC 020895).

Chapter 9 Questions

1. How many USA students enrolled in bilingual education classes in 1999?

2. What major changes came about as an outcome of the court case, Lau v. Nichols?

3. How did Plyler v. Doe affect bilingual education?

4. Why does the term "ESL" show up more in secondary education than elementary?

5. In elementary we normally see the term, "bilingual" used more often. Why?

6. *EXTRA CREDIT: Investigate current trends in bilingual education in your state in a few paragraphs.

Happy childhood times in Carolina with 2nd brother Ed and sister Louise. The author is on the right side, a rambunctious 12 year old with a loving family that made all the difference. Ed earned a PhD and teaches college. Louise is a busy mother and grandmother while running a thriving family business. Our oldest brother, David, is not pictured. He is president of an oil company in Oklahoma. A firm family foundation leads to solid values and great Doxography. Thanks Earl and Lillian!

Θ Chapter 10
BILINGUAL ED POLITICAL UPDATES

Bilingual education was once a red-hot political topic but not so much anymore. Although an occasional philosophical debate will rise up between purists of various factions within **NABE or TESOL**, still for the most part, the country seems to have finally made peace with this explosive issue by taking some very long-overdue measures, simply standing back to enjoy the federal funds pouring in, and putting new restrictions on long-term ESL programs. California and Arizona have been the most vocal in the bilingual education debate by both officially throwing out traditional, tax-sucking bilingual education programs once and for all by popular vote, California with Proposition 227 in 1998 and now Arizona. Both programs were voted out in heated political battles waged between Hispanic activist groups and mostly Anglo, English-only groups. They have mandated a one-year, intensive English class with English the only medium of instruction in 100% ESL class. No foreign language (native language) instruction is allowed. *Note: Several large school districts in Southern California have received waivers from Sacramento and continue bilingual services. In Texas and California the majority of students in public school are Mexican-American.

In some parts of the US it is very difficult to hire qualified teachers of foreign languages who can also qualify to teach under an official Teaching Certificate. A good example is Houston, Texas. In recent years Houston has experienced phenomenal immigrant growth, particularly from the Far East. Houston area school districts decided to implement a traditional "ESL style" bilingual program with only Spanish and English as the languages used in areas of large Mexican concentration; otherwise simply the ESL approach (all English). It seems to work well.

Lau v Nichols updated.

It may be surprising that when school districts find themselves in trouble over implementation and compliance in relation to their bilingual education programs, it is usually not because of methods or philosophy, but rather because of a clear violation of the Civil Rights Act. Yes, the 1964 Civil Rights Act is the key to enforcing provisions of the Bilingual Education Act of 1968 and 1988. School districts with huge numbers of second language learners sometimes, incorrectly, opt to give special treatment to these students in the form of a separate new building, or their own computer labs, inadvertently setting these students apart from their English speaking peers. This is illegal. The OCR (Office of Civil Rights) takes very seriously their charge to enforce equal and equitable educational opportunities for all, including LEP students. This is an integral part of the Title VI provision of the Civil Rights Act of 1964. This author has worked with several districts that have been sued by OCR and it is very ugly and embarrassing for the constituency. School boards are called into question, federal funds are jeopardized (but rarely withheld) and the community is embarrassed. It is indeed, a very big deal when this occurs.

In 1991 Congress authorized the **Office of Civil Rights, under Title VI**, to review school districts as to their compliance with Lau v Nichols from 1974. The policy update was primarily designed for use in conducting Lau compliance reviews designed to determine whether schools were complying with their obligation under the regulation implementing Title VI of the Civil Rights Act of 1964 which specified that schools were mandated to provide "any alternative language programs necessary to ensure that national origin minority students with limited English proficiency (LEP) students have meaningful access to all school programs" (www.nabe.org, 2002). It must be noted that this "Legal Memorandum" made neither specification nor mandate to any particular program of instruction. It would appear that politicians in the last decade were beginning to wash their hands of this sticky issue and stay within the safe limits of enforcing what was already on the books. Good move. Thus the debate over methods is relegated back to the local school districts where it rightfully belongs anyway. As stated elsewhere in this book, cosmopolitan regions such as New York and Houston are often caught in a bind by having to provide native language instructors if 20 or more students at one grade level need such a language provider. They would have to find qualified bilingual instructors for perhaps as many as 50 different languages! So they use a regular, intensive ESL program, thus continuing to comply with Lau, Title VI of the Civil Rights Act, and are performing a commendable job in reasonable fashion. Hats off to innovative visionaries at the local level and hats off to Congress for finally backing away from the intense language debate.

Backlash Across the Heartland

Phobias of foreigners taking over perhaps fuel the cause of English-only organizations. Other reasons include a call for national identity and a stronger sense of pride in Anglo-Saxon heritage. Some see such expensive programs as bilingual education eroding away Anglo dominance since Anglos have no need of such a program but are paying the largest percentage of taxes for it. But in regard to Anglo **xenophobia,** they are still vastly the majority by an overwhelming number of 200,000,000!

Several influential Anglo-based organizations have sprouted up as a result of the bilingual education debate. Their efforts have been fruitful with many states, officially passing legislation making English the only official language of government. It saves money from having to print documents in other languages, etc and is a very popular movement in many areas of the country. This backlash exploded in 1998 when Californians, angry at the growing influence of Hispanics and Spanish language, overwhelmingly voted out bilingual education via **Proposition 227**. Arizona soon followed their lead. Twenty-seven states have designated English as their **official language** and several more are considering similar legislation. Oddly enough, the United States Congress has carefully steered clear of this political "hot potato." In 1981 Senator Hayakawa from California proposed a law establishing English as the official language but it miserably failed. Most politicians simply are resigned to the idea, "We already have one basic language, English, and if that changes naturally, so be it." I agree.

What's Changed Since Teddy Roosevelt? In the last few years, **Alaska, Georgia, Iowa, Montana, New Hampshire, South Dakota, Utah, Virginia, Wyoming and Missouri** have enacted some form of official English language legislation (U.S.ENGLISH, Washington, DC). Is taking this English-only posture really viable? After all, America was and remains a grand nation of immigrants. The Articles of Confederation were drafted in German as well as English due to the widespread use of German in the British colonies. In fact, Germans accounted for 9% of the colonial population in 1776. The British, or Anglos, were by a wide margin, then and now, the majority.

The Continental Congress had no problem with English as the language of government since it was the majority language of the land. A few tried to introduce other languages into government, even Greek! Benjamin Franklin, frowning upon this absurd notion replied, "Let us speak English and let the British learn Greek." (Implying that we would not have to endure the same royal language as the King)! All attempts at changing English miserably failed as the dominance of our mother tongue has always prevailed since the founding of the country in 1607 at Jamestown. "God save the King!" English has always ruled America's tongues! We have nothing to fear in Spanish language or any other language in the future. If English becomes a secondary language at some point, who's to say? A language is not formed by a nation but a language indeed, forms distinct

155

peoples. Therefore, our brave, good people make us the nation we are today.

Immigrants have risen to highest ranks of government, business, and education. America is indeed the land of opportunity for all and that must include all their languages as well. But the question is, should the tax payer have to foot the bill for printing bilingual documents or pay for our children to learn a foreign language? (usually Spanish) Teddy Roosevelt said,

> "The one absolute certain way of bringing this nation to ruin, or preventing all possibility of it continuing to be a nation at all, would be to permit it to become a tangle of squabbling nationalities. We have one flag. We must also learn one language and that language is English."

2006 Update in Bilingual Education Politics

The Republicans are firmly in charge of the US education system and strongly entrenched in Texas and several other key Border States where the bulk of bilingual education funds are expended. With their rule comes **more accountability** as reflected in newest provisions of *No Child Left Behind Act.* Accountability affects bilingual students directly since they fall under the broader category of "Special Populations." They are certainly more at risk of failure or dropout than regular students. The Department of Education is also concentrating on a long-range literacy plan, beginning with 3rd grade on-level reading and in just about a decade, all levels K-12, must pass state tests at grade level.

Unfortunately such an ambitious program of achievement in the public schools is very difficult as well as time and resource consuming. As a result, Congress has recently backtracked on several areas of the original provision in keeping with numbers of complaints, especially from Border States such as Texas, New Mexico, Arizona, and California, with large Mexican-American populations who have difficulty passing state-mandated tests.

In summary, we have seen the results of intense political debate over bilingual education. The debate, at least for now, has died down, perhaps because Republicans are in control or because other issues are more pressing such as accountability for instance. Educators are more content than ever in the country's history although teacher's unions are weak, leaving most of the nation's 4,000,000 teachers nearly voiceless. Most states outlaw strikes by public employees. Organizations such as NABE which tend to be very racist, are beginning to tone down their pro-Spanish, anti-English rhetoric a bit, and one seldom hears much from the opposite camps such as USENGLISH anymore. Prognosis? The country is better off, settling for a more moderate bilingual education program of one year of intensive ESL instruction, and then mainstream the students into classes with certified teachers who are trained in LEP strategies. This is working at the moment with very positive results. *"All's well that ends well"* (Shakespeare).

Chapter 10 Questions

1. Discuss the modern trend in the USA of throwing out bilingual education programs on a statewide basis. Be sure to include the effects of California's adoption of Proposition 227.

2. What is "xenophobia?" Is it happening in your state?

3. How does this term, with its implications, still negatively affect bilingual education implementation in some parts of the USA?

4. Have you found that local leaders in your community support the goals of bilingual education? Why?

5. How many children are enrolled in bilingual education in the USA? Be sure to list your source.

6. In how many USA states are Hispanics now the majority of enrolled public school students?

7. What is the official language of the USA?

8. How many bilingual schools were operating in the USA prior to 1914? In what language(s) were they conducted?

9. What did Benjamin Franklin think of making Greek the official language of the USA?

10. What was the percentage of American Germans at the time of independence from Britain?

11. Should Anglo children need to participate in the bilingual education program? Why? Relate this to the fact that they are asked to pay the majority of taxes for this program, in a short paragraph.

Θ Chapter 11
THE MEXICANS ARE COMING!

Not since the days of Paul Revere have we heard this type of alarm. According to CNN (March, 2005), at least one million illegals invade the United States from across the southern border each year! As unbelievable as this may seem, basically nothing is being accomplished substantially different than always, to stop this. For the most part, this odd "invasion" is subtle and peaceful with hard-working people coming up from south of the border to work in the USA. But after 9-11 and new security concerns with terror cells lurching just south of the Rio Grande, this seemingly benign situation looks like it is ready to rip open at the seams! Citizens are looking for a solution from the federal government but despite billions spent and thousands of Border Patrol, still the problem grows each year. A grassroots effort has begun with a citizen's group called "Minutemen." They were auspiciously stationed along the Arizona border and near checkpoints in Texas during the summer of 2005 in a very public effort to draw attention to the problem of illegal immigration across the 2,000 mile porous border. Unfortunately, they are looked upon as being white racists by some political groups, although the head of the organization is Hispanic! So a counter group, dominated by Hispanics called "the Brown shirts," have taken up the challenge to mobilize and are determined to oppose the Minutemen.

Mexican-Hispanics constitute the largest ethnic culture in the USA and are subsequently the largest group crossing back and forth across the border each year. They also constitute the largest percentage of Hispanics residing in the USA, 70% (2000 US Census). **Thirty five million** persons self-identified themselves as Hispanics in the 2000 US Census. This figures to **12.5% of the total USA population**, 281 million. Of course this number is very conservative when one takes into account the often-reported possible 2 million undocumented illegal aliens, which if so, would raise the number to 37 million. Recent immigrants are naturally reluctant to speak with anyone associated with the federal government for obvious reasons so they are difficult to assess. An amnesty provision was included by Congress in the **1986 Immigration Reform and Control Act** (IRCA). Many immigrants now believe that residing in the USA, legal or not, will eventually pay off into legal status just as then. And so it probably will. In 2004, President Bush proposed a type of amnesty which was quickly pounced upon, even by fellow Republicans, as an unjust reward for earlier illegal entry into the country. So, at this point, in 2006, illegals continue to pour in at an amazing rate across the porous US-Mexico border. The federal government seems content to brush aside this amazing phenomenon, preferring rather to preserve a fragile but very vital economic relationship with Mexico, one of the top three trading partners with the USA.

The most recent US Census (2000) shows that Hispanic workers are migrating into the interior of the US in record numbers as American agriculture and industry demand more laborers. The percentage of change in North Carolina, for example, of the number of Hispanics residing there in 1990 and then 2000 is highly representative of recent immigration patterns. Over 30 counties in North Carolina, Georgia, and Alabama, gained 200% or more in number of Hispanics during this 10 year period! The stress upon local infrastructure, including education, police, hospitals and churches, has been handled adroitly by these states with the aid of federal monies and urgent training classes in Spanish language and Hispanic culture. In the largest hospital of the county of Pitt in North Carolina, several Spanish translators are on call at all times. And this is a very rural area of eastern North Carolina, 1500 miles from the border! Census data reveal that major growth in traditional areas of established Hispanic communities such as Los Angeles, Miami, Chicago and New York had much less population change in the numbers of Hispanics coming into these areas since 1990. By far the most popular sites for Hispanic workers and families were rural areas, mostly concentrated in the South from Arkansas to North Carolina. Even Texas experienced little change in Hispanic population, the exception being in about 10 counties only, which statistically is very small. Minnesota saw a tremendous gain in Hispanic migration as Las Vegas with a 200% increase from 1990 as well as northwestern Arizona. Even Alaska has one county with more than 10,000 Hispanics and several more with at least 5,000 (2000 US Census).

These patterns deserve scrutiny. Civic planners are scrambling to find adequate resources and funding for this massive influx of immigrants into the heartland. One very significant change affecting these areas is that they now qualify for federal funds from Washington in areas of Title I, VI and Bilingual Education. These funds can mean a tremendous difference to small, rural school districts. The dearth of bilingual teachers in rural areas gives way to an implementation of immersion ESL classes, often with amazingly very good results. The following anecdote relates an example of what often happens to language students.

Testimonial for Immersion

In summer of 2000, while keynoting an ESL conference in Knoxville, Tennessee, this author interviewed a Russian student named Igor. I was so impressed by the fact that this young fellow of 14 learned English in just one year. I promptly asked what ESL classes he attended. He had no clue what that was! He had been placed in an all-English, sink or swim class from day one. He testified that although frustrated for several months, he somehow pulled off the daunting task of mastering English in one year. He can carry on a basic conversation with ease with an understandably heavy accent, the only indication that he was a recent immigrant at all. <u>I wanted to throw out all my books and notes!</u> In one fell swoop this young Russian lad of 14 had shot down my best arguments for a very slow, deliberate transition from bilingual to ESL to the all-English mainstream classroom. (I quickly re-read Krashen!)

Mexican students impact bilingual education issues more than any other foreign language-speaking group in the USA, 35 million strong. They are the fastest growing minority in the USA at more than 40% over the last ten years! (2000 US Census). Mexican Hispanics are becoming well organized into political organizations such as MALDEF (Mexican American Legal Defense and Education Fund), which was founded in 1967 when the border was first closed to Mexican immigration (Vigil, 1990). Also, the Hispanic Chamber of Commerce boasts membership of professionals and entrepreneurs amongst Hispanics in the thousands, particularly along the US-Mexico border. Mexican-Americans are a vibrant and vital component of the US economy. Most Hispanics are citizens of the United States and have shared in defending this country heroically since first serving in World War II.

In summary, we have seen that Mexican-Americans play the leading role in Hispanic immigration trends in the USA. Furthermore, they should continue to impact American life and education in particular, if current trends remain. They spend billions into the American economy each year. Legalized American Hispanics are hard-working, quality citizens that deserve the respect of all Americans. Illegal immigration could potentially harm the country however, due to current trends in terrorism. So where will Hispanic influence lead? Undoubtedly Hispanic influence, in the near future, will lead to more bilingual education, more federal funds, and an infusion of much-needed working class people into the US economy. In the distant future, Hispanics will simply be acculturated into the larger American culture, having fewer babies, higher wages, taking a more active role in politics, and in general, they are likely to become professionals at probably the same rate as the general population, with little difference noted in who is "American" and who is not.

Chapter 11 Questions

1. 70% of all Hispanics residing in the USA are of what national ancestry?

2. How many Mexicans reside in the USA?

3. Discuss the implications of such phenomenal growth of Hispanics in North Carolina, Georgia, and Alabama, which have gained 200% or more during the decade of 1990-2000.

4. What is "language immersion?" List one current method which would be considered the opposite of immersion.

5. If you learned English as a second language, explain the process by which you mastered English up to this point in your development.

6. Politically, how much influence currently is available to Mexican-Americans, particularly in bilingual education?

7. List two national Hispanic organizations that are highly involved in the bilingual education issue.

Teacher inservice training is important but so is follow-up as demonstrated by Trainer Dr. Clark, interviewing a master teacher in Laredo ISD after a session on "Sheltered English" the day before. (2001)

Θ Chapter 12
PATTERN RECOGNITION

When we were children, we saw the world as a never-ending series of items, colors, shapes, and exciting new and delirious ideas. Sometimes those items and ideas were attached and collected; sometimes they were distinct and detached, even from one another. Thus, our journey into the wonderful world of patterns begins!

PATTERN RECOGNITION EXERCISE:

Look around you. Wherever you are, whatever you are doing, patterns exist all around. Can you point out a few right now? Take a moment and identify a few.

When a baby of only one year points to the big yellow arches and says, "Burger Daddy" what is going on inside his mind? This is a child who can barely utter a few words at a time and often those are misguided and barely intelligible. Correct use of language is still a distant challenge that he has just begun to attempt. How then, could this small toddler make the connection between the golden arches and a hamburger? Is he actually decoding information?

The answer lies within us all; every homo sapien born with a normal mind has a marvelous "pattern chip" imbedded within the brain. This is the natural ability to organize, categorize, and exercise data into small units or patterns. This innate ability causes babies to figure things out what is correct, what is dirty, what is wrong, what is pretty, and what is good (such as ice cream).

Piaget posits, "Logic precedes language." Does this make sense? Yes. Babies will cry if they feel threatened long before they can verbalize their fears. They simply sense a situation and react (without real language yet). This is truly an interesting phenomenon. Furthermore, babies can recognize objects, even emotions and ideas long before they can verbalize them. Humans are amazing code breakers, plus we enjoy the challenge! The inquisitive mind of humankind causes us to search for answers and the desire for a challenge, the quest, the "holy grail" as it were. This is true for young children as well, although they cannot speak for nearly one full year of life, are nevertheless, very active organizing, categorizing, and experimenting with their **world** until their **word** becomes activated within them.

Pattern Recognition: the Basic Fabric of Language Learning

Not unlike robots, everyday we function and operate in patterns—in set, fixed ways, whether we realize it or not. Humans seem to relish the thought of regulation, conformity, and boundaries of expression. Routines are a vital part of everyday life. Have you said something different this morning to your husband or wife that you have not said earlier this week? Have you even used the VERY SAME words? Probably so. 45% of the time we use only about 50 different words each day with a normal routine (Crystal). In other words we have very specific vocabularies for particular types of work. This is called "jargon." We use and manipulate this jargon a million different ways and are constantly bombarded with new vocabulary, pertinent to technology and innovations within a certain field. Once the basics of a certain jargon are learned, one should function quite well in that field.

Perhaps only in the academic realm must we consciously add new vocabulary as we constantly examine and investigate terms, modifying new ones to make sense and throwing out archaic ones, unnecessary to modern speech. Plumbers have a set vocabulary that must be learned. Doctors have their own vocabulary. All professions have distinct vocabularies that must be learned either in college or on the job. Even the humble grocery sack person down at the market probably had to learn some new terms that you and I need not know, yet he needs them in his daily routine to be successful at work. Language patterns are all around us and unconsciously affect 99% of our speech habits. For the new student of English, or even fluent speakers, the use of effective Pattern Recognition has rescued many students as they look for that edge in memorizing long lists of data for a test, or an adult who has complicated lists on perform on the job. Can we break out of linguistic discourse patterns? Not really. Conscientious efforts may be attempted but what is "set" cannot be easily modified because language patterns are very difficult to modify after puberty. This is the beginning of "fossilization" within a language system.

Social Registers

Depending on one's station in life—rich or poor, in a high position or not, we use language according to the dictates of our station in society. Have you ever noticed how rich people speak on TV? What about their servants? Notice a difference? How should you speak to your child? Is it different from the way you address your boss or your priest? Why? **Situational linguistic norms are determined by society and situation.** Interlocution standards are fixed patterns that are often difficult to duplicate in the ESL classroom, but nevertheless an attempt needs to be made. What if your students graduated from your class but knew not the correct situational vocabulary for a funeral, a church service, or a job interview? This would be disastrous. All of these special vocabularies need to be rehearsed in class and they usually are in Adult Ed classes but seldom in public school. Life situations are massive, complicated, yet extremely simple linguistic patterns. This paradoxical element in language and life can be remedied with large doses of social language and situational dialogue. The need to teach pattern recognition is very important indeed.

ACTIVITY 1: Look at this page. Take a pencil and circle every period. Then repeat this process for every letter /e/. What was discovered in your analysis?

of /e/ ____

of periods ____

ACTIVITY 2: Examine this sample of foreign writing. Repeat the same as # 1. Can you? Of course you can. Why?

Thelk von geliwpa. Itio cawiouwty con wethioic astho winx. Alsetha bin zintd und poqertero. Dint aiou oiu won nkoekn; wkkoi n non qiinnoeio. Qpoienbios xon dkehjlwer siondfs erhhkos knower hhsoi echo oih woi ioe oih w xhjios.

---

of /e/'s _____

of periods ____ Identify 3 patterns: _____

Were you able to identify patterns? Of course!

This is evidence that students can identify patterns in English even though they may not read the language with much fluency. See how easy it is? Students achieve instant success with this simple exercise, causing beginning students much needed self-esteem to tackle this formidable English language!

SUGGESTION: Bring some foreign language newspapers to class. Ask students to identify certain patterns. With a pencil handy, they can write directly on the newspapers as they identify patterns in letters, shapes, words, blank space, etc.

ACTIVITY 3: Count the # of letter F's in this sentence. You have only 10 seconds......Go!

FINISHED FILES ARE THE RESULT OF YEARS OF SCIENTIFIC RESEARCH COMBINED WITH THE EXPERIENCE OF A GOOD EDUCATION.

Stop! How many did you see?___

Most students only see a few letter f's because they read too fast, just skim the material, or they simply cannot see the f's in the words. Did you see six? That is the correct answer. Now go back again. Did you see them? NO tricks are used in this exercise. You probably saw only three, the ones in the longer words. But now go back and check carefully the **"function words"** which means the small ones. How many can you see now? Isn't that amazing! Although you are a fluent reader of English, you could not see all the letters of a very simple sentence. Wow! This goes to show how tricky English language is. The sound of /**f**/ in English can be /**v**/ or an aspirated /**f**/, which is most common. The brain automatically tells the reader that /of/ is not the normal /**f**/ sound because it doesn't "sound" like an /**f**/. Isn't that interesting? The brain not only reads, it also sends signals of SOUND/PHONICS to the optic nerve so that the eyes may be completely blocked to certain shapes if the brain tells it to block them out. It's that simple, yet amazing. Language must contain discernable, learnable patterns.

English is not entirely "symbolic." It also relies upon rote memorization, some true phonic relationships, and standardization of patterns, whether they make sense or not. Keep in mind that in English language, we have the letter name such as **"f"** but it can carry a completely different sound such as **"v."** Furthermore, the vowels in English have two basic sounds, hard and soft, but some have several real sounds. For example, "a" has three sounds as in "at, father, and ate." **Identifying patterns in both symbols and phonics are fundamental skills** to effective reading skills in children and beginner level adult students.

ACTIVITY 4: Importance of First Language on Second.

Directions: Try to translate this identical passage. Which language is easier?

FINNISH

Nayttaa silta, ettei maan paalla voida nauttia onnellisuudesta lyhyttakaan aikaa.

FRENCH

Il semble impossible heureux. sur la terre, meme peu de temps d'etre.

Write an approximate English translation of either one:

2. Which language was chosen?____ Why?

3. Most readers of this book will naturally choose French because it has patterns that more closely relate to English than Finnish. If you read Spanish, even CLOSER patterns are seen, ¿no? What method or with what prior knowledge was used to translate this passage? Some of you used Spanish. Some used other Roman languages. Excellent! For Spanish-speaking readers, this is a wonderful example of how Spanish can be helpful in **transferring information** into English on a test or other assignment. Bilingual speakers should use both sides of their bilingual brain. Spanish-speaking students in the USA often receive subliminal messages that Spanish is not as important as English, or even that Spanish is somehow inferior to English. This notion can

be dispelled with this kind of activity. Consequently, those who are literate in Spanish have the obvious advantage since French is a sister language to Spanish, both being "Roman" languages. This advantage adds an interesting twist to members of our readership who only read and write English.

Metacognition: Thinking About the Learning

Metacognition is "thinking about thinking or learning." As a valuable component of CALLA (Cognitive Academic Language Learning Assessment), researchers Chamot and O'Malley encourage English language students to think about their learning as well as participate in the normal role as learner. With this in mind, how did you feel when you had difficulties with the previous activities? Ponder the feelings that ESL students have each day, particularly at the beginning of their study of English, when hundreds or even thousands of other students in the school speak English effortlessly while they are struggling so hard to master it. Doxography incorporates the idea of literally asking your students, "Why do you…?"

Children know why they are not performing well, even though they may not **know that they know!** Thoughtful, gentle probing questions from a trained professional will help them clarify the reasons for their performance of tasks. Students have to be trained to think about their own learning and when they are made aware of it, a metamorphosis occurs that will remain with them all of their school days and they could benefit from this training in different avenues of their life in general, particularly in business and industry.

Remember the pattern for **iambic pentameter** from high school English? AAABB, or was it ABABA? How about the Periodic Elements Table? How could you memorize so much data? When memory was needed, it was certainly much easier if you had a pattern, right? Well, nothing has changed. If we can lead our students gently and effectively into the wonderful world of **pattern recognition,** we will provide a valuable service that will pay off, especially in testing situations where great amounts of data must be recounted.

ACITIVITY 5: Roses are Red

Roses are red. Violets are blue. Sugar is sweet, but not as sweet as ___.

Why is this little poem so simple to rhyme? Could it be that you are such an avid reader of English? Could it be that somewhere in grammar school you learned the PATTERN that we call rhyme? Yes. Rhyme is one of the best examples of language manipulation. All over the world children are taught using rhythm and rhyme. Aristotle taught that rhythm is natural in the universe. Rhymes have the ability to reinforce basic skills of natural cadence and intonation, the "singing" quality of a language. **The earth, stars and planets have rhythm**. Time itself is measured in patterns that respond to rhythm. A baby will go to sleep very quickly when a clock is placed nearby so that the rhythm of the "tick tock" is heard. Yes, rhythm is natural in the universe, our WORLD. Now, in the effective Doxographic-based classroom, we need to make it natural in our WORD, our language, as we use "doxos" (glory) in all lesson activities.

Children like hands-on experiences. Zeke and Beto are learning how to put a lawn mower together for the first time in 1992.

Chapter 12 Questions

1. Discuss Piaget's statement: "Logic precedes language." Are you in agreement?

2. David Crystal, OBE, posits that 45% of the time we use only about 50 different words each day. How can this be true?

3. What is a "social register?"

4. Examine the sample of foreign writing at the end of this short chapter. Underline every letter "e." How many can you find? Was this exercise easy? This exercise is a simple example of Pattern Recognition.

5. Why is Pattern Recognition so prevalent in almost every aspect of education and life in general?

6. Identify the term, "contextual clues."

7. Identify the term, "metacognition."

8. CALLA encourages a metacognitive element. How could this be used effectively in monitoring one's own development of language?

9. Give three examples of how rhythm is natural in the universe.

10. EXTRA CREDIT: Construct a model lesson using social registers as the objective.

Rock star Clark rehearses a musical number during a break at Universidad Valle del Bravo in Veracruz, Mexico. Music is a vital part of English acquisition in Latin countries.

Θ Chapter 13
TRANSFER SKILLS: DETAILS AND STRATEGIES

One of the most vital components of an effective second language acquisition program is transfer. When and how does one successfully prepare 3rd or 4th graders, or even 8th graders for the transition, as slow or as fast as it may be, into mainstream all English content classes? For our study here we will highlight a very unique and exciting region in the USA: **California, Arizona, New Mexico, and Texas.** In this study, we will look at some important ideas that relate to a different type of transition; a reading transition, one that affects nearly one million language minority students in this huge Spanish-speaking region.

The Mexican border region is the true "melting pot" and perhaps final frontier of the USA. Although situated on the US side of the river, many school districts have significant populations of Mexican-American students who speak Spanish as their first language. High birth rates (Chisman, 1989) and annual immigration, both legal and illegal, from Mexico, creates instability in the border region with disproportionate numbers of persons suffering from diabetes, child mortality, and poverty in relation to the USA mainland. All of these problems carry over and into the public school systems along the border.

Since language reflects culture and vice-versa, this poses a particular problem when it comes to the public school system as administrators attempt to run an **"American" type school** system to a population in which this model is not the typical American norm. They attempt to modify curriculum, improve test scores, and implement state-of-the-art programs that will enhance education and assure equity and excellence for all.

> Noble are the efforts but dismal the results of our bilingual education programs!

Children are brought into an education system where English is the dominant language and culture; yet their first language is a more indirect, passive, Latin-based language. The language dilemma is the **number one academic dilemma** facing school systems in the Border States region. The students are wholesome, fun and intelligent. The problem is English language mastery, not the students or their culture. The successful transfer of skills from a Latin-based to a considerably harsher Germanic-based language requires more than reading and writing drills in a 12-year school program. It requires a comprehensive approach that addresses transfer skills, assuring a quality chance at mastering English literacy on the state-mandated minimum skills tests, as well as end-of-semester exams, etc.

Furthermore, Mexican-American high school **LEP** (Limited English Proficient) students, whose categorization should not exist at all after several years of bilingual education, are routinely passed up the high school ladder until finally they either quit the system, or struggle through, only to end up failing the Exit test, ending their hopes of university or a professional career, feeling like a failure which they are most certainly not!

Many bilingual educators, particularly those located along the Mexico-USA border, are examining the influence of English-dominated texts and curriculum upon these students whose *first language and first culture* is Spanish dominant. The end product is an improvement of the quality of bilingual education programs. This in turn, is expected to help bridge the gap between oral Spanish and written/spoken English.

In a comprehensive bilingual education program, the native language is taught first, with emphasis on first language listening, speaking, reading, and writing, with second language developed gradually, after a full grasp of first language literacy has taken place. This approach is referred to in the literature as "Transitional Bilingual Education" with English literacy fluency as the major objective, but off in the distance, not a true reality for many years to come. Unfortunately some parents are not aware of this approach, preferring placement of their LEP children in all English classes. Results, although mixed, remain dismal when this approach is used in Border States.

Reading Transfer Skills from Spanish to English

According to bilingual education theory, a solid foundation in the native language will assure the best results in mastering the second language. But if the students are summarily opted out of the program, their mastery of English language skills could be greatly hampered in the long run.

This could be one of the reasons behind such high failure/drop-out rates among Mexican-American students, as high as **48% in some areas** along the border in Texas (Texas Ed Agency, 1994). After all, Spanish and English, as distinct language systems, have very little in common. However, general language-learning processes are very much "transferable." This leads to some important questions, which must be addressed when examining Border States issues:

- Are inherent differences between the two-language/culture systems inhibiting academic success in English?

- Are the consistent low scores in English reading comprehension a direct result of non-effective transfer skills practice/drills at the primary level?

- Can reading and comprehension transfer skills be strengthened at the primary level, thus ensuring success in English reading and therefore success on

State exit tests and beyond? (THEA and ACCUPLACER for college)

- At what age or language level of proficiency should the vital transition begin to take place? And, how should transition skills be implemented in the classroom?

With these questions forming a base, we begin our adventure into Reading Transfer Skills. For the purposes of this study we will define these terms thusly:

"Reading"=comprehending text in English

"Transfer Skills"=skills that enhance transition into second language

There are two divisions of Transfer Skills:

Literacy skills and Oral Language skills.

The student that has adequate literacy skills in Spanish theoretically holds a significant advantage over students with only strong listening and speaking skills. Oral skills are difficult to analyze and often, living along the border, students tend to pick up a mixture of the two languages at an early age, thus complicating the issue of bilingual education, often relegating an otherwise effective program into a weird type of "hybrid" program with the student neither mastering Spanish nor English literacy effectively. This has been an effective argument for antagonists of bilingual education for many years.

Code Switching, Tex-Mex and Spanglish

Research by Trinity University professor, Scott Baird, reveals that a substantial amount of evidence is needed to conclude that a separate language is emerging from the mixture of English/Spanish in the region. This mixture is commonly referred to as "Tex-Mex." Children can be heard saying, "Vámanos, let's go." "Cómo do you say your name?"

Furthermore, a more concrete dilution of the two languages is seen in the simple development of children's speech patterns as researched by this author (1982-1995) who discovered an abundance of English **developmental and interference errors** including the following:

Underwears, turn on the matches, someone is touching the door. What day are we? I have $5 to waste at the carnival, Turn on the matches, Would you buy me one? Who and who are going? This instead of these.

Keep in mind that these errors in English are caused by direct *"transliteration"* as opposed to *"translation"* from Spanish, which in itself, is a very valuable skill if developed using effective Transfer Skills strategies. In linguistic terms however, this phenomenon is referred to as "interference."

This author poses that if the LEP students were taught how to use their valuable Spanish language to bridge into English reading, the results would be astounding. However, most bilingual education programs are geared for REMEDIATION of poor English skills rather than support of positive transfer skills that can be taught and practiced. Their well-meant intentions are wrought with enthusiasm, yet test results from this region are resounding with a never-ending plethora of defeats, year-after-year, consistently performing significantly behind their heartland USA peers and Mexico heartland peers as well (Harmon, 1994).

Regardless of how educators view the problems revealed by low reading test scores, some foundational facts need to be carefully observed. One of these is language itself. Language is very fluid, most certainly changing, sometimes within a relative short period of time. One example is how the British pronunciation slowly exited from mainstream standard American English speech which took only about 200 years. Also, **Tex-Mex** is evolving in front of our own eyes.

"**Spanglish**" in Puerto Rico is following a similar "pidginization" of English as that which occurred in South Africa during the early 1800's. Communication, in a larger sense, involves all forms of language and vice-versa. Communication, however, can involve dynamics that have nothing in common with language per se. What we carry out and what we say may be two separate things but what we say is often just as powerful as what we carry out! "A study of the evolution of language involves two tenets: first, language as a means of communication is ordinarily thought of as being directed from person-to-person (social) and secondly, it is the means by which man encodes and decodes meanings with symbols" (Stauffer 121). What is your view of language? School educators need to be transparent in their near religious zeal they should share for language and its correct use in their schools from the highest levels to most elementary classrooms.

Functional Reading. By the time children are of school age the size of their functional speaking vocabulary is about 7,500 words in their native language (IBID). One can readily see that the breadth of the children's oral ability is certainly large enough to sweep them hastily into a regular reading program, so it would seem.

The issues complicated, however, when that child is being sent DOUBLE MESSAGES: *bilingualism and biculturalism* in society. Unconsciously we all are subject to hidden, discrete messages that are sent from our cultures: which are the best foods, clothing styles, social patterns, religious patterns, etc. And, of course, we are also taught intuitively which is the **"best" language**. This is the language that is naturally acquired at home with Mom and is indelibly linked into our minds at an early age as being superior and "correct." This is fine for any child and in fact, according to psychologists, is certainly normal and healthy for self-esteem and cultural personal identity. Unfortunately, the children who are exposed to a dominant culture such as is the case along the Mexican border, tend to suffer from a lack of these healthy links because they are bombarded by television and the pop culture with American values, American culture, and of course the American language: English!

Dr. Ray Graham, Chair of Department of Linguistics at Brigham Young University, stated in an interview in 1993, "No child raised in the USA cannot NOT learn English nor NOT be radically influenced by the tremendously powerful culture of the United States" (Distinguished Author Lecture Series, Region One ESC, Texas). This leaves us with many more questions than answers regarding how much dominant culture should students of one language be exposed to while attempting to learn their own native language literacy. In other words, the American culture is so dominant that bilingual education children will not want to wait for their schools to "transfer" them into English. More than not, students "jump the gun" and start reading simple English sentences in kindergarten to the apparent consternation of their Spanish-speaking classmates and teachers! But they are doing only what Dr. Ray Graham from BYU states is only natural since they are bombarded by a culture that simply won't wait for our almighty bilingual education program to catch up with Mother Nature.

This, of course, can lead to a major developmental problem in the classroom when the teacher requires answers in Spanish but the children prefer to respond in English. Are they punished? Is their grade lowered? Technically the class is featuring Spanish in K-3 so minimal English is required. When students launch into English too early and on their own, academic friction often results, leaving the younger children unaware of which language they are speaking. Kinder students in this geographic region have no concept that they are speaking two languages anyway. They communicate as efficiently as they can, whether in the language of the classroom (Spanish), or the dominant language of the pop culture (English).

Reading Difficulties

Learning difficulties, in large part, can be traced to reading difficulties, since all academic work is built upon one's ability to denote words, comprehend their meaning and purpose, and interact with various kinds of texts, graphic and otherwise. Simply put, most academic language problems are usually **reading problems.**

So we must take into account that Spanish-speaking children living in *Los Angeles, New York City, Miami, Phoenix, Nogales, El Paso, Laredo, Roma, McAllen and Brownsville,* are entering kindergarten classes with a vocabulary of perhaps over **7,000 terms** in Spanish, (based on Piaget's observations in French) and a certain number of terms in L2, English, which is, as yet, undetermined by research. Some of these students will be transferred out of an all-Spanish curriculum to an all-English curriculum by 4th grade, but then will remain labeled as "LEP" up to graduation. The question remains,

"WHAT EVER HAPPENED TO THEIR ACQUISITION OF LITERACY SKILLS IN BOTH LANGUAGES?"

Their oral language ability was strengthened through a myriad of interesting and fun activities. These skills were further enhanced by music and perhaps drama. But their literacy skills in Spanish are practically non-existent when they are transitioned in 4th grade. ¿Qué pasó?

Students in bilingual/bicultural high schools are seldom able to translate even a few sentences in Spanish accurately. If they had 4-5 years of all-Spanish curriculum in bilingual education, what happened? One theory is the old adage, **"If you don't use it, you lose it."** But the sad fact, in the case against bilingual education, is that they never had it to start with. Elementary children enrolled in an all-Spanish curriculum are not adequately prepared with Spanish syntax study to handle life-long literacy challenges in Spanish. Another theory, which rings all too true, is lack of teacher preparation. Teachers, regardless of cultural affiliation, tend to favor English out of the classroom for oral communication and 100% for written communication (other than academic or course). Therefore, theoretically, how prepared can a bilingual education teacher be who is not exposed to Spanish written communication on a daily basis in the **BICS** (Basic Interpersonal Communication Skills)? The answer is, they are not prepared and it is almost impossible to prepare them adequately in the USA. Then what is the answer?

Obviously bilingual education programs trudge along with horrendous results but the massive federal tax dollars keep pouring in, regardless. Where is the accountability? Basically speaking, no viable accountability measures have really existed until the Republicans introduced extensive legislation, bringing down the hammer, with the **No Child Left Behind** reauthorization bill in 2002. The federal government often prefers to see the bilingual program as an ethnic (euphemism for "racial"), cultural issue that must be dealt with by the Hispanics themselves, since they control the vast majority of funds earmarked for bilingual education. Congress is very reluctant to become involved in a political quagmire where their constituency along the border, for example, is 90% Mexican-American. This is only logical.

But nevertheless, some courageous changes must take place in order to bridge this knowledge gap in native language. Mexican-American teachers are called upon to perform basic Spanish skills in the bilingual classroom but are often incapable of doing so outside of standard greetings and common expressions that they have never seen committed to text. Pronunciation suffers, modeling is corrupted, and the end result in most bilingual programs is that students exit not having any real or even general knowledge of written Spanish. Thus, a common ground for building English literacy skills later in their education is rendered impossible.

Teachers want to know how to incorporate transfer skills in their Bilingual Education program.

STANDARD V. NON-STANDARD ENGLISH

Comparatively little has been written or researched on this topic one might find rather amazing. Standard English is a very poignant reminder to English speakers that a real, viable, regularized standard indeed exists today in our language, albeit one that is governed and moved by popular usage, not formal rules. With no formal Academy such as Spanish and French languages, English is left to its own devices in deciding what is "standard" or correct and what is not, with those devices being popular usage, popular writing, and pop culture in general. These are then published into certain norms which we then call "standard" English.

English language rules are driven not by design but by popular usage.

Spelling is forever plagued by this conundrum. My advice to new ESL/ELD teachers is simply to require a modern American English dictionary published in the USA. Have students consult the dictionary frequently, allowing them to understand the concept that the dictionary is our only reasonable "standard" for writing in this difficult but fun language. Also, a thesaurus is needed, to not only enhance readability and nuance for our sentence constructions, but simply to produce the language correctly!

English language very much has a standard set of guidelines for usage, divided into two main branches: oral and written. These are discussed elsewhere in this book. Teachers should realize that spoken and written language usages are very different and should be treated as such. How and what is spoken cannot be transcribed to the written page. Writing is almost always formal and oral language is almost always informal, so thus the most apparent difference.

One needs to keep in mind that the two main streams of English are **British and American** English formats. These are greatly separated by geography and history. Furthermore, our language is divided into smaller geographical regions with some really interesting variations in pronunciation, spelling, and everyday speech patterns. What is "correct" in one stream may not be in the other although we are so closely related.

Therefore, we are left to regularize the language as much as possible while maintaining a flexibility not enjoyed by most other languages perhaps. English teachers must set the bar high in writing while allowing for colloquialisms and changes in local speaking patterns, etc. Modeling correct usage and writing cannot be over-emphasized in this context as we ever strive for the illusive "holy grail" of perfect English.

The use of alphabets to depict language is a relatively new concept in human evolution. Why are they so important, yet so varied? Do they really regularize language efficiently?

Effective Steps to Bridge the Gap in Spanish Language Proficiency

1. Adopt texts and computer software, which are user friendly for Mexican-American students and teachers.

2. Encourage elementary students to not only converse in correct analytical Spanish (they already have the pronunciation), but also to WRITE correctly in Spanish.

3. Consider hiring teachers from Mexico who are well prepared in their own native language.

4. Pay. Increase pay for bilingual teachers who earn Masters Degrees in Spanish and/or take a certain number of hours in graduate level Spanish language.

If the Bilingual Education program worked, students would not only transfer their L1 skills into the target language, English, but would also graduate fully "bilingual" with bilingual literacy skills as well. Unfortunately this is not the case at all! Why? The program was set up to fail and it certainly is faithfully fulfilling that objective. Could the teachers use the same wonderful ESL techniques in the bilingual program in grammar grades? They could but are not given the resources or time to make this so.

In short, the problems within this megalithic academic program are at times overwhelming but not insurmountable. A considerable number of very capable educators are available on both sides of the border who could tackle the problems of bilingual education from a purely scientific viewpoint and offer wise, powerful solutions.

Maybe the words of Luis Machado would be in order here, "Today we have sufficient knowledge to increase the capacity of (intelligence) for every child in the world" (from Proceedings of 2nd International SEAL Conference, Hertford, Hertfordshire, England, March 2001). Is it possible to increase the intelligence, literal "brain power" of children from birth to early childhood? He says that this is possible on a much broader scale than we are currently using via formal education techniques in public and private schools. The parents are key elements in this intelligence-building process.

The logos (λογος) changes everything from the way mankind thinks to the way we interpret our world.

MODELS FOR EFFECTIVE READING TRANSFER CURRICULUM

1. A clear knowledge base and appreciation of Spanish oral tradition (semantics), syntax and writing format, and Spanish language literature

2. Adequately prepare students to become familiar with commonalities between the two languages

3. Adequately prepare students to become familiar with differences between the two languages

4. Conscientiously apply <u>rules of transfer</u> in all academic situations, as much as possible.

5. Avoid code-switching by the time students are in middle school grades via proper role modeling

New school administrators to the Southwest USA need to acquaint themselves with the culture and particular problems that are associated with this vast and burgeoning area of America. In many communities, education is the largest and most influential employer. "Knowing the ropes" can greatly aid in performance and initial success as the reins of school administration are taken. How does the school board feel about it? What is their slant? Who has influenced them in their thinking as to a workable theoretical framework for curriculum? And what about staffing? Are teachers experienced in current ESL/bilingual strategies? Are elementary teachers proficient in Spanish literacy as well as oral skills? These questions need to be addressed and many districts are doing so admirably.

HOW TO SET UP AN EFFECTIVE BILINGUAL EDUCATION TRANSFER SKILLS PROGRAM

1. Analyze the community population and student population. Find out where they are in respect to oral skills and literacy skills in English, the target language.

2. Analyze the same group in their native language.

3. Compare results and group students according to their abilities in Spanish literacy, not English. Apply the principles of your regular bilingual program. Be sure to emphasize heavy doses of Spanish literacy and literature into the curriculum while encouraging English oral practice, avoiding English literacy at the early grade levels until children have a firm grasp of native language literacy.

4. Train your teachers in phonetic differences between the two language systems. Encourage them to attend seminars, read the latest literature from Center for Applied Linguistics in Washington, TESOL (Teachers of English to Speakers of Other Languages.) Train teachers in Cognates, Contrastive Analysis, Linguistic Interference, and Transfer Skills. Avoid NABE (National Association of Bilingual Education). This group, although filled with many well-intentioned professionals, has nonetheless, been taken over by liberal political activists who are determined to make bilingual education a racist, biased Hispanic-dominated issue, far from its original tenets or philosophy.

5. When students are reading on level in native language, have them transfer into English literacy, using standard ESL methodologies such as Cooperative Learning, TPR, Games, Layered Learning, Language Experience Approach, Oral Reading, components of Krashen/Terrell's Natural Approach to second language acquisition, and most important of all, effective Reading Transfer Skills (see list in other parts of this book)

6. Monitor classes and student achievement and modify as necessary.

7. Evaluate results of State mandated reading test scores and modify program as needed.

The 3 M's in effective transfer language education:

MODEL MONITOR MODIFY

Model. Since language is largely learned naturally by mimicking, a good model is the best policy. Are teachers well prepared for their teaching assignments? Use pretend reading, free reading, skits and fun music including dance and songs.

Monitor. Teachers are the best at this. Encourage them to actively assess their language students on an on-going basis. Make it a part of their weekly discussion groups for lesson planning and Vertical Teaming efforts. Are your teachers encouraging Portfolios?

Modify. Change need not be something fearful when things need changing! If something is working and by empirical results is proven to work, CELEBRATE it! If it is not, nix it! Move on to something that is effective and gains real results. Visit other schools and see what is working for them. Modification can be extremely positive, not the opposite. This means a school is innovative and up to date. Curriculum needs to reflect both the local community needs and the larger community, particularly as it relates to the computer and Internet skills. Content can be "sheltered" but need not be remediated or "watered down." For example, when an item can be passed around the class to illustrate an otherwise complicated objective, why not use it instead of a proven method of failure for LEP's-lecture from an English text!

Comparative Analysis of Language Patterns to Reinforce Metacognition

This is a wonderful eye-opener to students who are making the transition from a native language to English (or vice-versa). Have the students look up definitions to commonly used nouns such as house, boy, girl, yes, no, and Monday; in Spanish, English, French, German, Russian, Portuguese. Students will quickly see the similarities of the Roman-based languages and the similarities of the German-based languages. Then, if Eastern languages are added, the same phenomenon occurs with these languages as well. It is fun and teaches a vital self-teaching, contextual reading skill that students can use.

English	French	German	Spanish	Italiano	Russian
No	non	Nein	no	no	nyet
yes	oui	Ya	si	si	da
house	maison	Haus	casa	villa	dacha
hound	chien	Hund	perro	cane	cobaka

*Can you identify any patterns?

English Spanish

Boy=muchacho Girl=muchacha (No transfer)

Automobile= automóvil bus=autobus (Evident transfer)

ENGLISH-SPANISH COGNATES (similar in root words)

English Spanish

Family=familia

Mama=mamá Papa=papá

*Did you notice simple transfer patterns?

Rosedale Free Church located north of London, was the scene of a memorable speaking occasion for Dr. Clark in 1998. Teachers are often seen as leaders in more than just academics and facts. Doxography involves many areas of real life. Church and school should work in tandem to provide a quality life for all.

THE SHORT AND LONG VOWELS CONUNDRUM

English has many vowel "sounds" but only 5 vowels, but the 10 most important sounds for the beginning English student are the short and long vowels.

The long and short vowels should not be underestimated in the kinder-first grade classroom (or any level when immigrant students enter classroom). These should be clearly visible in the classroom and periodically reviewed. Keep in mind that Spanish has no "short" vowels, only one set of sounds, period. Spanish phonics are highly consistent, always sounding the same. The short vowels should always be taught and drilled first. Most students probably already know the "alphabet" before entering into kinder. But beware! They are actually mimicking the long sounds for all 26 letters, whether vowels or not. An effective kinder and first grade teacher will reinforce the short vowels as soon as possible and keep these in front of the learning throughout the year.

Dr. Clark shares a happy moment with leaders of North Carolina Adult ESL Education, Sarah Loudermelk of Catawba Valley Community College (left) and Dr. Florence Taylor, (right). Dr. Clark was a contracted trainer for teachers in the Community College System of NC on five different occasions over a four year period, 1995-1999, and later presented at the Annual Conference in 2001 and 2004.

The "long" names of the letters of the alphabet

The names of the letters of the English alphabet are always said or sung as being "long." This may actually confuse new learners. Avoid where possible. Instead we recommend programs such as **"Sing, Spell, Read & Write"** (800-321-8322) and other programs that sing the phonetic sounds of the letters, including all possible phonetic variations, instead of repeating the long sounds only. Many potential headaches will be avoided early by using this method. The names of the letters and the sounds they make are often not the same or even similar!

McAllen, Texas, teachers are treated to a special guest speaker in Prof. Martinez, Rector and founder of Nuevo Laredo City College and La Universidad Internacional de Estudios Superiores in Reynosa, Tamaulipas, Mexico, shown here at the Holidome, 1998. He is a published author and very well respected academic in English language acquisition in his native Mexico. With the institution of NAFTA, Mexican teachers and USA teachers began seeing an increased need of mutual cooperation, especially in English and Spanish languages.

SIMILARITES OF ENGISH AND SPANISH PHONICS

Directionality. Both read and write from left-to-right.

Roman alphabet. Although the Roman alphabet letters are not pronounced the same as other languages that use this alphabet, still the letters are recognizable.

Capital letters begin sentences. A period ends them. *Be aware that the period in English reflects English/American culture, which means a very abrupt, sharp STOP! In Spanish, the period is little more than a continuation, a comma for all intents and purposes. Some Spanish writers use only commas in the place of periods altogether! Be aware that your students from Spanish will not understand this unless it is taught and emphasized. This will help to avoid many comma splices in future writing.

Same 5 vowels, at least in appearance, shape.

Both have some letters written above and/or below the base line: g,j,p,q,y

Both have silent letters: Eng: rende<u>z</u>v<u>ou</u>s Sp: a<u>h</u>ora.

Both have similar sentence structure:

Subject + Verb + Complement

Both have perfect tenses (have said = ha dicho)

Many idioms are similar "Birds of a feather, flock together." "Dime con quien andas y te digo quien éres."

Both have regular and irregular verbs. ENGLISH has go/went SPANISH has voy/fuí

This chart may be used to familiarize Spanish students with some association with the difficult soft vowel sounds with similar sounds in Spanish. Unfortunately few transfer links exist between English "soft" vowels and Spanish vowels.

ENGLISH   SPANISH

a as in apple   *no equivalent in Spanish so /e/ is often substituted incorrectly by Spanish speakers

e as in egg   e as in elefante This one will transfer!

i as in igloo   *no equivalent in Spanish

o as in opera   *no equivalent as an /o/ but as a Spanish /a/ Amen, alleluia

u as in up   *no equivalent in any sense. This is a schwa sound from Germanic roots in English language history.

The Tricky Schwa Sound: "Ah, the Inescapable 'uh' sound!"

Using the copy of the Pledge of Allegiance below, we will emphasize the significance of the schwa sound in English language. It is tricky for spelling, yet very simple to use in pronunciation after short drills. Keep in mind that the schwa or "uh" sound comes from our Germanic linguistic heritage and is everywhere, hidden in a vast majority of English vowel usage. It can appear in *every* English short vowel but *never* occurs naturally in Spanish, so it can be quite a hurdle for those coming from this language. The closest to the "uh" sound of the schwa is the "ah" sound of the Spanish /a/. However, this is still not the same sound so comparisons to this sound are meaningless.

I pledge allegiance to the flag of the United States of America, and to the republic for which it stands; one nation, under God, indivisible, with liberty and justice for all. *The word "I" is often spoken as a true long "I" and not as a schwa. We include it here since we so seldom lift the muscles of the jaws to properly make it a true "I".

194

PHONIC DIFFICULTIES IN TRANSFER FROM SPANISH TO ENGLISH

These sounds often cause difficulty in transferring from Spanish. Keep this in mind during phonics drills and vocabulary assignments.

a am, at-- no equivalent in Spanish

b baby-- tendency to soften the /b/to a /v/

ch chair-- /ch/ and /sh/ are often substituted for one another

d did does-- have equivalent in Spanish but when used as an initial sound, it is often pronounced as /dth/ or /t/, or /th/.

i him-- no equivalent in Spanish

j jump—T is is a silent letter in Spanish

ng sing--tendency to add a /k/ or /g/ sound following the blend.

s school--As initial letters they are often produced as /eschool/.

sh shoe-- No equivalent in Spanish

th then--No equivalent in Spanish

th thank--No equivalent in Spanish

d   In Spanish this letter has 3 sounds

z   In Spanish this is pronounced as an "S" only.

These sounds will not transfer naturally between Spanish & English: H R G J Q V Y Z

These diagraphs will not transfer naturally:

th---

---ck   kn—

--gh   wr—

--ng --nk

These vowel diagraphs/dipthongs will transfer naturally:

oy=toy/soy

ai=light/caigo

These will not: Spanish /ie/ as in "¿Quién?"

<u>International Phonetic Alphabet</u>. Should it be used in class? Not many instances can be identified where this otherwise fine linguistic instrument is needed in bilingual or ESL for grade levels K-6 classrooms except for occasional clarifications of pronunciation. However, for middle school and beyond where highly educated first language students may be enrolled, then the IPA would be helpful since most educated foreign students are already familiar with it. It is readily accessible on the Internet or usually at the front of a quality dictionary.

DICTIONARIES: What and When?

Obviously the dictionary is the cornerstone of language classes, period. That is why a quality library features an unabridged dictionary usually at the entrance. This symbolizes the immense importance of this instrument. Many weeks of excellent instruction could come from using simply the dictionary and no other text! Beginner level students absolutely MUST have an English-Spanish dictionary. Intermediate and Advanced level need to transfer into English-English dictionary.

Kids learn best by touching, trial and error, and large amounts of kinesthetic activities. As much as possible, the teacher needs to step back and let the students become the stars of the class, the "Sages on the stage" as it were.

SUGGESTIONS FOR BILINGUAL ACHIEVEMENT IMPROVEMENT FOR BORDER STATES

1. Mandate free English education for parents. Feasibility? Although this would certainly make an impact almost immediately for their children, most parents have a myriad of valid excuses why this would not work. Waivers would be given out prolifically and it would not work.

2. Switch to Dual Language curriculum. While still in its infancy in the USA, Dual Language programs have measured success in Canada. These programs still are not effective overtly in enhancing standard English language literacy skills; this is still a bilingual approach to solving a major linguistic need.

3. Throw away with bilingual curriculum altogether! Feasibility? Not likely since they are mandated by law (Lau v Nichols, 1974) and in some bilingual programs, the rate of English literacy achievement has matched and/or surpassed that of monolingual program students! (These are rare, but a few examples exist).

Keep in mind that California and Arizona have implemented this suggestion and switched to a more purely ESL approach. Results are promising but not yet conclusive.

4. Revamp the methodology and curriculum used to teach English reading to primary children whose native language is not English. This is the most cogent of all the suggestions above, but it still has an inherently subjective component because the question may be posed, "What is best for my school?" Whatever the solution for your school, we must keep in mind that we CAN have an effective bilingual education program along the US-Mexico border because we have the means, the methods, and the manpower to accomplish this but are we truly willing?

Chapter 13 Questions

1. Describe the typical bilingual program along the US-Mexico border.

2. Identify the term, "code switching."

3. Compare the terms, "transliteration" with "translation."

4. The bilingual program provides primary level instruction in Spanish first in order to build a solid language foundation, eventually transferring into English instruction and content areas. Why are graduates of this program not literate in Spanish language?

5. The author suggests seven steps for setting up an effective transfer skills program. Shorten and summarize each.

6. What are the Three M's in effective language transfer?

7. How can a comparative analysis of the two language being learned in a bilingual education program, support the learning taking place?

8. Identify the term, "cognate." List twenty cognates of Spanish and English.

9. List three similarities between English and Spanish.

10. Why is the "schwa" sound difficult for Spanish speakers?

11. List three sounds that will not transfer from Spanish to English.

12. Beginner level language learners should have what type of dictionary?

13. The author lists several suggestions to improve student achievement in language. Shorten and summarize each.

Θ Chapter 14
ADULT EDUCATION PHILOSOPHY

Mr. Rodriguez studies for the GED diploma with the author.
He passed with flying colors on his first attempt!
Adults are quick learners and highly motivated.

Enrollment in US adult education increased from 38% (over age 18) in 1991 to 48% in 1999. Fifty million American adults are involved in some form of adult education currently (National Center for Ed Statistics, 2002). Some take classes for leisure in order to keep up with technology, to attempt a new language, to return to college with a grandchild. Whatever the reason, adults are flocking back to college in record numbers and at older ages. But for our study here, we will focus on the more disenfranchised adults who are enrolled in **GED, ESL, or ABE** (Adult Basic Education) courses since they are the constituency which is in the greatest economic and philosophical need and for which this author enjoys a strong "Walshonian" affinity. (Attributed to the influence of Dr. Mark M. Walsh of Texas A&M University, Kingsville, Texas, from his 20+ years of selfless devotion to the underprivileged workforce enrolled in adult education both in the USA and in Latin America.)

Dr. Mark Walsh greets the author (left) on his induction into Phi Delta Kappa at Texas A&M University, Kingsville. (1991)

Adult education began in the USA as a rich man's club. For those in the know and the power brokers who needed an additional community pulpit, the beginnings of the Lyceum were very momentous and advantageous, although they certainly cannot reflect the humble nature of adult education currently. From the earliest Lyceum movement to Benjamin Franklin's noble attempts, the education of adults has held a position of importance, however subdued, in American society. According to InfoPlease.Com, a lyceum is "an institution for popular education providing discussions, lectures, concerts, etc. and, a building for such activities." By 1831 about 1,000 lyceums were in operation in the USA. This appears to be the favorite "medium of adult education in early 19th century America (Cambridge History of English and US Lit, VOL XVII).

"The lyceum organization, launched in Boston in 1829, included the town lyceum, state and national organizations. In reality the scheme never arrived at such complete general organization; however, it did attain universal popularity, very general distribution, and in some sections effective state as well as local organization" (IBID).

The use of oratory was viewed as the highest art form of rhetoric or verbal expression as it relates to education. Debate was a standard part of early US education. Members of Lyceum constitute a "Who's Who" of American politics, religion, and academia such as Greeley, Hale, Emerson, Garrison, Thoreau, Lowell, Willard, and Susan B. Anthony. After the abolition of slavery in 1863, black leaders such as **Frederick Douglas** and **Booker T. Washington** took up the daunting challenge to educate freed slaves. The Tuskegee Institute still shines as a testimony to these early efforts.

Another leader of note in adult education is **Malcolm Knowles** from Chicago. "His goal has been to advance the cause of the individual and of American democracy in the university and in adult education, in business and industry, and society generally" (Carlson, 1989). He is known as the father of andragogy, the teaching of adults. He published Informal Adult Education in 1950 which was also his Masters thesis. In it are contained 13 principles about methods, programs, and administration of adult education, published by University of Chicago Press.

Consistently under-funded however, adult education serves as a study in the indomitable spirit of local communities who usually take up the challenge of education America's adult population where the federal and state governments leave off. Thousands of volunteer hours and facilities are used each week across this land to educate parents, provide English as a Second Language and US Citizenship classes. Churches make up the bulk of free adult education classes but also many civic organizations pick up the slack also offer materials and/or volunteer hours to Literacy Volunteers of America or Laubach Literacy which is usually offered at public libraries.

Other leaders in adult literacy and related issues include **Paulo Freire** (1921-1997), Brazilian education reform leader. His efforts in Latin American adult literacy has earned him an eternal respect for all future generations of teachers of adults. He epitomized the very soul of —giving of one's self to the betterment of others. Freire's legacy of educational reform includes his own defining the struggle between a person's knowledge of the word and the world.

His writings, including **Pedagogy of the Oppressed, Cultures of Silence**, and others, gained him no friends in the government of Brazil; in fact, they landed him in prison and then exile. But eventually the climate for change occurred in Brazil and eventually his efforts paid off when Freire was asked by a new set of leaders in Brasilia who invited him to become Minister of Education for Sao Paolo, effectively giving him administration of two-thirds of the country's student population. He taught praxis, "a complex activity by which culture and society are created, and persons become critically conscious." This is the very heart of Freirean philosophy. He wanted to use literacy, knowledge of the word, to motivate individuals to change their world for the better. Is this not the epitome of adult education?

The need for ESL literacy propels the Freirean theory of liberation up a notch to pose this question. Is it right that we help adults acquire literacy in both the word and the world and they eventually graduate from our adult ed programs, only to end up a 21st century "slave" to globalization by having them work 8-5 in a factory? At what point does the "time=$" formula become translated into "*effort=more$<time*?" In other words, one's time is one's life. How much of one's life should be expected by the employer? Adult students lack empowerment, but adult graduates have it! They should be given OPTIONS within

society so that they are not tied to just one vocation. But if their Certificate of Completion reads, "Construction Trades" then what lateral transferability have they to seek something else later on? Very little.

The US Department of Education estimates that at least 10%+ of the nation's workforce consists of immigrants (2000). With immigrants comes the need for second language education in the adult classroom as well as the public school. The USA has traditionally been a nation of immigrants. English has been our strong unifying language, a leftover of our British rulers from long ago. Today, however, over 200 languages are heard from coast-to-coast as native languages enjoy rejuvenation in conjunction with Britain's "devolution" of parliaments and also of the English language even there! The "Received Pronunciation" is quickly and surely becoming "Estuary English" by growing numbers of British English speakers, according to the latest research at **Oxford University**. (Dr. von Heller attended Oxford Summer School, 2002).Although the dominant language of the British Isles by far, recent legislation in Parliament has funded language classes in Gaelic for Scotland and Welsh for Wales. The Assembly of Wales went so far as to proclaim both English and Welsh as proper languages for use in their national Assembly. Both Britain and America are going through 21st century changes that are often very similar, one affecting the other as it were.

As America grows older, industry is clamoring for a younger workforce to keep up with our service-dominated economy. We must place within the adult education curriculum viable components of a truer knowledge of the world to the level that the world has changed since Freire and Knowles so much that it is virtually a new world! Adult education is still behind when it comes to comprehensive training in computers and technology. Unfortunately the teachers are often computer illiterate as well, even in these modern times. Comprehensive training needs to be offered in the adult education curriculum that addresses 21st century needs with a

21st century format. That format is Doxography which takes into account the "liberating education" of Freire and adds the empowerment of technology to change our world. Indeed our world needs change. Monolithic, gargantuan corporations, in tandem with almighty governments, are impoverishing millions in the name of free enterprise and free trade. A person in Cambodia who is working for Nike making tennis shoes earns about $5 per day, a pitiful sum for a person's life and energy.

Unempowered hundreds of thousands will someday be able to read their word via Internet and Web radio and TV, learning 21st century ways in which to change their world for the better (NCES 97-269).Totalitarian governments love nothing more than to have a populace that is illiterate, poor, and in need of guidance. Adult educators need to focus on the persons in front of them and not fall prey to the larger concept of adults as being merely worker bees for large industry. For example, once this author was on a shuttle from the airport and struck up an interesting conversation with the chauffer. He passed my hotel and when I commented, he said, "I cannot stop there yet. I have to follow the whole route, even if no one is on the bus." When I commented that this was wholly a waste and time and illogical, he said,

> "I know you're right, but I'm not paid to think;
> I'm paid only to drive."

Adult educators have a wonderful opportunity to expand our current thinking from just teaching how to perform rote tasks, to teaching the joy, the "doxos" (glory) of thinking. Cognition with Doxography is marvelous and a powerful education tool in literacy. It is not difficult and best of all, it is natural because it glorifies God, and what could be more natural than that! As the Word was spoken and the worlds came into existence, so the learner can "speak" their worlds of knowledge into existence! Think of the potential!

Laredo educator, Felipe, and the author, are putting into practice a Doxography strategy learned the day before at a training session held at the beautiful La Posada Hotel.

Wall Street and the Doxos

Education is very much tied to making more money (Murnane and Levy, 1996). Both **performance and productivity** are viewed by industry as characteristics of "good workers." These values could eventually become inculcated by the recent adult education graduate as the "American value system" causing them to think of these factors as traits of their worth which of course, they are not. A construction worker who earns minimum wage in Houston, is not a "construction worker" but rather a "person who works in construction." However, a medical doctor is indeed a "doctor" because they earned the right to be called a doctor. The difference here is that when a daily worker is unemployed, they psychologically might relate their unemployment as a personal failure when it may have been just a glitch in the economy or an economic indicator from **Wall Street** that caused them to lose their jobs. A person should be known as a person of skills, not a person of facts. One can learn many trades, but personal qualities are inherent, stable and should only improve with time.

College students learn language twice as fast as high school students and five times as fast as 9 year olds (Duretta, 1972). Yes, adults learn language faster than children! Furthermore, Burstall (1977) found that adults are faster and more efficient learners of second language than children, except for pronunciation. Kids will outpace an adult every time in pronunciation. However, it is apparent that the public does not accept this message. Most would never agree, especially those parents who, after struggling with Arabic in Palestine for five years, return to America with their young children near fluent while they are still struggling with "Ke falik?" (How are you?) and "Alhamdulale" (fine). How can this be? It is because children are not exposed to the rules of language; they are instead exposed to the fun of the language without adult inhibitions and prohibitions (especially in learning the "bad words" which invariably will be among the first words learned)! In other words, they jump right into the language with the "que será, será" attitude so abundant in young children. However, no conflict with the research data exists at all. <u>Children are given "modeling" of the language, not rules.</u> Adults however, languish for hours in language labs learning syntactic constructions and formations.

In addition, research indicates that older students are better second language learners because they have achieved a higher level of cognitive development in the native language It appears that the amount of prior knowledge in one's first language and the ability to manipulate its constructive elements, greatly figure in the performance levels expected in the second language (Snow & Hoefnagel-Hohle, 1977). Therefore, adult students could be at a decided advantage over younger learners, depending on which of these factors come into play. Uneducated immigrants have a difficult struggle with English since most have never been given the opportunity to learn their own native language to any degree beyond survival level.

Some believe that **Doxographic philosophy** fits more effectively in adult education than at any other age level. Where else is witnessed such a "hunger and thirst" for literacy? The philosophy and altruistic attitude of adult education programs lend themselves readily to Doxographic philosophy. The Doxographic designed adult education classroom is one that involves all facets of the adult student's life including: family, social, religious, government, the law, and community interests. Only when adults are satisfied with themselves and with their situation in life, can they fully comprehend their world. Anticipation and anxiety lead to distraction both in and out of the adult education classroom.

Furthermore, adults are very sensitive to what the teacher "features" towards the students. Students care much more what you, as a teacher think of them, than what you know about the material being presented. They are persons first and foremost; not just numbers to fill an administrative mandate or state requisite for contact hours. The Doxographic trained teacher sees adult students as those who are worthy of an education, peers, not underlings seeking the crumbs off the table of life. In the adult classroom they can become kings, receiving Shakespeare and Tolstoy, learning and reciting the greatest poetry, singing the most beloved songs and hymns, learning to appreciate the finest artistic achievements of mankind. Learning how to get in touch with one's word and then changing one's world for the better—these are all components of the Doxographic adult education classroom.

Each year millions of American adults enroll in community education or university. The driving force currently in local adult education programs is the great influence of Mexicans who are seeking US Citizenship and/or ESL classes. Some are working towards a GED either in English or in Spanish. Heartland states such as Tennessee and Minnesota are actively recruiting and enrolling migrant workers.

Yet results from American adult education are dismal at best. In a recent assessment of adult literacy skills, 20.8% of the adult population in the USA had only basic, or "level one," reading and writing (prose) skills. Compared to most of the other countries assessed, the USA showed a great concentration of adults scoring at the lowest literacy level (level one) across the prose, document and quantitative literacy categories. However, the USA had one of the highest concentrations of adults scoring at or above level 4 on the prose scale" (National Center for Ed Statistics, 1994). See chart below:

Percentage of Adults Scoring on % Levels of the Prose Literacy Scale: 1994

COUNTRY	LEVEL 1	LEVEL 2	LEVEL 3	LEVEL 4
Canada	6.6	24.8	36.4	22.3
Germany	13.8	35.3	37.3	13.6
Netherlands	10.4	29.4	44.7	15.5
Poland	42.7	34.3	19.2	3.7
Sweden	7.2	20.7	39.8	32.2
USA	20.8	24.4	32.8	22.0

Note: Prose literacy relates to the knowledge and skills required to understand and use information from texts, including editorials, news stories, poems, and fiction.

Prose Level 1 tasks require the reader to locate and match a single piece of information that is identical to, or nearly identical to, the information given in the text.

Prose Level 2 tasks require the reader to locate one or more pieces of information from the text and to compare and contrast information.

Prose Level 3 tasks require readers to search the text to match information and make low-level inferences.

Prose Level 4/5 measures how well readers perform multiple-feature matching, use specialized knowledge and make text-based inferences from more abstract text sources.

National Center for Education Statistics, 1994, Department of Education

---

Why are adults returning to school? Recent studies indicate that most return to better their economic position. Some are mandated by law or by a court to seek courses related to citizenship and/or English language. Adult ESL programs are one of the most popular in the USA, particularly among the Spanish-speaking immigrant population. Their children quickly pick up English in a few years while the parents rely upon their children as translators for most of their life. The vast majority of immigrants never darken the door of an adult education program. Low economic status causes many to attend classes; by the same token, it is the #1 excuse as to why they cannot attend classes also. Many have to work at night or are simply too tired to attend. Other more practical reasons may include:

1. they may not have clothes that are appropriate,
2. babysitting problems,
3. lack of dependable transportation.

The future looks bright for America's adult education programs but more funding is urgently needed. American industry is in greater need than ever of an effective, educated, English-speaking workforce.

English teachers in Mexico are eager and ready to learn the latest methods and strategies. The author sits to the left of the Rector of La Universidad Valle del Bravo in Reynosa, Mexico, in 1999.

Chapter 14 Questions

1. By what percentage was enrollment in adult Ed programs increased between 1991 and 1999?

2. By 1831, how many "lyceums" existed in the USA?

3. Identify: Malcolm Knowles, GED, LVA, Paulo Freire

4. What is the estimated percentage of immigrants in the USA workplace?

5. Research is decisive in reporting that adults learn language faster and more efficiently than children. How can this be true?

Θ CHAPTER 15
ESL STRATEGIES

Dr. Clark uses the piano to illustrate the importance of music in the classroom for San Benito, Texas, teachers, summer of 2004.

In this chapter we will explore several highly acclaimed strategies that are in current use in ESL, both for k-12 and adult education. We are defining Strategies as coming under the domain of "Methods" and Methods under the domain of Approach, and Approach under Philosophy.

Strategies>Methods>Approach>Philosophy.

A school board or administering body determines the *philosophy* to be used in the overall English language program. This philosophy is then taken to be the official *"approach"* of the school. Then the practitioners (teachers), who usually sit on curriculum committees, begin to determine the overall *methods* to be used. Then comes the *strategies* which are very student-based and must be accurate in meeting the varied needs of the students.

These terms are used interchangeably in the literature so one should not worry too much about the specific order as given here or if a "stage" is skipped by the curriculum people in the school. The main objective is merely to organize a language program that is readily accessible by all, thus fulfilling the letter of the law, and to formulate a program that meets the needs of the students.

Probably the term, "strategies" is used the most in ESL literature for lesson plans and kinesthetic activities in the classroom. We will now examine a few of these.

Layered ESL Instruction for the Multi-Level Class

Multi level adult classes are the norm in adult education. Few programs have the luxury of same level ability classes due to funding and/or staffing. Levels of proficiency may range from preliterate to advanced, all within the same classroom. This is every teacher's worst nightmare. When this author was challenged with this dilemma with nine languages represented on four different levels, I quickly turned to others with more experience. One of those who helped me was Dr. Wayne Pate who served as a consultant in Adult Education with the **Texas Education Agency.** He trained us in Layered Instruction. While this approach is not as well known as Cooperative Learning or Language Experience Approach (LEA), it is the most effective of all approaches that I have tried when faced with the dilemma of teaching multi level classes. The results have been very positive.

The beauty of a layered approach is that only one lesson prep is needed. This one lesson plan is used for all levels with extensive modification for each level. Students are seated according to their level of language proficiency with the most advanced in the back and the beginning level in the front. The teacher begins with the beginning level and presents a short lesson, using the targeted vocabulary and/or objective material of the lesson. This is then repeated to the next level and so on. The advanced level will receive much more sophisticated constructions of both oral and written language via assignments, etc., and everyone will improve as a result of hearing the new material several times in a low anxiety setting where a particular group will only be called upon one time.

SCHEMATA FOR LAYERED LEARNING
ADVANCED STUDENTS (at back of classroom)
INTERMEDIATE LEVEL
BEGINNER LEVEL (up front)
Teacher

Costumes are a definite hit in Sheltered English classes. Helen Hilton from McAllen schools, especially enjoyed participating in this workshop along with the author (the Arab sheik of course).

WHAT IS SHELTERED INSTRUCTION?

Sheltered Instruction is a method designed to modify content material for Limited English Proficient students, involving many different types of activities and learning strategies. Dr. Jim Cummins is perhaps the most prominent name associated with this ESL Approach.

FOR ELEMENTARY: Sheltered Instruction is helpful for all subject areas, but is especially well-suited for the metric courses such as Science and Math. Elementary students are in process of making the TRANSITION from Spanish-to-English so activities are geared toward this end. Sheltered activities can be presented in any language. Games and activities are encouraged in English with Spanish directions as necessary for full student participation and comprehension of the subject matter being studied. In essence, Sheltered learning forms a bridge between the first language oral skills and second language literacy skills as second language literacy skills are carefully constructed and developed for eventual mastery of TAKS Reading which should lead, in short order, to mastery of all classes.

FOR SECONDARY: Secondary students have usually made the TRANSITION from Spanish-to-English, at least enough to be mainstreamed into classes that include both **EP** (English Proficient) as well as **LEP** (Limited English Proficient) students. Most Sheltered English materials are published with secondary students in mind. Activities range from raps, numbered heads, corners, competitive games, to intense interaction with graphic organizers, only to name a few. Secondary students are more proficient in how they gather and manipulate data so teachers are keenly aware that secondary students must be challenged accordingly and in a manner that does not embarrass them. Using Sheltered English lessons promotes self-esteem while building language skills and content material simultaneously. With this in mind, **LEP** students should have ample interaction with **EP** students at all levels. This interaction, regardless of how slight it may be at first, is a tremendous esteem booster for them and greatly aids their development of local speech patterns. Finally, this type of approach allows **LEP** students the opportunity to imitate reading and writing patterns of **EP** peers.

QUESTIONS:

1.   Have you used Sheltered instruction? __yes __no

2.   If so, how? _____

3.   ELEM: When is the Sp-Eng transition begun for your LEP students? __2nd __3rd __4th __other _____

Sheltered English and a Metacognition Approach

ESL learners, whether adults or children, come into the classroom with distinctive linguistic needs, desires, and goals that need to be fine-tuned like a fine stereo system. They want everything on the English plate and are eager participators in their own learning, yet lack the metacognitive skills to accurately think about their own learning in order to be successful. One way to ensure that students work to their potential and at their particular level of language comprehension is by using a "sheltered approach."

First and foremost, a **sheltered approach to language** causes students to feel more comfortable about their new learning situation. After all, they are naturally at a disadvantage, linguistically, or they would not be enrolled in the class anyway. Although well accepted that first language requires an active process of construction where the need and desire to communicate is easily acknowledged, the level of proficiency and rate of acquisition is much more evident in learners of second language (Wong Fillmore, 1991).

Some have suggested that the input of a student's own thinking into the actual process of language learning is paramount to an effective strategy for ample second language acquisition. "As teachers we only fool ourselves if we think we can teach language skills or literacy without integrating students' own ideas, purposes and dreams into the teaching program" (Enright and McCloskey, 1988). Self-confidence also plays a significant part of one's ability to think about one's own learning (Cummins, 1989). With this in mind, educators find that a sheltered approach in which students are actively engaged in their own learning processes is very beneficial.

Sheltered English encourages special modifications of regular content area courses using techniques that are common in ESL classes. These include--use of cognates from first language, visuals, kinesthetic activities, role-playing, drama, Total Physical Response, emphasis on socio-affective filter and others.

♫ Music While Writing

Substantial research has been conducted to conclusively draw a direct correlation between certain pieces of classical music to retention of information and scholarship, particularly the use of **Mozart**. Having said this, let us examine the role that quality pieces of music play in the mind of the writing student. If a certain type of music is played consistently, or even one particular artist, the students will subconsciously convert the external, physical audio signals into brain waves that will convert to **memory** sensations, causing them to forever associate that same music with the writing tasks that were being performed at the time of the class. Why is this important? As a positive memory-triggering device, this can be very helpful. Brain research indicates that the more attachments available in which information can cling, the better chance of that information remaining longer in the mind.

Sheltered English Philosophy and Related Methods

Sheltered English serves as a bridge between the ESL/ELD class and the regular content classes. Of course along with the regular classes comes preparation for state tests necessary for graduation. These are only permitted in English. Most content classes are not geared for the special language needs presented by LEP students (Early, 1990; Mohan, 1986). Content teachers such as English, History, Math and Social Studies, are highly trained in their teaching area but they are not usually well-prepared for LEP students. Classes are taught in English with no allowances for reading deficiencies. To make the situation worse, some courses in middle and high school are heavily "text-driven" such as Social Studies and Science.

LEP students are under tremendous pressure in two realms of language: academic and social. They want to fit in quickly with American society as soon as possible, and they need to master academic language to graduate and pass the state test. Many children of immigrants are eager to learn English and they usually receive firm parental support. Some, however, come from poverty-stricken families that often struggle economically just to survive. These children qualify as Chapter I, Title I recipients for reasons wholly apart from language.

Chemistry, Geometry, Social Studies, Lit—all require massive quantities of language via texts, reference materials: maps, the globe, Internet, dictionaries, encyclopedias, CD's, data bases, almanacs, etc. In the effective sheltered class, plenty of media opportunities should be available for students to use. Media releases the teacher from the limited vocabulary of a text and opens students up to a very interesting and challenging avenue of learning as well. Also, computer-assisted language learning (CALL), allows a student to review and remediate as many times as necessary. The computer never gets tired.

Thematic Units at Home

Themes are all around us from birth. Remember "Grandma's Coming?" Our moms would frantically prepare food and clean the house before she arrives. Everyone would be affected by the important thematic unit until grandma was gone and we could relax again. The next one would of course be, **"Relax, Grandma's Gone."** We would go back to our rooms and throw off the fancy clothes, take out our toys, and go back to regular life. These are important thematic units in our childhood. We learned huge amounts of valuable vocabulary from these little "units" from our siblings, parents, and friends. Students enjoy thematic units since they are easily related to real life as well, only in a school setting.

COLORED WRITING BANDS STRATEGY

The Writing Process must be considered and carefully included into any successful writing program. One interesting technique that is being successfully used throughout the world is the **Colored Writing Bands**. Dr. von Heller devised this technique to clearly show the steps of the writing process by using colored bands which are worn on the arms of the students. Green is for brainstorming and any techniques used Pre-writing. Yellow shows that the student has graduated into the Rough Draft Writing stage after Pre-writing is concluded. Students enjoy the bands and they serve as simple status symbols which can be worn not only in class but Dr. von Heller encourages them to wear them out of the class to advertise and celebrate their efforts with other students, many who think of writing as a tedious, relentless chore. The third band is purple, representing the Editing and Revising stage.

Then, the final band is placed around the wrist which is Red for Final Draft stage. This is the most coveted of all colors and is only worn when the instructor has verified that all the other stages are successfully completed. "Awarding" the red band can be made into a fun activity, celebrating the arduous process that the student has endured and mastered. All the other bands may be kept by the students and placed on as they progress through the Writing Process except for the red which can only be "awarded" by the instructor. This puts a final touch on the whole methodology employed and gives it an official stamp of approval. Students usually "buy" into this technique with great enthusiasm.

Students will tend to compare their "status" by the color of bands, teasing each other which serves as great bonding and peer encouragement. Types of bands are not important so long as they fit loosely around the wrist although the looser the better, especially with children. Teachers of children need to check with their supervisors before implementing this technique due to safety concerns. The choice of colors is not important either so long as their use is consistent from the beginning of the course to the conclusion.

Who says that staff development cannot be fun? These outstanding Brownsville, Texas teachers are practicing how to use "Audiowhispology," a Doxography technique, in their classes.

Thematic Units in Content Areas

A thematic unit is a unified attempt at incorporating one central theme or concept into different academic disciplines via classroom activities throughout the entire school for a certain period of time. Of course, just one teacher could have a thematic unit for their classroom as well. As students change classes in high school or even subjects in elementary school, new vocabularies have to be absorbed. Consequently, students actually learn many different "dialects" during their school career. For example, in the normal high school day, students may have a schedule like this:

♠ Scienceze: H2O, Co2, periodic table, hypothesis, AC-DC current, solar system, stratosphere

♠ Historeze: chronological order, Neanderthal Period, libertarianism, the Suffrage Movement

♠ Englisheze: hyperbole, subjunctive mood, periodicals, passive and active voice, punctuation

♠ Healtheze: epidermis, hypothermia, reproduction, allergies, nervous system

♠ Computereze: Diskettes, modem, CD-Rom, external drive, hard drive, zip drive, keyboard, monitor

♠ Matheze: theorem, equation, decimal, A2+B2=C2, Pythagorus, fractions, dividend

Staff members of the Clarkheller Institute seen here are (l-to-r) Carlos Garcia, Dr. Clark, and Prof. John E. Hatridge, Professor Emeritus, Honorary Chair of Queen Elizabeth II Literacy Foundation, 1996-1998.

One can readily see the need for unity of purpose by incorporating vocabulary into one central theme. Some schools have modified this format to include only a wing of the school or just a grade level. Any format that is functional is fine. Having each class pre and post tested on basic vocabulary and comprehension of the unit can easily assess the ultimate product. Results can be outstanding. The psychology involved is that no longer can the student use the ploy, "But Mrs. Johnson doesn't do it like that!" Pitting one teacher against another is old as the hills but Thematic Units and Team Planning destroy this ploy with more learning and language development as a result. At secondary level our students are attempting to learn "Scienceze" and "**Historyeze**" without filling in the appropriate English language gaps. Nothing of consequence results from this segregated approach.

While allowing for specialized jargons in the different classes is quite normal, still an overall awareness that language is being developed school-wide, must become apparent in the whole faculty. Without the conscience efforts of the different faculty departments, this development will not flourish and the end results will be those as already reflected in Border States and amongst high school students in Los Angeles and New York City, abysmal and plummeting each decade! This author contends that a conscience effort needs to take place to change our way of thinking about learning and one of those ways in to consider assigning Thematic Units throughout the entire school with a great emphasis on vocabulary development. One excellent source for further reading is chapter 13 "Literature and the Curriculum is <u>A Thematic Approach of Legacies: Using Children's Literature in the Classroom</u> by Liz Rothlein and Anita Meyer Meinbach, Harper Collins College Publishers, 1996.

SAMPLE TOPICS FOR THEMATIC UNITS:

Spring	Family
Earth Day	Water
Mother's Day	Dinosaurs
Patriotism	Ancient Egypt

Doxeze Vocabulary (The Glory of Positive Words)

Having seen that school curriculum is naturally divided into specific jargons, let us turn our attention to another aspect of jargon which changes attitudes, increases interest, and makes the school workplace simply better. This jargon is "Doxeze" the glory of positive words. This is the language of encouragement, self-esteem, and people building as it were. Each and every school classroom can be turned into a positive experience with the right vocabulary. The teacher may have to rehearse these words and the students need to become acquainted with them as well, but the end results are worth the effort.

A good place to begin affective learning is with what we say. Often, positive comments are not natural to many people, especially teachers. A kind word goes a long way with kids and learners in general. Each Doxography lesson should be started with the saying of **a motto**. A motto is a formal thing, one that brings unity and will never be forgotten. After that I start each lesson, even on test days, with some type of positive, uplifting literature, either a poem or just a wise saying which takes only a minute or two. Sometimes I end my opening comments with a joke, even if they refuse to laugh (especially at 8am!)

Again, the power of the logos is everywhere and apparent in all walks of life. "This isn't your best work but at least you used your time wisely and the paper appears somewhat organized. Now I want you to try it again and remember to follow directions carefully. I know you can meet your goals. Think positive. You're a smart person!" These **Doxeze words** were said by a high school teacher just this week! How impressive! This student is not a top performer but at least she left the teacher's evaluation feeling that her work was not in vain and could certainly be improved. Will she give her best for this teacher? Absolutely! Doxeze words work! We like them and students also.

Kinesthetic Activities

Competition and participation are vital experiences of growing up. Athletics and field games come naturally to most children. With this in mind, a controlled spirit of competition can be highly effective in promoting both academic achievement as well as language acquisition. The learning curve takes a wild swing upward when kinesthetic learning takes place. **Drama and skits** are excellent activities for increased participation and positive interaction with otherwise timid risk takers. Physiologically the brain is stimulated, blood circulates more rapidly which means more oxygen and energy. It is indeed, an academic "win-win" situation for all. Who does not like to see something instead of hearing about it? And, how much better still is having the opportunity to actually touch and handle real objects! Bring a football to your next ESL class and pass it around. Talk about it. Ask questions. Look it up on the Internet. What are the dimensions? When was it invented?

Hollywood Highlights! The Use of Drama in the ESL Classroom

Kids love drama. Here is a simple suggestion for use of drama in the ESL classroom. Divide into teams. Teacher assigns an objective from the text. It can be a word, certain topic, item, or entire section for the text. Students have to act it out, without talking. They give only gestures to indicate the topic or to illustrate an event (as in history). Once the objective has been met and item guessed, that person or group must direct the whole class into a short writing activity, describing the objective in correct detail as required by the teacher.

Lectures or **"Sage on the Stage"** strategies are not conducive to effective language learning. Drama lessons reduce this dilemma by encouraging all students to become involved in the content without rigid amounts of text to read or instruction to listen to. Writing at the end of this simple activity causes students to think cognitively and to organize their thoughts on paper, which also causes longer retention of information.

Another interesting activity is for the teacher to assign an objective from the text, same as above. Then each group has to compose a 12 line dramatic dialogue. Here is a silly example from high school:

Example from Science class. The topic is WATER.

H. Hi O, what are you doing?

O. Not much, but I need you.

H. Why?

O. Without you I feel so lonely and dry.

H. So dry? What do you mean?

O. Yes, because without you I can't become something wet and wild!

H. What's that?

O. That's water of course!

Wasn't that fun? And think of all the learning that took place. All students participated? Make sure that everyone takes part; if not, modify rules so that all are included, or at least peer pairs. Students want to be motivated, even in language classes.

Bingo!

And how could we ever forget Bingo? Any shape, any topic; Bingo is always a hit! Content area classes, which can be very daunting, can be modified greatly by using these simple strategies and activities. With this in mind the use of groups for all activities is highly recommended with a mixture of proficiencies within the groups. (Unless using Layered approach).

MIX IT UP!

Research indicates a positive correlation between second language acquisition proficiency and exposure to the target language, even if exposure involves indirect interaction with interlocutors of the target language. But how can interaction of ESL students with native speakers of English exist when ESL classes are often segregated? This is a problem within the structure of the school day scheduling that can be solved by including ESL students in vocational classes, athletics, P.E. and electives such as Art, Music, and Drama. The good news is that direct interaction is not necessary, just accommodation in at least two class periods per day.

Direct interaction between learners and native speakers of English may not be absolutely necessary for learning to take place. Some learners appear to be able to pick up the target language simply by observing teachers and peers (Cummins, 51). Furthermore, **Lilly Wong Fillmore** poses, "It appears that what is essential is that learners have access to language that is appropriately modified for them, and is used in ways that allow learners to discover its formal and pragmatic properties" (1991, 64) This is the good news. So access is the key, not direct interaction with other speakers. How can the curriculum allow for more access to meaningful language then? Are we encouraging ESL students to participate in school sports? Pep rallies? Assemblies? We should. Enright and McCloskey posed the importance of interaction throughout the normal school day:

Students fully develop second language and literacy through using the second language in many different settings, with a wide variety of respondents and audiences (including themselves) and for a wide variety of purposes…(Enright & McCloskey, 1988, 21).

The proponents of **CALLA**, (Cognitive Academic Language Learning Approach) **Ana Chamot and Michael O'Malley**, 1987, believe that early exposure to content subjects in limited formats of English greatly enhance future all-English, mainstream content classes. Although ESL students are given valuable vocabulary and structure, they are seldom given adequate preparation in academic content areas. Cummins poses that as much as five years may be needed to acquire a level of academic proficiency comparable to their English speaking peers. With this mind, a long-range comprehensive plan must be followed in the tracking of ESL students.

Their progress has to be monitored for many years, even after students appear to be "comfortable in English" (Cummins 54). This is so very important, because unlike others in the school population, language students are highly mobile, often migrant farmers, and are susceptible to changing their situation very quickly during both the school year and during their school career at one particular school. To have them start all over at beginning level, year-after-year is a disgrace to the public school system, but this is often the case when border students migrate to states within the USA that are not aware of the latest trends in ESL Assessment or they simply lack sufficient numbers of ESL students to form a bona fide ESL language program. Migrant students face obstacles that are not common among the majority of American school students. Migrant children face culture shock and find it difficult to make the necessary adjustments to succeed. Some US high schools, for instance, may be larger than even the entire town that the migrant student is from! Plus, the entire American school structure is somewhat alien to that of an all-Hispanic school in New Mexico, Texas, or Puerto Rico (Mounts, 1986).

Strategies for Migrant Students

Migrants are seasonal workers who follow crops or other seasonal industries. Texas has the largest migrant workforce in the country, consisting almost entirely of Mexican-Americans from the border regions. These workers provide a valuable service for the economy and are highly sought after from roofing contractors in New York, to tobacco farmers in North Carolina.

Most migrants follow a traditional annual trek northward during the spring months and return in autumn, well after the school year has begun. This causes major disruption in the classrooms unless an accommodation is made. How would you like to start with an enrollment of 14 and after six weeks, suddenly 10 more are added!

Some children of migrants are enrolled in both northern states and in their home state. Therefore, several key migrant states, including Texas, have a tracking system in place which helps alleviate the many problems associated with record-keeping of migrant students. The obvious problem is of course, that many students simply choose, for whatever reason, not to enroll in classes, especially if their work takes them to several states. **Texas Migrant Council**, Head Start and a host of other governmental agencies are helping and using resources to support migrant families. Texas is home to the largest group of migrants in the USA and most of them live along the USA-Mexico border in the lower Rio Grande River Delta, a densely populated region, extending from Brownsville to Mission.

Teachers are keenly aware that as many as 1,000,000 illegals pour across the border each year, many who are going to send for their wives and children later (CNN, March, 2005). The need for migrant education will only grow over the next decade. Are we prepared? Which strategies will work best with migrant students? A wide variety of strategies would be successful, but Doxography recommends a Sheltered approach with any method that stresses vocabulary development, self-esteem, and group work.

Enjoying the Mexican tradition of smashing confetti-filled eggs on unsuspecting guests, the author is loaded with ammo at a Resurrection Day party at Canterbury Estate on the Tex-Mex border.

Culture Clues Language Training Method

Another Doxographic strategy that is highly effective with LEP students and migrant students in general, involves culture and language together. It is called *"Culture Clues Language Training."* The philosophy underscores cultural understanding and self-esteem while reinforcing valuable English language vocabulary skills. Students are asked to accomplish a variety of skill-building tasks, depending on age and ability. These tasks begin with culture modeling on a broad basis and culminate in self-esteem exercises and a myriad of group activities. The results are amazing! Here is a sample from Culture Clues Language Training:

Students draw a map of the globe. Then the USA, then their state, and finally their local area (if a model is available). After this process is complete with explanations of the importance of "Who you are where you are" lessons, students divide into groups and are given one specific cultural clue after they have chosen what culture they are going to study.

Finally, after this process is completed in groups, students are given worksheets that contain pictures of different people in different situations of life, not vocations, but situations including a tragedy, a funeral, and a happy event such as a party. Students discuss their feelings as a group and finally on an individual basis. By the end of Cultural Clues Language Steps, students have evolved improved their English vocabulary as well as in self-esteem.

Newspapers in the Classroom

This strategy is growing in popularity in classrooms from Gifted and Talented to everyone else. **Audrey Eoff**, noted training specialist and conference speaker from Weslaco, Texas, says, "Using the newspaper is probably the most effective means of reaching all children of any level, with valuable information while supporting their literacy skills as well as objectives in math, social studies, and science." And this author concurs wholeheartedly. The newspaper is current, can be written upon, discarded, and is a renewable "textbook" that is always current. Lessons include looking for numbers, cities, certain words, clues, dates, styles of writing, print ad photos, writing commercials, etc.

Cooperative Learning

Without a doubt, cooperative learning projects increase the interactivity of all students to some degree. Rotation of assignments of Leader, Recorder, Evaluator, etc., also adds to the excitement of this method of instruction. Hispanic children and adults work especially well in this context as they are more prone to be more comfortable in social settings rather than individualized as most Anglo students tend to prefer. Much has been published on this method and is widely available in books, journals and on the Internet.

Language Experience Approach

This strategy is based upon the idea that students learn best while being exposed to substantial doses of the target language via modeling instead of direction instruction. The teacher writes the words of the students as they devise either a story or other type of narrative. Then the students copy the sentences from the board, insuring that the language is accurate, thus learning from listening, speaking, and last of all, writing (via copying).

The Research Method

Doxography encourages this as a preferred method for language instruction because the material used is real, not contrived from a textbook. Students work in groups on projects of real interest, often which they choose themselves as a short interview of their hobbies and goals with the teacher. With the Internet readily available, students will learn about their field of interest while earning points for the class as well. Thus, Doxography is truly taking place because the *learning originates with the learner*.

One way to use the Research Method is to challenge students to find a problem in their local classes, school, or community and then research it. Then they formulate a short survey and interview X number of people. Combining the survey results with the general investigation, students devise solutions to the original problem. The success rate for this type of project is usually very high because of the interest the subjects raise, and also, groups can divide up the various components.

Here is a standard format used in Doxography for the Research Method:

The Problem (identified in a short page)

The Need (2-3 pages of research)

The Survey (students explain why they devised the questions as they scored and how they conducted their survey)

The Findings (students report their tabulations of the survey with charts to depict each question from the survey, and their general impressions from the investigation)

Conclusions (students summarize their research)

Solution(s) (student devise solutions to the problem researched)

Works Cited page (an annotated bibliography)

The author assumes the role of Mark Antony, offering the crown to Julius Caesar (Danny) a migrant student from Donna, Texas. Drama is a wonderful stress reliever as well as an unforgettable experience for the students. Have you tried this in your classes?

The Product Method

Today's world of business relies upon printed products at every turn--reports, affidavits, resumes, manuals, etc. American graduates are losing ground to countries where this method of language acquisition is utilized to a large degree such as India, Japan, and Malaysia. Students need to actually "produce" a product in English on paper, typed in higher grades and handwritten in lower grades. Work produced that does not promote Doxography will not be fully appreciated by the student who produced it nor the instructor who requested it. This translates into the same scenario in the future with the boss not being pleased as well. If we can instill the desire to produce REAL **world products**, simple though they might be at lower grade levels, the end result will be more positive attitudes with many "affectives" realized from Doxography, and overall, a true win-win situation.

The Product Method is very simple, yet extremely rewarding. Technically speaking, most work carried out in a classroom is related to this method naturally. Here are some suggested activities for implementation:

ELEMENTARY:

Adopt a pet from the newspaper or T.V. Draw their picture. Give them a name. List how you are to care for them. Assign each group member a responsibility for the pet. Have each member illustrate the responsibility. Then they must write a caption under the illustration. Check spelling! After the "evaluator" of the group has checked the work, submission goes to the teacher for the final process: evaluation.

SECONDARY

Find a job you want from the Classified Ads of the newspaper. On one page, write the skills needed for the job. Then illustrate the main function of the job. Next, write a mock resume and a letter of intent. Submit for evaluation.

Rehearsal Memorization Strategies

Ever been to a "dress rehearsal?" Very formal and exciting, right? This same experience can be duplicated in the classroom with extremely positive results. Rehearsal of information is a proven manner of storing data in long term memory of the brain. Why is so much "learned" in school so quickly forgotten or discarded? While many answers are possible to this conundrum, still the Doxography teachers realize that the most logical answer lies in production of the language at the best possible speed and with the best possible results.

Whether a poem, thought for the day, motto, or saying, students need to rehearse oral language each day, each class, each hour. No excuses! Why does Buckingham Palace have a press office which releases prepared statements? Why doesn't the Queen simply invite reporters in and say things off the cuff? Why doesn't the President? The answer is clear: these world leaders know that their words must be rehearsed ahead of time to appear professional and in charge of the language. A misspoken word could cause great damage. Why can't we teach this strategy to our students as well?

Using certain life situations common to all such as parties, weddings, funerals, bar mitzvahs, or ceremonies at church, have the students to investigate the very best words and sentences that they should use in these situations. Then rehearse over-and-over until they are memorized! Then when the situation arises, they will not have to stumble for words.

The words will be filed in their cerebral cortex under whatever situation and they will look like real pros!

Poems are wonderful rehearsal tools for supporting the target language. Start with simple ones like *"The Raven"* and work up to *"The Highwayman"* and see what happens. The human mind is capable of enormous application of memory if information is rehearsed enough to become a "part" of the mental threads that reserve information in tact. And who wins as a result of rehearsal of language? Everyone involved! Why? Because their teachers used a simple Doxographic tool, rehearsal memorization.

Audiowhispology Technique

The art of listening involves discerning discreet tones, whether loud or soft. One way to gain the attention of students is to whisper. **Audiowhispology** involves the use of whispering while teaching as a modification technique to keep students alert. Students can become so accustomed to the "teacher voice" which is usually louder than normal speech, that they tune out instruction completely. After all, younger teen students listen to very loud music while at home, in the car, and certainly at concerts. Teachers have tremendous competition in this area.

The use of a microphone cannot be underestimated, particularly in a language classroom. Moreover, as a technique for delivering important information, audio-whispology is an excellent choice as a change of pace. For example, the instructor says, "I want you to write down the six steps of the writing process" Then start the list in a whisper. "First of all..." What would happen? Students might think it a joke at first. But more importantly, they would immediately pay closer attention and probably lean forward as if to hear a juicy secret from a friend. The end result would be effective listening which hopefully will lead to effective learning, another interesting technique used in Doxography.

Business is using audiowhispology. Once this author was introduced to a sales team and taken into a large noisy room to listen to a sales presentation. After we were seated around a small table, the sales rep launched into a well-choreographed presentation with flip charts and pictures. I could hardly hear a word he was saying so I had to get closer to the table and lean towards him. I kept thinking, "Why doesn't he just speak up louder?" Looking around me I realized that this same thing was happening at all the little round tables. What a trick! By near whispering, the sales staff were actually creating more interest in their product by causing us to have to pay closer attention. And although I was not interested in the product, only the free gift, I nevertheless can recall much of the data covered in the 30 minute presentation to this day! Audiowhispology works!

<u>Reconfiguring the Negative Mind Activity</u>

Children are bombarded with negative images and ugliness each day via TV and movies, video games, and the news channels. These images naturally form negative psychological messages in the brain and psyche which could be largely responsible for anti-social behavior. Doxographic methods can be used to counter this trend. Reconfiguring the Negative Mind Activity helps students learn to think and speak more positively. For example, while examining the Gettysburg Address, students should highlight any words they perceive as positive. Rehearse these words orally. In each major lesson activity, stop and rehearse positive terms, ideas, messages that are contained within the text. Students are smart; they quickly begin to improve attitudes and behavior with this type of positive reinforcement. This may seem to be an oversimplification of a complex psychological issue, but this author's results have been very effective. I urge teachers to try it.

Life is beautiful! "All the world is a stage..." said Shakespeare. The author believes in spirituality all around us, particularly in the physical world, one of exquisite beauty and loveliness. Let us strive to bring out the loveliness in each and every one of our students as we behold the beauty that is "la dolce vita."

Chapter 15 Questions

1. Briefly summarize the relationship between philosophy, strategies, methods, and techniques in second language acquisition.

2. Draw a small chart illustrating the concepts involved in Layered Learning.

3. Why is Cooperative Learning so effective?

4. List three important strategies that can be used with Sheltered English curricula and explain why you chose them.

5. Are newspaper projects an effective tool to use in an English language or ESL class? Explain.

6. Identify LEA.

7. Why would the Product Method be so useful with students who are studying business?

8. List three components of the Rehearsal Mem Method.

9. Explain the philosophy behind Audiowhispology technique.

10. Sheltered English allows academic material to be "sheltered" by approaching material carefully and methodically, using charts, graphs, pictorials, etc. Is this approach effective? Explain.

11. In philosophies of pedagogy, which are the best ones? "Sage on the Stage" or "Guide on the Side"? Why?

12. Do you think the "departmentalization" of American schools was a negative thing? Why?

13. What about theoretical approaches that support the use of "Thematic Units?"

Θ CHAPTER 16
MODERN EDUCATIONAL HISTORICAL PERSPECTIVES

School "factories" have blighted true education reform.

Unifying the Campus: "Blue Light Specials in Room 301"

Not unlike a huge Wal Mart, American schools have become compartmentalized and departmentalized. English teachers teach English, Science teachers teach Science, and so on. But this is a relatively recent innovation in American education. Prior to World War II many schools consisted of one-room schoolhouses where students of all ages were under the same roof, with the same teacher. Each age or grade level received adequate information and instruction while the other groups listened in while working on their own assignments quietly. The absorption and transference of knowledge was tremendous! First graders learned of world wars, horrible battles, and new and extensive use of vocabulary from listening while the teacher was with the other groups. Imagine it! The entire class was one giant Cooperative Group!

With the enormous prosperity of the USA after WWII came new construction of school facilities and the pouring in of mass amounts of money for educational reform. Free and compulsory education up to the age of 16 became the law of the land. With these changes came the introduction of compartmentalized schools. Teacher colleges such as Peabody in Nashville, began to offer majors in one or two fields instead of a "general" college degree, one in which the teacher was expected to teach everything from math to

239

proper eating manners! Eventually specialized teachers and classes developed, much as one now prefers to go to a "specialist" physician rather than a general practitioner. And thus were begun separate classes for the different subjects. The basics of reading and writing expanded also to include Home Economics, Vocational Education. Physical Education became big with the impetus given by the youthful American President John F. Kennedy in the 1960's. By now, "changing classes" had become a status symbol of growing up and moving up into high school.

Next came departmentalization of subjects. The English department acquired its own wing and a "department chair." The idea caught on and American schools became mini Wal Marts with a department for every subject imaginable. Schools are now fully broken up into not only small political units but also into small, manageable units of time called "class periods." Usually a class is one hour long. Why? Most likely this paradigm began simply because 60 minutes are in each hour and an hour is the only large division of time on the clock; nothing more. With block scheduling, that period of class time is extended. Often, the most commonly heard reason against extended class periods is simply that teachers have no desire to be stuck in the same room with the same students for so long. The normal reason usually is, "I run out of things to do." This is reasonable perhaps but will not be dealt with here.

A much larger issue is at stake with the **compartmentalization of American schools** and that is chopping up English language development. All teachers are English teachers, unless they teach 100% in a foreign language course, which is unlikely. This is the one true constant in public education. Over the years since WWII, schools became so efficient at teaching specialized subjects that eventually a "territorial mentality" caused faculty to seldom if ever converse other than with their own department members. And it would be unthinkable in an emergency situation where a math teacher would have to use one of the Science classrooms! "What about my posters? What about my desk? I'll lock it up tighter than Fort Knox. That'll show 'em!" But whose classroom is it anyway? We are all in this wonderful world of education together and we would be better off thinking as a whole instead of a segregated unit of learning.

Academic Teams and Vertical Planning

Fortunately, back in the 1990's, schools began to see the error in the massive herding of students and began to incorporate the academic team approach, one that has met with significant results and somewhat improved discipline. A typical team is composed of the English, Math, Science, and Social Studies teachers of the same grade level. They meet periodically to discuss at risk students and issues that arise. By using the team approach, students are less likely to fall between the cracks in our massively overpopulated middle and high schools in Hispanic regions of the country. Hispanic high schools along the Mexican border towns of Brownsville and Laredo, regularly boast of enrollments up to 3,000 in one high school. Can you imagine the problems associated with that many students! Academic teams are wonderful and should be applauded.

School Within a School and Magnet Schools

Along with the Academic Team concept came another recent innovation, sometimes powered by industry, that middle and high schools should look more to practical application of skills and gently begin to acculturate students toward a career goal. This led to a separate "school" with a separate staff and principal, within the larger school. Some of these schools are specialty schools such as one that this author visited in **Laredo** funded in part by a major airline company. Students received incentives to earn high grades, take additional science and engineering courses that could eventually lead to a promising career with the airlines industry. This author applauds this innovation in education.

Other magnet schools are specializing in medical fields, teaching fields, with excellent results.

As far as the second language learner is concerned, they are not left out either. The desire to strive for excellence will filter to their LEP (Limited English Proficient) classes as well, causing them to want to compete with non-LEP students for these promising career choices as well.

How Can We Unify and Strengthen our Efforts?

- ❖ Vertical teaming within the district
- ❖ Departmental training within the school
- ❖ National Council of Staff Development offers flexible training sessions that are catered to the needs of the faculty.
- ❖ Regional Education Service Centers are tax-funded training facilities that are located throughout the USA. They work under the auspices of the state education agencies or directly with Department of Education in Washington.

Why are band students consistently better learners? Why are they better behaved? Could it be that the discipline and connectivity of working in a unit provide skills that are learned intuitively? Yes. The Arts provide lessons in life that are not contained in textbooks or education manuals. Schools should support the Arts, particularly Music Arts education.

Chapter 16 Questions

1. How can we best unify our efforts on one single campus?

2. Is departmentalization effective? Explain.

3. List three positive outcomes derived from Academic Teaming and Vertical Planning?

4. Magnet schools are often unjustly referred to as "nerd academies." Is this an accurate assessment? Why? Explain.

Questions for Essays:

    a. Can a school be too large to be effective?

    b. Compare and contrast the one room schoolhouse of the last century with our mega high schools.

    c. Are specialized campuses successful? Why? Will the trend continue?

Costumed as Hamlet, the author poses with an outstanding South Texas College student who is enrolled in his literature course.

COMPUTERS AND THE LITERACY CONNECTION

Sixty six percent of teachers use computers for instructional class time. Forty-one percent assign practice drills that involved computer programs (FRSS 70, 1999). Without doubt, the computer is an effective tool in the modern classroom, especially for ESL as well as foreign languages. The computer offers students tremendous flexibility to learn as fast as they want. No more waiting for someone to catch up with the class. It also offers extensive auditory and writing practice, often with instant assessment. And best of all, computers offer ESL students individualized attention.

Computers empower ESL students to be in charge of their learning to a large extent. The teacher can serve as a model and a guide which is more correct than the traditional lecture approach anyway. Plus, computers never get tired or are distracted. Computers need not modify for the different levels of language competencies within one class. Without doubt, use of computers in education has revolutionized the American classroom. Computers are the great equalizers in that they are true examples of "equal opportunity" for all that know how to manipulate them. They have no prejudices, black or white, English speaking or not, smart or low performing, young or old. However, **only 23% of US teachers reported feeling well prepared** to use computers. 40% use computers to create instructional materials yet a whopping 34% use computers for tedious record keeping, and 23% for email use. The good news is that less than 1% of teachers reported no access to Internet or computers during the school day (IBID).

Studies indicate that elementary teachers were more likely than secondary teachers to assign students practice drills using computers (39% vs. 12%). They were also more likely to have their students use computers or the Internet to solve problems (31% vs. 20%). Secondary teachers, however, were more likely to assign research using the Internet (41% vs. 25%). Teachers in **lower poverty schools** districts were more likely to assign students work involving computer application, research using CD-ROMs, and research using Internet to a moderate-to-large extent than teachers in the highest poverty schools. And, perhaps obvious, is the fact that this study found teachers with more professional development in computer use, assigned computer work more in and apparent direct proportion to their own skill and experience base (FRSS70,1999,http://nces.ed.gov/pubs).

Victoria Lee and Sloan Avery excel at everything "electronic!" Kids have an uncanny innate affinity for computers, text messaging, and all the latest in electronic devices and gadgets.

On line courses.

Another wonderful recent innovation is **online coursework.** Courses are convenient allowing students the flexibility to attend class anytime, day or night, from anywhere Internet access is available. Classes are flexible; this eliminates conflicts with vacation or work schedules. Online courses offer convenience to those who are not able to attend classes due to illness or physical limitations. And, courses are equal in credit value as a traditional sit down course.

Universities such as the University of Phoenix are offering **100% online degrees** with interaction with professors possible via email and instant access in "real time" formats. What was unheard of just a few years ago is now becoming a norm at college campuses across the world—classes are going to the students instead of the students going to the classes.

Drawbacks to online computer courses are perhaps obvious: lack of camaraderie and eye-to-eye contact, physical interaction, and lack of participation in group presentations. One must be highly self-disciplined and motivated to complete online courses successfully. Sometimes ideas expressed by media are more difficult to comprehend than in person where the entire range of delicate language and body language nuances can be experienced more fully.

COMPUTER ASSISTED INSTRUCTION FOR SECOND LANGUAGE LEARNERS

Students of second language come in all shapes and sizes with a myriad of different needs and wants as we all. One feature, however, stands out above the rest and this is an earnestness to master the target language, usually English, so that they can quickly become integrated into the American workforce, ah, the illusive "American Dream" for which we all aspire. The reason we say, "usually English" is because a new phenomenon is developing America, one that calls for Spanish as a 2nd language. Quite a demand has grown recently for Spanish classes across the country. While many view Spanish as a luxury language, using it mainly for travel or buying things in Latin America or Spain, still other adult students need Spanish because of business. Due to the massive influx of Spanish-speakers into the USA, many Border States colleges are offering an increasing number of

Spanish language courses. Business leaders are now becoming more and more aware of the tremendous economic impact that this wave of immigration is causing. The **Hispanic Chamber of Commerce** estimates that billions are spent each year by the millions of Hispanics residing in the USA. When the word, "billions" comes into play in our economy, business leaders sit up and take notice. Bilingual labeling is becoming the norm in border states in order to attract and hold Spanish-speaker business.

Furthermore, the earnestness with which the second language learner comes into the classroom can be readily harnessed by the conscientious teacher by utilizing a wide variety of teaching techniques since not everyone employs the same learning style. "One size surely does NOT fit all" in the language classroom. Thus, teachers are turning to more hands-on demonstrations (kinesthetic) activities, as well as **Higher Order Thinking Skills**, to aid them in leading their language students through the veritable "minefield" of syntactical twists and turns, apparent in the English language.

How can teachers best harness the latest in theory and the best of application? One very positive manner is to use **Computer Assisted Instruction (CAI),** also known as **Computer Language Learning (CLL)** for language applications. Why computers? Obviously, the business world and industry rely heavily upon computers for almost every aspect of their livelihood. Moreover, **computers never tire**, are reliable, and accessible 24 hours.

Furthermore, computers offer to the timid second language learner the advantage of anonymity and equality along with every other student, both foreign and native. Computers are the great equalizers of the 21st Century, bringing the world of technology to their fingertips.

Although many adult second language learners are not usually adept with considerable computer skills, most children of second language are; the exceptions being those who are not educated and perhaps from underdeveloped countries. Adults, however, are generally quick learners and react well to challenges, especially when they know that they are improving their skills for specific reasons, such as job placement for example. In addition, they have a decided advantage in Higher Thinking Skills and should readily adapt to the keyboard with the least amount of instruction combined with a pinch of patience from the instructor. Research studies indicate that adults who use Computer Assisted Instruction in any subject area are more likely to 1. *Attend class more often.* 2. *Gain greater self esteem* 3. *Achieve more academically* than those who are taught with a traditional "Direct Instruction" approach.

The largest CLL (Computer Language Learning) system is from the Berlitz Company. One of the earliest companies to really understand the need and tremendous earning potential of second language learning, the **Berlitz** Company has provided language instruction in dozens of foreign languages for over 30 years, founded by Maximilian D. Berlitz of Providence, Rhode Island, in 1878.

"The organization now known as Berlitz International, Inc. was founded in 1878 by Maximilian D. Berlitz in Providence, Rhode Island, USA. Descending from a long line of teachers and mathematicians, Maximilian Berlitz grew up in the Black Forest region of Germany. He immigrated to the United States in 1872 and arrived prepared to teach Greek, Latin, and six other European languages according to the strict traditionalist grammar-translation approach. By replacing rote learning with a discovery process that kept students active and interested, it solved many of the problems that had plagued language instruction in the past"(www.berlitzsc.com). Language has never been so accessible at any other time in history!

While most manufacturers of software and audio-visuals for language basically re-invented the Berlitz method of listening and speaking, one stood apart in methodology from the rest. **Rosetta Stone©,** trademark for the product manufactured by Fairfield Technologies of Virginia, has somehow returned to the most simple principle of second language acquisition: *show and tell*, and turned it into a million dollar winner! While simple to use, from showing images and hearing simple terms, to more sophisticated writing lessons later, Rosetta Stone© is one of the most effective on the market.

The main reason for the worldwide success of Rosetta Stone has been its simple format, using the highly popular Natural Approach. Students see only 4 images at a time at Level 1. A voice over is heard each time a photo is selected, reinforcing the most basic of all language skills--listening. Stephen Krashen, eminent language researcher, posits that four language skills are natural in humans. The order of their mastery generally occurs in a similar sequence, regardless of language:

LISTENING, SPEAKING, READING, WRITING.

Rosetta Stone© and similar products utilize this research as they allow students to progress with a natural curiosity and growing skills in the new language as opposed to the more traditional Audio-Lingual Approach which uses minimal visual reinforcement. The result of using a Natural Approach within a computer software program is more authentic replication of phonics, highly retainable images, and the advantage of repetition as much as needed. The computer never tires! Eventually literacy skills are slowly introduced as the student has sufficient lexicon to proceed by adding words near the photos so that the mind "reads" the words even before the student understands how to read them (if the characters are in a totally foreign script such as Arabic or Hebrew, for instance.) Thus, the overall outcome can be truly inspiring and rewarding for both student and teacher alike.

Computer and satellite technologies have certainly brought the whole world closer together by raising very concrete questions about how we learn and in what language(s). How has this affected language and even more important, how we teach it? Are computers merely imitators of what we see as "language" or the "written word" or are they slowly becoming the creators of language by changing how we perceive communication in general? What about the future? What does it hold for language and language acquisition on a global scale? Why has English become the de facto international language?

After all, what is language? Is language a set of distinguishable symbols set in a certain meaningful order? Is it a group of words that when put together in certain ways, make sense to the hearers? Perhaps all of these. Perhaps none of these. But for the six billion people on the earth, language is probably best described as simply "Me; it is who I am."

Chapter 17 Questions

1. What percentage of teachers use computers for instructional purposes?

2. Who use computers for instruction most? Elementary or secondary?

3. List two advantages and two disadvantages of online courses.

4. Do you expect that online course enrollment will increase? Why?

5. What is CLL? Why has this accelerated worldwide?

6. List three positive components of CLL.

7. What company is the world's largest provider of computer-based English language acquisition?

8. Why is Rosetta Stone software so effective?

9. EXTRA CREDIT: How has the Internet affected k-12?

Pete Stoll is a gifted educator while Teri, his wife, serves as a government official on the Texas-Mexico Border; close friends of the author, both working to make their community stronger.

Θ CHAPTER 18
INTONATION OF ENGLISH LANGUAGE:
"Singing English."

This study is based upon the idea that learning English can be made simpler by showing students not only the grammatical format of the language, but the intonation as well. Some languages sound more sung than others. Chinese and Arabic sound to English speakers as very tonal and "sung." In fact, some languages have to be literally sung in religious services such as Hebrew and Arabic. Even the Roman Catholic Church and Anglican sometime sing the liturgy in Latin or English, so the idea is both functional as well as theoretical. In our study here we shall use the "music of English" to emphasize *stress, intonation, cadence, and inflection.*

All languages in one form or another have these four elements. Language contains rhythms to help join the countless formations of words and phrases possible. Just think of the possibilities that rhythm affords to speakers!

Modern day speakers of the popular European languages are not as prone to "sing" their tongues as in the 1940's for example. When one views a movie made in that period, the obvious singing **tonal qualities** of Spanish, French, and Portuguese come alive and are very entertaining. People who live in Mexico City are still famous for their pitches up and down of Spanish. Even in Mexico they are famous for this phenomenon. As Italianos are said to speak with their hands, so the "Chilangos" (those who live in Mexico City) speak with their emphasis on pitch.

Well one might ask, "Does English also sing the language?" Of course we do. The British sing one certain way, the Americans and South Africans another. We are all proud of the way that each of us has developed certain tonal peculiarities of the Queen's English which in Britain is referred to as RP (Received Pronunciation).

What is the difference in the following sample? Mary *LOVES* me! Mary loves *ME!* Quite a bit, wouldn't you agree? The way we emphasis stress determines meaning. We call this SEMANTICS. English language offers the speaker the opportunity to say the very same words but by using different stress, change the entire meaning! Comedians often use this method for an easy laugh. Puns are popular from Britain to Bombay, Miami to Melbourne!

Dr. Clark von Heller has developed a series of easy to follow steps for teaching intonation for new language learners which are as follows:

STEP ONE: Discuss samples of stress that we use in everyday simple speech patterns. "Hello, how ARE you?" "Fine, and YOU?" Stress determines meaning in many contexts.

STEP TWO: Have students divide the following words in syllables. Then have them identify the syllable of the most stress.

EX: instructions	in/struc/tions	2
1. tomorrow	_____	__
2. comfortable	_____	__
3. cafeteria	_____	__
4. hopefully	_____	__

STEP THREE: Explain the difference between Primary and Secondary stressed syllables.

Have them identify them in the list that follows:

Example: secondary   se" con da' ry   (we are using " for Primary and ' for secondary)

1. tomorrow   _____

2. investigation   _____

3. manipulated   _____

4. ingenuity   _____

STEP FOUR: Number and Stressed Syllable. Have the students identify the number of syllables in words and then identify on which syllable the Primary stress falls by indicating 1st, 2nd, 3rd, 4th, etc.

EX: instructions   3   2

1. organization__

2. looking__

3. heavenly__

4. incredible__

STEP FIVE: Draw five lines across a paper, separated by about 1 inch, repeated eight times. Between the lines or "musical notation paper," we will insert the words and see if the students can identify the stressed syllables by actually drawing a musical note, or a small dot if desired, right above the syllable, going as high as they think the stress should go. NOTE: Students should avoid beginning at the highest line on the first syllable. The middle line is more reasonable. That way they have the choice of going up or down on the subsequent syllables/words.

EX: or ga ni za tion

See how the notes go up and down with the stress?

Now, practice writing the "music" or stressed syllables.

_♪_____

_____♪_____

looking   transportation   perpendicular

The point is to see if the students can properly "hear" the stressed syllable, a marvelous tool in their oral language development.

STEP SIX: Now we progress to phrases of common English expressions to listen for stressed syllables. We will utilize the same musical score to "write the music" as we hear it in English for the phrases:

___♪_____♪_____	
_____♪_____	
_♪_____♪_____	

Hel   lo,   how   are   you?   Fine, and you?

Chapter 18 Questions

1. What components are involved in "singing" of a language?

2. How is the intonation of English different from the Roman-based languages? Spanish would be of particular interest.

3. Using Dr. von Heller's technique of "writing" music as students say new words, expound on how this would help students conceptualize accented syllables and words.

4. Working with a partner, formulate several phrases that are particularly difficult for ESL students to enunciate properly. Write the phrases under the five musical lines and annotate them as you hear them naturally.

5. EXTRA CREDIT: Expand Dr. von Heller's technique to include five terms from another language.

6. EXTRA CREDIT: Compare research from Mozart with research conducted on other types of music in how they affect learning.

The author enjoys a reflective moment while watching a TV show in Los Angeles at the home of college friends, Larry and Cindy Carr in 1994.

Θ CHAPTER 19
INTERESTING FACTS ABOUT ENGLISH IN
RELATION TO OTHER LANGUAGES

"When that Aprille with his shoures sote
The droghte of Marche hath perced to the rote,
And bathed every veyne in swich licour,
Of which venture engendered is the flour."

(Chaucer, *The Canterbury Tales*)

Aren't You Glad You Speak English!

Russian has no equivalent for "efficiency, challenge, engagement ring, have fun, or take care" (New York Times, June 18, 1989).

Spanish has hundreds of cognates with Arabic! All words in Spanish that begin with "al" are of Arabic derivation, including the name for Allah preserve in the Spanish, "Ojala."

Italian: have 500+ terms for different types of macaroni, English has one! (without an adjective)

Japanese: have no definite or indefinite articles nor future tense

Eskimos: 50+ words to convey meanings about "snow" but no word that simply means "snow."

German: Seven words for "you" (du, dich, dir, Sie, Ihnen, ihr, euch)

Japanese & Korean: must distinguish the social position of a person before certain forms of "thank you" are correct. For example, "arigato" is the simplest way, but some in Japanese society would consider this rude if their position is a high one. They would prefer to hear: "makotoni go shinsetsu de gozaimusu" which means "what you have done or proposed is truly and genuinely kind and generous deed."

An Abbreviated History of English

English is part of the Germanic family, which split into three branches. These were North Germanic (Scand. Languages), West Germanic, (English, German, and Dutch to name the largest), and East Germanic, whose three component languages: Burgundian, Gothic, and Vandalic have since died out.

Latin's influence weakened greatly when in 813 Charlemagne ordered that sermons throughout his realm be delivered in the "lingua romana rustica" and not the customary "lingua latina." But Latin remained a literary giant with many well-known books written in Latin up to the 16th century.

The Anglo-Saxon and Norman Legacies

The Anglo-Saxon's legacy lives on in English with the days of the week, named from their pagan Germanic religion:

Monday for the Moon

Tuesday for "Tiw"

Wednesday for "Woden"

Thursday for "Thor"

Friday for Woden's wife, "Frig"

Saturday for Saturn

Sunday for the Sun

The Norman Invasion of England in 1066: Added 10,000 words to English of which about ¾ are still in use today! Some examples are: justice, jury, felony, traitor, petty, damage, prison marriage, sovereign, parliament, govern, prince, duke, and baron.

Kings of England used French language for the next 300 years as the lingua franca! French was the language of the British Parliament from 1066 until 1392.

85% of the 30, 000 Anglo-Saxon words died out under the influence of the Danes and Normans. That means that only about 4,500 Old English words survive to this day, about 1% of words in the Oxford English Dictionary. Examples include: man, wife, child, brother, sister, live, fight, love, drink, sleep, eat, house, to, for, but, and, at, in, and on (Crystal, The Encyclopedia of Language, Cambridge University Press).

According to McCrum (Story of English, 61) "Every one of the 100 most common words in English today is Anglo-Saxon."

The Normans were considered cultured while the native British people not, so we have these distinctions: a lady perspired and expectorated while a servant girl sweated and spit. A farmer today still looks after his Anglo-Saxon cows, calves, swine, and sheep, but once they are served up appetizingly in a restaurant, they magically become: beef, veal, pork, and mutton (Farb, Word Play, Bantam Books, London, 1973).

Shakespeare

coined 2, 000 words and phrases, including:

one fell swoop, in my mind's eye, more in sorrow than in anger, to be in a pickle, bag and baggage, vanish into thin air, budge an inch, play fast and loose, go down the primrose path, the milk of human kindness, remembrance of things past, the sound and the fury, to thine own self be true, to be or not to be, cold comfort, flesh and blood, foul play, tower of strength.

Evolution of English

Undertaker > mortician > funeral director. Television > set > TV

Grammaphone > phonograph > hi-fi > stereo > boom box

Kelvinator > icebox > refrigerator > fridge. haven't any>haint any>ain't

Settee > couch > sofa. "God bless ye">Goodbye

Lad > boy > kid > punk > young man. going > gonna

Θ CHAPTER 20
LANGUAGE PRE-TEST

Name _____ Date _____

1. English is most closely related historically and linguistically to

    German   Latin   Spanish   French

2. English is approximately ___ percent Latin-derived.

    0%   75%   60%   100%

3. The "mother language" of English is: ("mother" used figuratively)

    Latin   Greek   Hebrew   Sumerian

4. The "grandmother language" of English is: ("grandmother" used figuratively)

    Latin   Greek   Hebrew   Sumerian

5. What language group invaded and conquered England in 1066?

    Romans   Italians   French   Germans

6. What is the significance of the year 1611?

    a.   The translation of the Doomsday Book into Middle English
    b.   The translation of the Bible from Hebrew/Greek, into English by King James
    c.   English is made the official language of England by King James

7. One of the earliest literary works that set English as a bonafide language was:

    a.   Canterbury Tales by Chaucer in the 1300's
    b.   The English Bible in the 1600's
    c.   Shakespeare's works in the 1500's

8. The term "Romance" language comes from:

    a.   the term for "Romeo" as in Shakespeare's play

    b.   the term for "Roman" as in the Roman Empire

    c.   the term for "Romano" as in a famous Italian cheese

9. Which one does NOT share a Roman-based alphabet?

    Latin   French   Russian   English

10. Which ones read from right-to-left?

    Greek   Hebrew   Chinese   Arabic

11. From which ancient language was the first occurrence of the term "alphabet"

    Greek   Hebrew   Chinese   Arabic

12. When is "the" pronounced with a long sound?

    a.   before a vowel

    b.   before a consonant

    c.   before a diphthong

    d.   all of the above

13. What is the "official language" of the USA?

    English Spanish   French   German   None

14. When the Continental Congress was designating the language to be used for official documents/proceedings for the new country (USA), which language lost by just one vote?

    English   German   French   Dutch

15. Spanish language today is still influenced by what invasion of Spain?

    a.   the Jews in 1492

    b.   the Arabs in the 8th Century

    c.   the British in 1776

16. List four examples of foreign language influence upon Spanish. (Note: only one is truly "Spanish")

Tamale   ojalá   mañana   filete   hot dog

17. Looking back at #16, list the language from which the term derives:

   Tamale _____

   Ojalá _____

   Mañana _____

   Filete _____

   Hot dog _____

18. Americans have traditionally viewed what modern language as being a language of wealth and high social status?

   Spanish   French   German   Italian

19. Who would be considered Shakespeare's counterpart in Spanish?

   De la Fuente   Dante   Cervantes   Octavio Paz

20. What is the fastest growing first language in the USA?

   English   Spanish   French   Russian

21. What is the fastest growing second language in the USA?

   English   Spanish   French   Russian

22. From 1066-1400, the English kings and nobility were related to and spoke what popular second language?

   a. German people and language

   b. French people and language

   c. Italian people and language

   d. Welsh people and language

23. From the 1700's to the 1930's, the English kings and nobility were related to and spoke what popular second language? (Note: George I and Edward VIII are prime examples.)

   a. German people and language

   b. French people and language

   c. Italian people and language

   d. Welsh people and language

24. Which is used most in written English language?

    vowels   consonants   both the same amount of usage

25. What is used most in written English language?

          a   e   i   o   u

26. What is the most widely used English word?

      I   you   me   the   and

27. Which classroom learning strategy has been shown to be very productive, particularly with Hispanic students?

  cooperative learning   independent research   Learning Centers

28. Who is considered to be the most highly accredited researcher in the field of ESL?

  Krashen   Cummins   Bloomfield   Piaget   Vgotsky   von Heller

29. Which of these two age groups can learn language quicker, allotted the same time/experience frame?

        Children   adults

30. Which two of these common words are disappearing from the English language?

  past tense of come   past tense of do   past tense of am

31. When two languages are used interchangeably, often unconsciously, it is referred to as:

  code-mixing   code-linking   code-switching   code-coding

32. Children, at what age, who are exposed to two languages, realize that they have two distinct languages and not just one mixture of both?

  three   four   five   as yet undetermined by current research

33. Children who are exposed to two language systems will sometimes experience difficulty in separating them in proper usage. What is this called?

    a.   interlingual errors

    b.   linguistic incompetence

    c.   interference

    d.   linguistic ambiguity

34. Comparing English to Spanish, list two sounds that will not transfer.

   /z/   /th/   /b/   /d/

35. When two languages are compared in order to facilitate second language learning, it is called:

   a. interlanguage comparison

   b. bilingual competence differentiation

   c. comprehensible input

   d. comparative analysis

36. Which one of the following is NOT a part of all worldwide language systems?

   lexicon   phonology   writing   alphabet

37. List two examples of language or "communication" that are not written or spoken in the traditional sense:

   _____

38. English writing style is described by discourse researchers as which of the following:

   a. indirect and evasive

   b. elaborate and effusive

   c. "direct and confrontative" (Dr. Maria Harmon)

   d. circular and inventive

ANSWERS TO PRE-TEST

1. German. German is our closest modern linguistic relative because of the invasion, off and on, of the Danes, Germans, (Angles & Saxons), and Norse Vikings during the early centuries before England was a united monarchy.

2. 60% *sources vary

3. Latin (Its relationship to English is profound and technically a direct antecedent language of English. England was conquered by Rome.)

4. Greek (Again we use this as the answer only to generate commentary on the importance of Greek in the ancient world and its massive impact upon ancient alphabets and literacy. Technically no such concept at "grandmother" language exists in sociolinguistics nor applied linguistics. Chronologically of course, Greek preceded Latin.)

5. French. William, Duke of Normandy, a part of northern France, succeeded in fighting for his claim to the English throne in this year. He defeated King Harold at the Battle of Hastings on the coast of England, October 14, 1066. This is significant in the evolution of English language. French became the official language of government and commerce for nearly 300 years!

6. b. King James, the successor to Queen Elizabeth, made an incredible contribution to the language by incorporating 17th century English into this, the most popular version of the Holy Bible that has ever been printed up to this current date. The language is flowing, gentle, and very poetic.

7. a. Chaucer's writings had a tremendous impact upon the evolution of the language by preserving the language of the common people or the "lingua franca." This is definitive proof that English was a separate and viable language by this epoch.

8. b. As the Roman Empire broke up into smaller national units and states, derivatives of Latin evolved into dialects which we identify now as "Roman." These are: French, Spanish, Portuguese, Romanian, and Italian.

9. Russian uses the Cyrillic alphabet.

10. Hebrew and Arabic read from right to left.

11. Hebrew. The first letter of Hebrew is alpha and the second is beth. (alpha-beth). *Some hold that Phoenician was the first.

12. a. before a vowel. Example: the egg, the elephant, the ostrich

13. None. Although 27 states have adopted English as their legal language of government, still the USA is composed of hundreds of language groups and has never considered this issue in modern times. Note that the Continental Congress almost adopted German as the official language of the new nation.

14. German. See above.

15. b. The Arabic language is prevalent in Spanish. All "al" words are of Arabic origin with the "al" referring to "Allah." Also, the word, "Allah" is incorporated into the popular Spanish term, "Ojalá" which means, "hopefully."

16. "Tamale" is from Nahuatl, the language of the Aztecs

"ojalá" is Arabic

"filete" is from French

"hot dog" is English

Only "mañana" is truly of Spanish origin

17. (see answers for #16)

18. French. America has always held a firm "West-East" view but has never adopted a "North-South" political or linguistic view until the 1980's with massive migration of Spanish-speakers from Mexico and Latin America.

19. Miguel Cervantes was a contemporary of Shakespeare. He penned "Don Quixote de la Mancha." This definitively set Spanish as a world class language.

20. Spanish. The reason is that although the majority of USA consists of native English speakers as their first language, Spanish speakers are the fastest growing language group (2000 Census) and they naturally teach their children Spanish first in most cases.

21. English. The reason is because Spanish speakers are the fastest growing language group in the USA and because of their enrollment in ESL classes, as well as other immigrants, English is the fastest growing second language in the USA.

22. b. French. See #5

23. a. German people and language. The Georges (Hanoverians) were of German ancestry as was Queen Victoria. Edward VIII spoke fluent German and met with Hitler prior to the war. The association with German ancestry was so embarrassing to our present Queen that she

continues to use the revised dynastic name of "House of Windsor." A clear example is her youngest son, Edward, who prefers the simple name, "Edward Windsor."

24. Consonants, simply because they are the majority

25. e (according to Dr. David Crystal of Cambridge, <u>Encyclopedia of Language</u>)

26. The (source is Dr. Crystal)

27. Cooperative learning. Hispanics are naturally very socially inclined and group oriented.

28. Krashen is perhaps the best known and most widely respected today, with Jim Cummins and Tracy Terrell (deceased), along with a host of other respected researchers including Collier, McClowskey, Maria Harmond, Lilly Wong-Filmore, etc.

29. Adults. The key here is "allotted the same time/experience frame." Children learn naturally and intuitively via much experience and interaction with others. Adults usually are sequestered in a lab, memorizing patterns in a most unnatural manner. With this the case, the children will outpace adults. But, if given the same opportunity, naturally adults, with superior experience in logic and learning skills, would outpace the children.

30. Past tense of come and do. If one carefully listens to media trends and music, one will undoubtedly arrive at this conclusion although this has not been proven by research. Noticeably, modern Anglophones are referring to the past tense of **come** as in "he come yesterday" and past tense of do as **done**, as in "he done it yesterday." Although this is NOT correct, unfortunately it is becoming, slower but surely the norm in English speech.

31. Code-switching. An example would be "My teacher viene a mi house mañana."

32. As yet undetermined by research. Children are naturally unaware that two separate "systems" of language exist around them, for example, if they live on the border. At some point, however, they will begin to gravitate toward one as being dominant and the other as subordinate to it, although for some, a mixture of the two will be an apparent lifelong pattern.

33. Interference.

34. /z/ /th/ No /z/ sound exists in Spanish alphabet; it sounds like a /s/. The /th/ or "theta" simply does not exist. Therefore "theater" is "teatro" etc.

35. d. comparative analysis.

36. Writing. Some linguistic groups have yet to set their oral speech into an alphabetic type of sound-sight relationship.

37. Body language, Braille and perhaps "flag language" as used on ships, and of course, sign language. (answers may vary)

38. "Direct and confrontative" (Maria Harmon, Cal State, Fullerton)

This means that English language appears to be a very direct, almost harsh language when compared to Latin-based Spanish and other languages. Furthermore, when analyzing writing Dr. Harmon found that Mexican-American children had significant difficulty dealing with this abruptness required in English writing.

Standing in front of the statue, "Christ of the Ozarks," Dr. Clark strikes a similar pose while on family vacation in Eureka Springs, Arkansas in the summer of 2004.

⊖ CHAPTER 21
POWERPOINT MASTERS FROM TEACHER TRAINING SESSIONS REGARDING LANGUAGE ACQUISITION

First and second language acquisition are both highly complicated branches of linguistics. Dr. Clark von Heller has spoken to outstanding faculty and staff in America, Puerto Rico, England, Israel, Peru, Mexico and Turkey. The following pages include various charts and simple to use transparency or Powerpoint masters. For more information regarding the format and use of these pages, contact us at clarkvonheller@yahoo.co.uk.

Starting with a global view of over 6000 world languages, this chapter reveals via charts, fascinating information gleaned through the years and presented to teachers. Lessons games, and fun exercises are also included that teachers can copy and use right out of the book with minimal formatting. As will be quite evident, much of the data contained in these charts, deal with the symbiotic linguistic relationship of Spanish and English since Dr. von Heller's principal research is concerned with these two languages.

WORLD TONGUES

AMERICAS	938
ASIA	1840
PACIFIC	1216
EUROPE	18
MIDDLE EAST	67
TOTAL:	6170

Source: Summer Institute of Linguistics, Dallas, Texas
WYCLIFFE Bible Translators, 1990

PIAGET's* Four Stages of Mental Growth

Age 2 gaining motor control and learning about physical objects

Age 2 – 7 pre-occupied with verbal skills

Age 7 – 12 deals with abstract concepts such as numbers and relationships

Age 12 – 15 begins to reason logically and systematically

List three actions that you see in your student that are "age appropriate."

*Jean Piaget. (1896 – 1980) Sociólogo y pedagogo suzio. Investigó la psicología genética, la evolución mental del niño. Autor de El lenguaje y el pensamiento en el niño.

MAJOR DIFFERENCES IN ENGLISH & SPANISH

1. Writing: Spanish has diacritical marks: (ñ, á, é, í, ó, ú)

2. Aspiration: English is more aspirated.

Example: Say the words, "I need you." Hold up your hand in front of your mouth. Feel the air?

3. Speed: Spanish = Up to 9 syllables per second

   English =Up to 7 syllables per second

4. Culture: Culture and language are inseparable!

Example: In Spanish, we say, "Mi reloj está caminando (walking) rápido."

Whereas in English we say, "My watch is not running fast." Notice the difference as to speed.

5. Space & Time: In English, when someone is knocking at the door, we say, "I'm coming." In Spanish we say, "I'm going." Anglo speakers prefer more physical space between them than Hispanic speakers.

LINGUISTIC TERMS

1.   Compound Bilingual – an individual who translates from one language to the other usually because the second language was learned under those circumstances; does not keep language systems separate and experiences considerable interference between them.

2.   Content Words – Usually nouns, adjectives, verbs, and adverbs, i.e. words that have a "dictionary meaning" contrasted with function words.

3.   Coordinate Bilingual – an individual who has two separate language systems, usually learned under different conditions, which cause minimal interference with each other. They can switch at will; independent of each other.

4.   Degree of Bilingualism – how well an individual knows the languages he uses.

5.   Dialect – the variety of language spoken by members of a single speech community either regional or social.

6.   Diglossia – a situation in which each language is typically used in, and is considered appropriate to, different types of situations (home vs. outside, particular topics, certain roles, etc).

7.   First Language (native language) – the first language learned by a child, usually the language of his home.

8.   Function Words – words used to signal grammatical relationship (prepositions, article, and auxiliaries).

9.   Idiolect – the unique speech of any individual.

10.   Interference – how one of a bilingual's languages influences his use of the other – the use of non-native sounds, constructions, or word choices as a result of influence from the native language.

11.   Lexicon – the vocabulary or words of the language.

12.   Morpheme – the smallest recurring unit in a language, which carried meaning ("cat" is one morpheme; "cats" contains two morphemes).

13.   Morphology – the study of the structure of words.

14.   Phoneme – the smallest unit of sound, which makes a difference in meaning in a language (/t/ and /d/ are phonemes of English because they make a difference in meaning in such combinations as tin:din and not:nod).

15.   Phonology – the sound system of language.

16.   Phonotactics – the pattern of distribution of sounds in a language.

17.   Second Language – a language learned subsequent to a speaker's native language, sometimes the language of school or of the wider community.

18.   Syntax – the way words or morphemes are related to each other in a sentence (their arrangement).

19.   Target language – the language that is to be taught.

20.   Articulation – the production of differing speech sounds by altering the shape and size of air passages in the vocal tract.

21.   Balanced Bilingual – an individual who is equally skilled in the use of two languages.

Dr. Clark filmed the documentary, *"The Three Invasions of England"* with Buckingham Palace as a backdrop, in 1998. esidence.

274

USEFUL ESL ACTIVITIES

CLOZE WRITING Ex: The _____ boy went to London. (shark, little)

Ex: Literature selections from classic novels, Shakespeare. Fill in the blank while listening to an audiotape

LEA. Language Experience Approach. Students generate a story. Teacher writes it on board. Students should not copy until all is finished and reading is reviewed thoroughly. Then students copy story exactly as it appears on board. At teacher's direction, whatever teaching objectives can be extracted from the "sample." Students write and react to their own work.

MUSIC. It's affective and very effective as well!

RHYMES/RAP. Right brain.

READ ALOUD. Nothing takes the place of the human voice for pronunciation and reading practice. Follow along reading is effective in learning to read. "A story a day keeps the ugly TAKS scores away!"

COOPERATIVE GROUPING. Small groups are very effective with almost every group of language learners imaginable! It is social, fun, interesting, and the learning is reinforced in several ways, including peer review, responsibility and accountability.

SUSTAINED SILENT READING. This method is okay but it must be monitored carefully for best results. Use with a comprehensive WHOLE LANGUAGE program

LIGHTING. Make a spotlight with the overhead projector and call for an impromptu drama! Kids love it! Everybody's a ham.

LAYERED LEARNING. If multi-level groups are in one classroom, stagger the level of instruction/assignments for each group while using a THEMATIC APPROACH in that the same objective is covered, only with different ability level techniques used.

JOURNAL WRITING. Start in native language while encouraging students to move into English when comfortable. After a few weeks, count the number of English terms attempted and reward students for trying to use their new language.

ILLUSTRATIONS. Everyone loves to draw, regardless of degree. Stick figures are fine. Drawings are non-threatening and fun. Drawings tend to generate more language.

FIELD TRIPS. Teachers and students have to venture out of the classroom. Whether to the school library, the auto mechanic shop, "behind the scenes" tour of cafeteria, or even the local grocery store, your ELD/ESL students will enjoy the natural excitement and "real learning" experience.

GUEST SPEAKERS. Select a variety of accents and topics. Prompt your speakers to bring a short film, slides, or other visuals if possible. Take notes of vocabulary, etc., so that the post-debriefing with students will be more meaningful. Watch their expressions when you bring in a fireman or policeman. Students will definitely acquire "Comprehensible Input" from these encounters.

RESEARCH STRATEGY (See chapter 15)

THE PRODUCT METHOD (See chapter 15)

REHEARSAL MEMORIZATION STRATEGY (See Ch 15)

AUDIOWHISPEROLOGY (See Ch 15)

MATH ACTIVITY

Placing English Language into Math Terms

Students probably already know this information in first language. This exercise allows them to be very successful at something they already know, yet now they can learn the mathematical terms in their second language. Also, they are developing vocabulary skills as well.

Objective: Make a chart with 100 squares. Your task is to find various ways to say the same number. Directions: Draw a dog in 10 squares, draw a cat in 25 squares, draw a car in 30 squares, and draw an airplane in 35 squares.

Discuss and enter all the ways that each item can be explained:

Fractions _____

Decimals _____

Percents _____

Item	PERCENT	DECIMAL	FRACTION
Dog			
Cat			
Car			
Airplane			

1. Which items, when put together, cover 60% of the squares?

2. Which items, when put together, cover 4/5 of the squares?

3. Would cars and dogs together be closest to 0, ¼, ½, or 1?

4. What item is 25% of the whole?

5. What item is 35% of the whole?

6. Which two dictionary words would make up 70%?

KINESTHETIC At-Desk ACTIVITY

In order to show how easy it is to acquire a second language by using kinesthetic learning and bilingual research, we use an example of Bingo in German. Directions: The leader will say the term several times as the students repeat it. Then the leader will "act it out" so that comprehensibility is achieved. Then we play simple Bingo. Whoever wins has to call out each term and give the definition. If the correct definition is not given, even for one term, that person loses! We are using terms from a familiar theme: Christmas. A German dictionary is needed for non-German speakers.

DEUTSCH BINGO

Der Kaiser	Geschenk	der Stadt
die Hirten	die Welt	Sterndeuter
Die Sohn	das Kinder	die Engel
Die Tannenbaum	der Stern	Stille Nacht
Die Mutter	Christus	Gott

If the leader knows German and uses these real terms in correct context of the Christmas story, students will be amazed at how they not only retain them, but also quickly learn the pronunciation!

Short Story/Essay Template

This format allows students to "fill in the blanks" at the proper cues. ESL students are reluctant to write. This offers them a "template" as a safe, easy method to generate English writing.

HOLLYWOOD HIGHLIGHTS

1. Students get into groups.
2. Create a short, one page story about Pete, Mary, and Joe while incorporating a lesson objective in the narrative.

Title of this story: _____

Once upon a _____

(where?) (setting)

_____

(who?) (protagonists)

_____

(when?)

_____

(what?) (¿Qué pasó?) (story line action) (Sequence of events)

_____

(description of characters, settings, etc)

_____

(conflict)

_____

(how?) (resolution/denouement)

_____

(conclusion)

_____

Team Challenge:

3. Locate the topic sentence or "key phrase" of this story and highlight it.

4. Highlight all describing words (adjectives/adverbs) with yellow highlighter; then copy them below. _____

Congratulations! You are now on your way to becoming a successful writer in English! Now, as a group, formulate your own story with the same elements (cues).

SELF-DIRECTED LEARNING CHOICES

This Doxographic lesson attempts to challenge students to become accountable for their own learning with minimal guidance from a teacher with minimal guidelines. Students decide on how much practice they need to master an objective. For example,

1. "And now students, please look up at least 15 of the 20 vocabulary words. Take out at least five that not needed or already known."

2. Of the five essay questions, choose two that you think are your strongest topics to defend or oppose a position.

PROJECT: Choose from 5-10 elements in the Periodic Table which you believe are probably most prevalent in your geographical area. Research and bring findings to class within 14 days.

You may present findings orally (5–7 Minutes) <u>YOU CHOOSE HOW YOU WANT TO LEARN THE OBJECTIVES OF THIS UNIT BEST.</u>

*in a written paper (3 – 5 pages) citing from 4 – 6 references

*produce a short video on Internet (5 – 7 Minutes)

*produce a PowerPoint presentation of 5-9 slides.

*produce a musical format to present information (3 – 5 Minutes)

*invite a guest speaker to address your findings (not a student!)

*show a slide show (using 10 – 20 frames)

*produce a short video on VCR format (5 – 7 minutes)

You may work in groups of 3. Turn in roles of each participant with documentation to prove work by each.

*<u>You choose</u> the documentation format.

*Please <u>choose</u> a grading matrix or other format for grading purposes.

GOING BEYOND: Why is giving choices important?

Who becomes in charge of the learning with this approach? Why?

How can this approach be applied to the world of business and workplace?

COMPARATIVE LANGUAGE ANALYSIS
EXERCISE IN DEUTSCH

Berlin, den 10, Dezember, 2005

Lieber Mark,

Mein Name is Barbara Braun. Ich bin funfzehn Jahre alt. Ich bin Schulerin und lerne schon zwij Jahre Deutsch. Mein Hobby ist Musik. Ich spiele gern Klavier, aber nur klassische Musik.

Mein Bruder heibt Bill. Er ist achtzehn Jahre alt. Er ist grob und schlank. Er spielt Gitarre und singt nicht schlecht. Er spielt oft Rock.

Mein Schwester heibt Mary. Sie ist erst elf Jahre alt. Sie ist klein und dunn. Sie spielt sehr gut Geige. Oft is sie doof. Sie ist aber noch ein Kind.

Meine Mutter ist Apothekerin. Sie arbeitet von Montag bis Donnerstag. Am Freitag, Samstag un Sonntag is sie zu Hause. Das ist naturlich schon. Sie ist ser musikalisch. Sie spielt Klavier und Geige.

Mein Vater ist Elektriker. Er arbeitet viel und kommt oft spat nach Hause. Abends hort er gern Musik, und er kocht (er kocht gern and gut!). Er spielt Klarinette. Am Wochenende machen wir oft Musik, meine Mutter, mein Vater, maine Schwester, mein Bruder und ich. Das macht viel Spab.

Was machst Du gern abends? Spielts Du Klavier oder Gitarre? Oder was? Horst Du gern Musik? Wie findest Du Klassische Musik? Treibst Du gern Sport? Tanzt Du gern? Hoffentlich schreibst Du bald.

Harzliche Grube,

Barbara

> What language is this?
>
> In what format is this communication?
>
> Translate a paragraph
>
> How was your assignment planned out for your success?
>
> What prior knowledge was used?
>
> What language that you speak, looks very similar to German?

PUNCTUATION RULES RAP

By Dr. Clark von Heller

Punctuation rules, should get your attention

The words are not hard, and they can save you from detention!

Two sentences are joined with a "but" or "and."

But don't forget the comma; it's used throughout the land.

One more place, the comma has been.

Is after a clause – that tells us when.

The question mark, what? What did you say?

It follows a question; that's the only way.

Take the period, the point, not hard to understand

It appears at the end of a statement or command

The exclamation point, is used for Watch out!

It follows something exciting and you better not pout.

The dash – the dash – it's here and it's there

If you need to make a pause, use it everywhere

Quotation marks are easy; they have no reservation

About hanging around, outside my conversation.

The colon likes to show, a list of goodbyes

A long list follows, those little snake eyes

It's cousin, the "semi," will not be outdone

It likes to take a break; and let's have some fun.

So when you're writing and writing and can't do it right

Mind the punctuation, cause an F can be a fright!

FRENCH VOCABULARY TEST

How much French is in your vocabulary? You might be surprised. English contains hundreds of French words. Take the test and see how much you know. Answers are located on the next page. No peeking.

1. soup of the day	a. buffet
2. a place for autos	b. Chevrolet
3. a bubbly French wine	c. entrée
4. the waistband worn with a tuxedo	d. Champagne
5. fish cooked without bones	e. boutonniere
6. a warehouse	f. debut
7. all you can eat meal	g. cologne
8. the main dish of a meal	h. debonair
9. ice cream on top	i. depot
10. lotion	j. fillet
11. a military officer	k. bouquet
12. a small flower worn by a man	l. cummerbund
13. a boyfriend	m. chalet
14. a popular American auto	n. avant garde
15. a coming out party for a girl	o. lingerie
16. a game of chance	p. rendezvous
17. ladies underwear	q. soup de jour
18. small size for ladies	r. chandelier
19. of a serious nature	s. heifer
20. a house	t. detour
21. a bunch of flowers	u. roulette
22. goodbye	v. garage
23. a meeting	w. beau
24. handsome, suave	x. bon voyage
25. current, cutting edge	y. a la mode
26. an abrupt change of course	z. Colonel
27. fancy light fixture	aa. demure
28. female bovine	bb. petite

ANSWERS TO FRENCH TEST

1.	q	15.	f
2.	v	16.	u
3.	d	17.	o
4.	l	18.	bb
5.	j	19.	aa
6.	i	20.	m
7.	a	21.	k
8.	c	22.	x
9.	y	23.	p
10.	g	24.	h
11.	z	25.	n
12.	e	26.	t
13.	w	27.	r
14.	b	28.	s

PHONICS PRACTICE

This is an oral exercise. Have students sound out the words and combinations just for the fun of it. English needs to be "sung" or sounded out. Phonics exercises are very valuable and should be incorporated into every lesson. Explain to them that some of these combinations are not bona fide English words.

1	2	3	
Tight	Tis	Fill	Feel
Right	His	Sill	Seal
Might	Bis	Dill	Deal
Sight	Lis	Mill	Meal
Fight	Dis	Kill	Keel
Light	Mis	Pill	Peel
Night	Fis	Ill	Eel
Fright	Ris	Hill	Heal

4	5	6	7
Bought	sink	through	further
Taught	link	throughout	whether
Wrought	brink	throat	weather
Fought	fink	Three	Nether
Sought		Thrive	Heather
		Thrill	Tether
		Threat	

8	9
There	zinc
That	zebra
Than	zero
They	Zap

FUNCTION WORDS & CONTENT WORDS

One way to help ESL students is to teach them the difference in spotting short **"function"** words such as prepositions, which merely take the reader from one word to another, and the **"content" words** which have so much more impact and innate definition. Content words carry the message of the language.

FUNCTION WORDS: shorter (it, and, in, be)

CONTENT WORDS: longer "The general rule is that they have to contain at least three letters."

For that reason, if a content word only has two letters, we either double the final letter or add a final /e/. This increased length cues the reader that the word is a content word and thus carries some of the essential meaning of the sentence.

For example **/in/** is a function word, but **/inn/** is a content word. Similarly, **/be/** is a function word, and **/bee/** is a content word. These variations in spelling, which violate the demand that words be spelled like they sound, actually help readers by giving them syntactic cues.

Grammatical function word = /be/ (verb)

Content words ex.= /bee/ (noun)

*Prediction of word meaning by position (context) is not exclusive. Readers also quickly learn to predict meaning by distinguishing the difference between "function words" and "content words." Are you aware of the difference?

*See Kenneth Goodman's research into Whole Language for more information.

EXERCISE: Take a passage from a text and have students determine which words are function words and which are content words. This aids in the identification of the subject and verb also.

Spanish Exercise in Contextual Clues

Using Spanish language skills, try to determine what the patterns are in order to understand this passage. This passage is about a queen.

AMADA LA REINA

Habiá una vez una reina llamada Amada. Su nombre representaba lo bueno que era ella. Todos los dx su rxinzdo lz zmzbzn. Lz Rxinz Zmzdz lxs hzcíz unz tixrrz mzgicz. Hzbíz juxgos y muchzs golosinzs pzrz comxr. Todos sx divxrtízn xn lz fixstz mzgicz. Lz Rxinz Zmzdz y su rxinzdo cxlxbrzron lo buxno dx lz vidz. Y tuvixron un finzl fixstz, a mxnos qux un díz llqqzzbl oioxpqr pbxx y xe wplix bn sz ybxzzwwowwom.

Written by: Rose Mary Ayala, Los Fresnos ISD, Texas

Exercise:

1. Copy each line carefully, substituting the correct vowel for the incorrect spellings.

2. Porqué puedes divinar las palabras cuando está mal escritos?

3. These stand for what? X = _____ Z = _____

English Exercise in Contextual Clues

KINGDOM OF JOY

Once upon a time, in a land far, far away, a kingdom existed of sheer joy and imagination. The king was so nice that he decided to givx a hugx fxast for all the pxoplx. Xvxrything was just wondxrful until a hugx mqnstxr appxarxd! "Whzt shzll wx dq?" crixd thx king. His chixf sqldixr syid, "I will gq up thx mquntzin znd kill thx bxzst!" Hx did znd thxy livxd hzppily xvxr zrbble.

Which words make no sense at all? _____ Why?

What reading skills were employed to figure out this word scramble?

What about prior knowledge? ___ yes___ no

What about word shapes and patterns? ___ yes___ no

LEARNING ENGLISH THRU SONGS

Directions: Students will copy each line. Look up any terms that are new. Caution them that a translation is almost impossible for an artistic piece or even poetry. Translation should not be attempted! Then have them to sing it aloud for pronunciation practice. They will surely enjoy it.

SHE'LL BE COMING 'ROUND THE MOUNTAIN

She'll be coming 'round the mountain when she comes_____

She'll be coming 'round the mountain when she comes_____

She'll be coming 'round the mountain_____

She'll be coming 'round the mountain_____

She'll be coming 'round the mountain when she comes._____

We will kill the old red rooster when she comes_____

We will kill the old red rooster when she comes_____

We will kill the old red rooster_____

(repeat 3 times)

TEACHER CHECKUP:

1. This is an example of
__right brain activity
__left brain activity
__both right & left
__affective component of a State-mandated Bilingual Education Program
2. Going Beyond!   What other types of musical techniques could be used in effective language class? (Specify age or language level in your design)

THE LASTING HERITAGE OF LATIN

Latin language is a study in itself, but as it relates to ESL, Latin needs to be deliberately studied carefully. More English words are Latin-based than from any other organized language system. Keep in mind that although English and German are more closely related, still the influence of Latin in vocabulary and "official" English words is overwhelming. Latin roots/stems still affect English today in larger measure than any other language system, ancient or modern.

I. "The Roman alphabet is the most widely used on earth."

(National Geographic, August, 1997)

II. "English historian, Peter Salway, notes that under Roman rule, England had a higher rate of literacy than under any British government for 14 centuries" (IBID).

Sample Latin phrases:

carpe diem, per diem, alma mater, alter ego, antebellum, habeas corpus, ignoramus, in extremis, ipso facto, persona non grata, per capita, prima facie, quid pro quo, sui generis, sine die, vice-versa, a.m., p.m., i.e., A.D., ad lib, ad nauseum, IBID, op cit, etc.

WRITING GRADING MATRIX

							WRITING DATA				Student _____		
							use of period						
							verb tense						
							Use of capitals						
							Fragments						
							run–ons						
							Spelling						
							Punctuation						
							Paragraph placement						
							Sentence structure						
							verb/pronoun agreement						
							General format						
							Adequate title						
							clear thesis						
							solid supports and evidence						
							A clearly stated conclusion						

WRITING GRADING MATRIX

Discourse Patterns and the Influence of Culture

The discourse pattern refers to the logical arrangement of ideas of an expository text or of an oral presentation for the native language of the writer/speaker. That is, logic is not universal. The logical arrangement of ideas is **culture-bound** (Kaplan 1972, 1980).

1. The importance of discourse pattern to literacy skills

a.   decoding is lowest level of reading

b.   writing will not be comprehensible

2. Discourse patterns in various languages

a.   English (linear discourse pattern)

3. American English Linear/Deductive → Thesis at beginning

a. British English Linear/Inductive → Thesis at the end

b. Asian languages (Korean, Chinese, Japanese, Thai, Vietnamese)

 c. Semitic languages (Arabic, Hebrew)

d. Romance languages (Spanish, French, Italian, Portuguese, Romanian)

 Developed by digression/repetition use of many adjectives (Hyperbole)

e. Russian

4. Situational – can be used confrontationally as in English but changes with each situation

5. Implications for educators: Discourse pattern is tied to literacy skills. Students cannot read nor write standard American English if they are unaware of the discourse pattern expected in their expository compositions or in informational oral presentations. We have to teach students the discourse pattern of American English along with subject area content.

(Taken from lecture notes presented by: M..R. Montaño-Harmon, PhD. California State University, Fullerton, 1994, and Kaplan, 1972, 1980).

293

ESL BINGO GAMES

Games will enhance the fun and interest of an ESL class. Bingo is a universal game that is easy to play and its versatility allows for all types of language objectives to be taught while the students are "playing!"

Step 1: Choose a topic or lesson objective.

Step 2: Divide into groups. Have each group devise five cards with the vocabulary from the text, dictionary, or their own heads!

Step 3: Play Bingo! Be sure to select a Caller from each group as the game progresses. Check for pronunciation from the Caller as well as from the Winner. The person who "wins" has to prove his ability with the row of information by explaining the information contents in the winning row, and/or pronounce each correctly, or otherwise forfeit the prize and Bingo continues. Ex. If one square reads, "Say the Pledge of Allegiance," and the person cannot, then no winner is declared and the game continues.

EXERCISE: Please decide on a topic/objective now, follow the steps and let's illustrate how it's done in ESL Bingo!

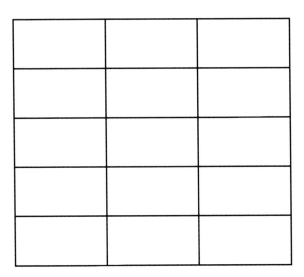

TOPICS: Photosynthesis, Egypt, H2O, Capital cities of USA, Capital cities of Europe

TIME LINE EXERCISE

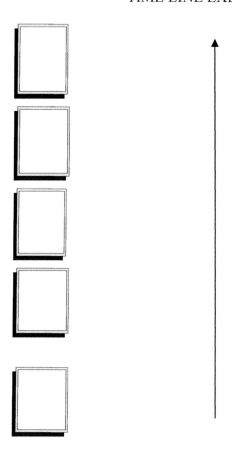

Have students record significant events from their own life to illustrate and reinforce the concept of left-to-right sequence and cause and effect.

This also is important for beginning level English students because it reinforces linear thinking and Western logic which involves complex syllogisms such as If A=B, and B=C, then A=C.

KWL CHART

This is an organizational and metacognitive chart. Often classes are rather mundane and routine, causing students to "block out" important information. The KWL allows for quick reference of "real" information placed in a secure, methodical manner. At the conclusion of the class, students should fill out their KWL chart. Students write down what they already know about a topic. What they want to know, and then, what they learned.

Topic: _____

Class: _____ Date: _____

Know	Want to Know	Learned

Selected Transfer Difficulties Between English and Spanish

Grammar & Culture

Spanish has diacritical marks (café, mañana)

English has several sounds for some vowels, whereas Spanish has only one.

In Spanish, the concept of "hard" and "soft" vowels is non existent.

Discourse and Writing Patterns are distinct and different:

*Spanish = circular, informal, extensive elaboration

*English = direct/confrontive 1-2-3 very linear

Placement of adjectives (White House-la casa blanca)

No capital letters for certain proper nouns in Spanish

(lunes, febrero, otoño, norteamericanos, or estadounidense)

Placing periods after names and underlining them in correspondence or when signing a document.

In Spanish, no word exists for "chairperson." They use "presidente."

Spanish has "tambien" (also) and the opposite "tampoco" sort of like (and them never also!)

TIME AND SPACE

Spanish-speaking countries use 24:00 clock and metrics. (24cc, 13m)

Spanish speaking countries use Celsius.

Spanish speakers tend to stand closer than English language speakers.

Spanish speakers would answer a door, "I'm going," but English speakers would answer it, "I'm coming." This is a matter of point of view.

In Spanish a watch "walks fast" but in English "runs fast."

CULTURE

To ask a person to come closer, Spanish (and Arabic) speakers will motion the hand downward; English upward.

To note the size of a child, a Spanish speaker will use two fingers pointing outward at the desired indication of height but will use the full hand extended for distinguishing the height of an animal. In English we have no such distinction.

Mexican-American men will seldom allow another man to stand directly behind them while standing in line.

Mexican-American men will seldom wear a hat, even in the rain unless it is a traditional cowboy hat and these are usually only worn by older men.

Neither Mexican-American men nor women normally use an umbrella for any reason. In Puerto Rico, however, I noticed ladies using parasols to counter the hot sun.

Mexican-Americans, both genders, seldom smoke.

Mexican-American women seldom wear fancy hats in Protestant churches but in Catholic, often, usually with a veil.

Mexican-Americans prefer items given directly into the hand, not placed in front of them whereas Americans prefer to have things placed down to be retrieved at will.

(*A more extensive investigative study of Mexican-Americans is contained in Dr. Clark von Heller's book, Mexican-American Culture, 1990).

CLASSROOM ARRANGEMENT CHART
FOR INCLUSION OF LEP STUDENTS WITH EP's

(EP=ENGLISH PROFICIENT)

TEACHER (front of room)

EP	Low	Low	Low	Low
EP Team 1 Leader		LEP	LEP	LEP LEP
EP	Mid	Mid	Mid	Mid
Team 2 Leader LEP	LEP	LEP	LEP	
EP	High	High	High	High
Team 3 Leader LEP	LEP	LEP	LEP	
EP	EP	EP	EP	EP
Team 4 Leader				
*LEP=Limited English Proficient *EP=English Proficient*				

Team Leader sits on the side to assist in pronunciation and other tasks for the row.

Team Leaders can be rotated as students gain more language during the course.

This chart is based on the assumption that the lower levels will gain by sitting closer to the center of instruction. Also, if the teacher employs "Layered Learning" techniques, the EP's will be called upon first with the same instruction repeated so that even the lowest achievers are able to hear the lesson repeated several times before they are called upon.

TECHNIQUES TO USE FOR SLOW READERS

- Control rate of speech, reducing speed if necessary while attempting to maintain normal rate.

- Avoid abbreviations and out-dated idioms in oral speech.

- Stay consistent with instructional terms each class.

- When re-writing materials, present the main ideas in a clear and simple manner.

- Have the topic on the board in large letters.

- Try to relate the materials to prior knowledge or experience.

- Link key vocabulary to some form of visuals.

- Use a simplified but not artificial approach to test items; avoid ambiguous language.

- Avoid highlighters, especially with girls. They tend to "paint" the entire passage, rendering the use of the highlighter moot.

- Encourage students to run their finger along the word line as they read but make sure that they are trained NOT to stop at each difficult word.

- Encourage students to annotate academic passages with a pencil by taking marginal notes.

ENGLISH AND SPANISH COGNATES

For Beginner Level ESL (if students are native speakers of Spanish), this is a wonderful way to instill self-esteem and build upon what learners already know about their first language as they begin their conquest of English. This author has effectively used this method in the opposite spectrum as well with Anglos who were nervous about beginning Spanish classes.

curioso	curious
delicioso	delicious
famoso	famous
furioso	furious
generoso	generous
correctamente	correctly
finalmente	finally
probablemente	probably
rápidamente	rapidly
usualmente	usually
acción	action
asociación	association
atención	attention
información	information
nación	nation
democracia	democracy
diferencia	difference
frecuencia	frequency
servicio	service
silencio	silence
actividad	activity

GEOGRAPHY SITER EXERCISE

Modern curriculum challenges students to know their culture and their world. This activity is intended to be a gradual exercise in which students are exposed to what is known, what is unknown, what is concrete, and what is abstract via a simple demonstration of geography. This exercise uses global learning, starting with a small, known geographical area and working outward. This exercise is especially appropriate for ESL and LEP students. They should work in groups. Oral language should be emphasized and enticed out of the new learners as much as possible.

First we start with the school. Eventually we work outwards to the state and then the country. Finally we teach the geography of the entire globe!

Part 1: The School

Part 2: Home and Community

Part 3: The State

Part 4: The USA

Part 5: The World

Today we will demonstrate Part 3: Major Cities in Texas

MATERIALS: Markers, place cards, and a transparency with a map of the State of Texas.

PROCEDURES:

1. Divide into groups

2. Assign group roles: principal, teach, coach, custodian

3. Announce the topic: "The Map of Texas." Tell students that the principal is lost! Where is he? Our mission is to find him!

4. Assign the teacher the task of writing the name of a Texas city on a place card.

5. The custodian must make sure the place card is clean.

6. The coach takes the place card and then with the principal, they must decide where the assigned site/city is in relation to the entire State of Texas. (Ex. Austin, Laredo)

You might want to use famous sites also, i.e. the capital, San Jacinto Monument.

7. After all the coaches and principals are satisfied with their positions, the coaches return to base.

8. The teacher of each group is given a "secret" map of Texas with the position of their principal clearly indicated. The groups make the evaluation of whether the principal is standing in the right place or site (with help from the real teacher of course).

9. Applaud the results and then repeat, substituting the coach of each group who is lost during a recent out of town football game! Where is he?

*Then repeat by having the teacher become lost on Spring Break and the custodian to become lost while on a trip to buy school supplies, etc. Students can have loads of fun while learning English!

The author takes a break from visiting Westminster School to tour Kensington Palace, the home of Princess Diana. (1999)

POETRY ANALYSIS-O-RAMA Poetry Appreciation Unit

*This unit implements standard practices in appreciation of poetry by taking one piece of poetry, reading it, and then filling out these probing questions to help students truly think about the work being analyzed.

1. Examine the title as you write it below. What language? What does it really say? Playful? Ironic?

>

2. Look at the author's name. Write it. Is it a typical English name? Foreign? Nom de plume?

>

3. Look at the poem. How many stanzas? ____

4. Format Review: Is this a Sonnet? Haiku? Does it contain special features? If so, describe them.

>

5. How is it printed on the page? Standard? Weird? Explain.

>

6. How are the words printed? Are capital letters in the right places? Are spellings unusual?

>

7. How many lines in each stanza? ____

8. List any examples of:

Alliteration
Repetition
Metaphor/Simile
Imagery

9. Analyze the rhyme scheme and list it here: (aa,bb,cc, etc.)

10. Count the # of words in each stanza. Compare/contrast. Find any patterns? Be specific.

11. Verb Search: Find any verbs that repeat. Why are they significant? Be specific.

12. Verb tense. Were any changes noticed in verb tense in the poem? If so, where? Why? Why not?

13. Noun Search. List each of them. (5 points each)

14. Adjectives Search. List them. (5 points each)

15. Count the # of re-occurring alphabet letters if a pattern emerges. How many letter /e/? How many letter /o/?

16. Explain any apparent patterns emerging from your research so far.

17. List any type(s) of rhyme: initial sound, middle sound, terminal sound, internal rhyme.

18. Tone/Theme. How does the poem affect you as a reader? Sad? Happy? Other?

19. Interpretation. What does the poem say to you? (on your own paper)

20. What impression have you formed of the poem after reading it at least three times? (check off ones applicable)

___ liked it ___ disliked it ___ weird ___ interesting

___ made me cry ___ morbid ___ melancholy ___ pensive

___ sullen ___ mysterious ___ inspirational ___ sad ___ happy

___ made me smile ___ made me think ___ strange ___ fascinating

CHAPTER 22
CLARKHELLER 35 WRITING RULES

1. Use MLA stylesheet. Essays and compositions must completely fill two pages or more. **A Works Cited** page must be included if sources are used in the paper. Font must be New Times Roman, 12, with margins set at 1 inch on all sides. Black ink only. Avoid bold or italics unless called for in MLA or APA or by the instructor.

2. Essays and compositions require **Readability Statistics** on top right side of first page, under last name and page number.

3. **Title & Thesis**: The first letter of each significant word must be in caps, centered, and double-spaced from body of paper. Avoid bold or larger fonts. **Thesis.** Make sure that it is short, clear, to-the-point and listed as the last sentence in the Introductory paragraph.

4. **Redundant phrases.** Avoid "I believe" and "In my opinion." Your name is on the paper. Restating this is redundant and not needed. For example, "I believe abortion is wrong." Not needed. Simply state, "Abortion is wrong." We know this is your belief if no source is provided otherwise so the "I believe" is unnecessary.

5. Avoid overusing the word, "I" in general. However, "I" is needed for first person narratives, testimonies, etc, where it is very important but even then, used sparingly.

6. **Contractions.** Never use them in formal writing unless in a question or taken from a direct quotation.

7. Use the pronoun "one" instead of "you" at every plausible instance unless the sentence would appear awkward and contrived without it. Keep in mind that commercial writing requires "you" but not usually required in formal writing.

8. There. Never use it unless referring to a position or place such as "over there".

9. Keep subjects/predicates next to each other. This helps to avoid fragments and run-ons.

10. Avoid the "he/she" formation. Simply avoid gender entirely if clarity is fine.

11. Verb tense. Maintain consistency in the same sentence and usually in the same paragraph.

12. Avoid superlatives: all, everyone, nobody, no one, always, never.

13. TIME FRAME. Never begin a sentence with a time frame unless it is immediately followed by a predicate.

"Yesterday we went to the movies." Change to "We went to the movies yesterday."

14. Avoid dangling a preposition at the end of a sentence. "He knows where I am at."

15. A comma must follow a dependent clause that begins a sentence. "If we go tomorrow, then we should leave by 6am."

16. A COMMA SPLICE must be avoided. This occurs when two clauses are connected incorrectly with a comma instead of a period. Avoid! Simply use a period to be sure. Semi-colons are not clear so avoid unless an avid grammarian.

17. A FRAGMENT is a partially constructed sentence. Fragments cause the need for further, needless questions such as "Who?" Constructions need to be clear.

18. A RUN ON sentence is a horrible construction and cannot be tolerated! Simply learn to place periods at the end of a complete idea. Lengthy sentences are fine for variety and impact, but be sure to review them to make sure the meaning is clear by identifying the main subject and predicate.

19. Avoid DO and "Got" or any derivative thereof such as get, got, gotten, do, did, done, unless used in the construction of a question or direct quotation.

20. Proofread and Edit. By submitted this paper, you are demonstrating that it is a FINAL DRAFT. It must contain no errors.

21. A single sentence cannot serve as a paragraph.

22. Use paragraph indentions often at the inclusion of any new idea or twist that supports the original thesis.

23. **PRONOUNS.** Try to avoid overuse altogether to improve clarity. For example, "in your writing" could change to "in the writing" with no compromise to integrity of meaning. "He rode his bike to his house with his lunch" is a clear violation of overuse of a pronoun. "He rode his bike while clutching a sack lunch" is better.

24. UNCLEAR MEANING! Consider re-wording. Check the syntax. Translate it into your first language and see if it makes sense.

25. **DUPLICATION** of content words in the same sentence is prohibited.

26. IT. Avoid beginning a sentence with this pronoun. Simply substitute what you are talking about in its place.

27. Avoid beginning a sentence with a dependent clause or a word that begins with "ing" if a Beginner Level student. Going home and leaving early,... Change to "I had to go home so I left a bit early."

STYLE RULES: USE THESE TO INCREASE CLARITY AND BEAUTY!

28. Use a tight balance and variety of Passive & Active voice verbs. This helps to keep the reader alert and interested in your writing.

29. Descriptive words. Use clear descriptions but avoid "cute" metaphors and similes. Save these for fiction, not formal adult business & industry types of writing where they are hardly ever appropriate.

30. Repetition. "He worked and worked on the science project." Used occasionally, this construction is very pleasant to the English reader.

31. 1-2-3 Punch. "She saw it, grabbed it, and ran with it."

32. Quotes. Quotes will increase your grade in an essay. Keep all punctuation inside the quotes.

33. Alliteration. "shape up or ship out" "spic and span" "the slithering snake"

34. Use supporting evidence: examples, statistics, charts, photos, and any type of real data to support points in the essay.

35. Rhyme. Use it effectively in compositions. Ex. "The fish wriggled and swiggled to free itself out of the net."

Buckingham Palace serves as a reminder to the author and all English speakers that ours is indeed a wonderful, royal linguistic heritage. More Americans are descended from the British Isles than all USA minority groups put together. Viva English! God save the Queen!

EXPLANATION OF
35 CLARKHELLER WRITING RULES

1. This rule covers the format of compositions and longer papers using MLA format.

2. Essays require **Readability Statistics**. MSWORD provides this feature under "Tools" but you have to go into Spell check and click on Options. (Make sure that an error is in the document; otherwise Options will not appear on the screen.) In Options, go down to the bottom left side and click on "Readability Statistics." That's it!

3. **Title**. Students have a tendency to "cutzie" up the title. This should be avoided. Same font, no bold, etc.

4. **Avoid redundant phrases**. Students like to take ownership of their writing and this is very good. But use of "I believe" and "In my opinion" actually weaken a position paper or argumentative research since it is apparent that the opinion is the author's since the name is clearly presented in MLA format (or otherwise) at the top right of the paper! Often, the "I believe" syndrome is used as a crutch for lack of investigative research on the topic.

5. Avoid over-use of the word, **"I."** Although very effective in position papers and commercials where first person testimonials are vital, overusing the first person pronoun causes a paper to lose effectiveness and featureship. Occasionally fine, often no!

6. Avoid **contractions**. In formal speaking and in formal writing, contractions are to be avoided. Change "don't" to "do not."

7. Use the word, "one" in place of **"you"** if at all plausible. The British have a propensity to use this term which is usually a bit too formal for American writers to follow. Nevertheless, use of "one" instead of "you" allows for a third person perspective which can be very helpful. In literature we refer to this as the "omniscient" view. Many instances, however, such as writing instructions and process essays, call for the use of "you." If this is the case, it is better to embed the second person within the text as understand rather than spelling out the word "you." For example, "When working with the metal strips, be sure to cut carefully." This embeds the second person sense without having to spell out "you" so much.

8. Never use **"there"** except as a position or place. Instead of writing, "There are thirty students are in this room." Simply write, "Thirty students are in this room." The subject is "thirty students" not "there."

9. Keep **subjects and predicates** next to each other. For second language learners, this rule is of particular significance to their success in English writing. Students often write lengthy sentences such as this: "My mother who is from Mexico and works at the grocery store, is also a very good cook." While this sentence is not incorrect, it is nevertheless awkward at best. By placing the

subject and the predicate next to each other, the result will be a clearer idea: "My mother is a very good cook, she is from Mexico, and works at a grocery store." While three ideas are included in this barrage of words, they are much clearer when subject and predicate (Mother is) are next to each other, even if a period in needed to break long ideas into shorter ones.

10. Avoid the **he/she** construction. This should never be used! Simply re-word sentences to avoid having to specific gender or pronouns at all. Instead of writing, "He/she will benefit from the work," simply write. "Each person will benefit from the work."

11. Maintain consistency with **verb tenses**. This should be apparent and basic for all writers. Once a verb tense has been established, it needs to be maintained in the same sentence. Of course, many exceptions occur in fiction works in particular. Verb tense is usually the same for an entire paragraph although again, it really does not have to be, for special effects, usually used by more advanced writers.

12. **Avoid superlatives**. While spoken English enjoys using these all the time, still in writing, we must be more selective about these constructions. Writing is a more static, permanent form of communication, one that cannot be explained or defended beyond the printed text. Therefore, clarity is of paramount. Since we could not possibly know each person on earth, to write, "All people like ice cream" is simply not necessarily a fact or even possible to prove. We could write instead "Most people love ice cream."

13. Avoid beginning a sentence with **a time frame**. For example, *"Yesterday we went to the movies."*

14. Avoid a **dangling preposition or verb** at the end of a sentence. Dangling prepositions are not needed and look very awkward. "Where is he?" is sufficient. Adding the "at" will not clarify. "I am as old as he" is correct and needs no additional "is" at the end.

This construction places "Yesterday" into the false role of SUBJECT in the minds of most students, often causing significant confusion. The subject must answer the question, who? or what? So "Yesterday" could not possibly serve as a subject in this sentence. To avoid this situation, simply avoid the time frame at the beginning of the sentence and place it at the end. For example:

"We went to the movies yesterday." This construction is clear and easier to understand.

15. **A comma** must be used somewhere after beginning a sentence with a subordinating conjunction such as "If we all go now, we will…" or "Since we are all here, we can…"

16. **Comma splices** must be avoided. Students can easily understand the concept of independent clauses since these form the backbone of English text. Explain that a comma is worth 5 cents and a period is worth $1,000. Simple exercises will usually clear this pitfall up rather easily.

17. **Fragments** must be avoided. One of the worst possible constructions for the beginning language student, the fragment must be explained in comparing ORAL

language with WRITTEN language. Fragment use in popular American writing is unfortunately being widely used in popular culture as reflected in magazines, newspapers, and novels. So although a clear line exists between harmful fragments that rip apart thoughts in a text, still, if a short, meaningful fragment can be used to bring the message home, this is not only permissible but actually quite constructive in most contexts. "She opened the gift gingerly. *Giggles aplenty from all the students.* Was she ever in for the shock of her life!" The use of the fragment here accents the excitement that this text needs for clearer comprehension. Therefore, fragments are useful in some cases. However, **Limited English Proficient students** should not be allowed to use fragments. These students should stay safely within the confines of standard English syntax until after State Mandated Tests are out of the way first. Oral Language Development should form a base upon which literacy skills in English can be built.

18. **A run on sentence** must be avoided. Lengthy sentences can be tricky for LEP students. Often these cause run-on constructions.

19. Avoid using **do, did, done, get, get, gotten,** unless used in the construction of a question or used from a direct quote. These verbs are ugly, often unclear in writing and are thieves! Example: "He did the homework." Or "He completed the homework." Which sounds more professional? Students should use synonyms to replace DO. Sentences will be much more effective and clear. This verb is an English thief, stealing other more viable verbs that would convey much clearer messages to the reader.

"Joe did the bathroom before leaving for Monterey." No! The bathroom cannot be "did!" This idea is absurd! No such thing exists in English language.

"Jose used the bathroom…" Yes.

"My student did a good job on the State Test last year." No!

"My students performed well on the State Test last year." Yes.

Other examples include: *"He did the work."* This sentence is unclear, especially if communicating via email or telephone, not being in the presence of the speaker. In this case, by inadvertently using the ugly thief verb, "did," the writing reduces accuracy of the thought intended. What type of work was it he did? Also, which is most important? The fact that the work was accomplished or the fact that HE did the work? The main point of this sentence is the work, not the person who did it. Therefore, by placing the word, "work" closer to the beginning, the meaning becomes clearer. So, "The work was completed by him." The negative syntactic point here is that now the sentence is in PASSIVE VOICE! To remedy that problem, we can simply modify the sentence to read: "He completed the work." Why not modify this construction like this? "He completed the repairs on the A/C (or the homework, or whatever the outcome was).

Also, avoid the word, **"Got"** or any derivative thereof (get, gotten). Got specifies no clear information, leaving the reader at an obvious disadvantage in some situations. The English lexicon provides a wide variety of effective verbs that could take the place of "got" and help the comprehension of intended meaning. Use thesaurus and synonyms to strengthen the text. Instead of "He got wet," say

"He was wet" or "became wet." If none of these convey the power of "got" then rephrase the sentence completely. "He fell into the pool."

20. **Proofread & Edit**. English teachers are avid gluttons for punishment, taking home stacks and stacks of papers home to "be graded." Actually they are not just grading, they are editing. Big mistake! Why should students need to learn the rules when they know they have a safety net to edit each day? Proofreading & Editing are standard tasks of the writer, not the evaluator. Teachers are the final evaluators but not editors.

21. A single sentence cannot serve as an English paragraph. Clear and succinct is this rule. Paragraphs should be as long (or short) as needed, but one sentence cannot adequately convey enough meaning to warrant it being set off with an indention or otherwise to note it as a complete paragraph.

22. **Use paragraph indentions** often. Paragraphs offer variety on the written page as well as transition and clarity. Paragraphs also allow the larger text to be read faster. Finally, paragraphs send the eye of the reader to the first sentence naturally which is usually the topic sentence.

23. **Avoid personal pronouns** as much as possible to improve clarity. Use real names or describing words such as "The priest"" or "Rev. Smith" instead of "My priest" since technically no one can own a priest although he may actually be your priest. Instead of "your writing" use "the writing." This allows for third person perspective. The exceptions are listed in #7.

24. **Unclear meaning**. To have unclear messages in a paper is possibly the worst error possible. Consider re-wording, revising, or simply scrapping the entire idea and starting again. Consider asking a peer to help.

25. **Duplication**. Content words should never be duplicated in a simple sentence. In a complex sentence, however, often duplication is needed and permissible. Keep in mind that function words such as "the" and "and" may be duplicated as needed.

26. **Avoid beginning a sentence with "It"**. This construction tends to lessen the intended effect of the sentence and idea contained therein. For example,

"It is such a beautiful day that I think I will go for a walk in the park."

If we substitute "Today" for "It," the sentence is made stronger, thus:

"Today is such a beautiful day that I think a nice walk in the park would be great."

While this main idea in the sentence is clear, yet it is weak in other areas (#25, Duplication of words should be avoided). When we take out one of the word, "I," see what happens.

"Today is such a beautiful day that I think a walk in the park would be just wonderful."

By eliminating the first "I," we have transformed the sentence without reducing the impact of the main idea. Another way to modify this sentence while retaining the original idea would be:

"A walk in the park would be just wonderful since today is such a beautiful day."

27. **Avoid beginning sentences with a dependent clause**. Limited Proficient English students often have difficulty in writing clear sentences due to confusion with the location of SUBJECT and PREDICATE. This rule takes this into account and can be a significant help in overcoming this syndrome. Spanish tends to lean heavily upon dependent clauses in Spanish, especially in the subjunctive mood. For example, "Si Diós quiere, voy contigo mañana." I would have the absolute beginner students rearrange this to read, "Voy contigo mañana, si Diós quiere." Although certainly not incorrect, the dependent clause often causes the student to lose track of the true subject of the sentence, thereby causing confusion in the eventual construction of the larger sentence. If the subject and predicate are clearly written at the beginning of a lengthy sentence in particular, students usually have no trouble in identifying the main idea of the sentence. *"If the United States continues to help Afghanistan, the election will be a success."*

The main idea of this sentence is that the election in Afghanistan will be a success. The secondary idea is the involvement of the USA. By placing the independent clause first, Standard English Sentence Formula (Subject + Predicate + Complement) is strengthened, thus: *The election in Afghanistan will be a success if the United States continues to help."*

28. **Passive and Active** Voice verbs. Active voice verbs act upon the object. Passive voice verbs act upon the subject. Ex. "The boy hit the ball." (active) "The ball was hit by the boy." (passive) Most passive voice verbs use the verb "to be" or "have". The Internet and handbooks offer simple lessons on how to use active and passive voice to achieve a tight balance of each for effectiveness and control.

29. **Descriptive words.** Use of metaphors and similes is very popular in English writing, whether fiction or not. Encourage students to occasionally place these in their writing, although sparingly. If over-used, writing appears contrived and frivolous.

30. **Repetition**. We enjoy repetition in English. Famous speeches include examples of repetition. "I came. I saw. I conquered." (Julius Caesar) English adores patterns. "Tomorrow and tomorrow and tomorrow creeps in this petty pace from day-to-day" (Shakespeare's <u>Macbeth</u>).

31. **1-2-3-Punch**. English readers enjoy triads whether in simple words, phrases, or even three sentences back-to-back. "She peered into his eyes, took him by the hand, and said, "I do.""

32. **Quotes**. Use of quotations is a simple and effective manner to increase credibility in a paper. By quoting someone, the writer shows humility, needing the words of another. By quoting, the writer displays a high level skill in English.

33. **Alliteration**. English readers enjoy this literary device as well. If not abused or overused, alliteration can increase the joy of reading. Alliteration sounds out the language by using phonics that are similar either as an initial, medial or final sound in order to create a sense of sound. Ex. "The *slithering snake snarled* at me."

34. **Use supporting evidence**. Support is needed for the points contained in a composition or even a paragraph. An example, chart, statistic, or testimony, adds welcomed supporting evidence and will cause a paper to score higher.

35. **Rhyme**. The use of small amounts of rhyme and rhythm can be effective, even in formal works. "The President tried his best to *wring out and wrangle* a deal with Congress."

Students who learn with strategies of Doxography gain vital components of the target language, English, by imitating the classic writers who have preserved the "logos" into their writing. Here these Hispanic students are acting out Shakespeare's *Julius Caesar*, improving their English while broadening their liberal arts curriculum objectives. (Donna High School, Donna, Texas, Rio Grande Delta Region, 1980's)

ANALYZING WRITING PRODUCTS

Students need to visualize writing as a product that can be physically analyzed and manipulated for improvement. Use of simple charts as these can be highly effective teaching tools.

	PARAGRAPH 1	PARAGRAPH 2
# of words		
# of periods		
# of sentences		
# of capital letters		
Most frequently used verb		
List Active Verbs:		
List Passive Verbs:		
Tabulate average # of words per sentence		
Tabulate average # of letters per word.		

STATE MANDATED ASSESSMENT WRITING GUIDE

What are evaluators looking for?

*This model is based on the Texas State Test/TAKS

VOICE

Voice is the heart and soul of a composition, the veritable "magic" that causes a reader to enjoy the text or not. The manner in which a writer embraces an idea, develops that idea thoroughly, and elaborates clearly, using a tight balance of Active and Passive Voice, convinces the reader of the clear intention as expressed in the topic sentence. The voice of the composition carries a sense of how the verbs are being acted upon or are carrying out the action of the characters or storyline subjects, whether animate or inanimate.

ORGANIZATION

Organization is the glue that holds all principal parts of a composition together. Writing that exhibits strong organization begins with a resolute lead in and wraps up with a strong "broche de oro" with the concluding sentence. In between the writer takes care to construct carefully upon the last sentence, always working toward an apex or turning point at which the composition is then slowly drawn to a viable and credible conclusion.

WORD CHOICE

Word choice is the use of effective, precise language that moves and motivates the reader. A solid vocabulary will provide impetus and strength that propels the text through personal examples and illustrations, quotations, metaphors, and a host of literary devices, in order to force a response from the reader, whether grief or delight. An effective choice of words should follow the natural flow of the topic. If the topic is about animals, sounds should be intentionally used in expressions that mimic the animal itself such as "slithering" if talking about snakes or "whispering" if talking about butterflies.

SENTENCE FLUENCY

Sentence fluency serves as the "nuts and bolts" of the language. Use of interrogatives can grip the attention of the reader for example. Declarative sentences have a propensity to become lackluster unless combined with solid, definitive description and action verbs that push the subjects forward into a solid "Subject + Verb" relationship that is entertaining and gets the intended message across at the same time. Exclamations are essential to instill the immediacy of the moment! Wow! The writer needs to let the Jeannie out of the linguistic bottle to allow creativity to flow along with positive, forceful selection of types of sentences, type frequency, and length.

CONVENTIONS

Conventions are usually relegated to that of mechanics only. But conventions convey the awareness of color, tone and texture of the language as well. Writers can "let loose" their inhibitions on the TAKS test by using creativity to underscore their use of effective voice, organization, word choices, and sentence fluency. The result will be a remarkable paper, one filled with appealing use of fluency, fluidity, and fun!   *{12.0}

(*This number represents the readability grade level of this text. For more on Readability Statistics, check the Table of Contents in this Guide.)

FREQUENCY: THE SCIENCE OF WRITING BY NUMBERS

When is a good thing too much? When it comes to effective writing, this is usually not a problem. "Practice makes perfect." Sentence structure is the basis for all we attempt in text whether writing by hand or by artificial means. That structure must be acted upon in the same manner that we act upon every other facet of life such as eating and sleeping. Too much or too little of either can cause severe problems.

When a student learns to tally words, sentences, periods, commas, or even a certain word, that student is more likely to become sensitive to the elements of effective writing.

FREQUENCY SAMPLE 1: SENTENCE LENGTH

"The postman set it on the front porch along with some other mail. The postmark was blurred so we couldn't make it out. "Who sent it?" my mother wondered aloud. All the kids stopped playing in the yard and ran over at the big brown package, just sitting there looking so out of place on the concrete slab, next to the porch swing. "Can we open it?" Memito cried. "Of course not!" protested mother, picking it up gently and giving it the good old "one over," turning it up and down, trying to figure out who might have sent this mysterious Christmas package." (Taken from von Heller's *The Package*, 1998)

How many sentences? ____ How many long? ____

How many short? ____ What is the ratio of long to short? ____

# of words in the entire passage? ____

# of words in sentence 1 __ sentence 2 __ sentence 3__
4:____ 5:____ 6____

Write the formula for sentence length in this passage: (Use S for Short and L for Long) Ex: **1S+1S+1L**

FREQUENCY SAMPLE 2: WORD LENGTH (Use the same passage)

# of words in Sentence. 1_____ Sent. 2 _____ Sent. 3_____

FREQUENCY SAMPLE 3: VERB LENGTH (*Do not count Infinitives as verbs for this exercise.)

First, we need to underline each verb in the passage. Count the number of letters in each. Find the average length of the verbs.

# of letters of the shortest verb:

# of letters of the longest verb:

FREQUENCY SAMPLE 4: PREPOSITIONAL PHRASES

First, we need to put brackets { } around each. How many?

FREQUENCY SAMPLE 5: MODIFYING WORDS (adjectives and adjectives:

List number of modifiers:___

"Computations" and "computers" share the same root word. Having students to manually compute their English language is an excellent learning lesson for them to understand the importance of frequency which should naturally lead to better, more effective English writing.

INITIALS WORD GAME

Divide into teams and try to guess the phrases. The objective of this is Communicative Competence (Oral Language Development). Put textbooks away. It's time to play!

Encourage the students to guess out loud. Even with wrong guesses, this may cause someone else to "catch on" and guess the right answer. It's fun and very effective. These clues include content area clues such as $H2O$ as well as cultural items such as famous English nursery rhymes and Passing Go in Monopoly, etc. Example: 12=M in a Y (12=months in a year) *Answers on next page.

1. 50=S on the A F
2. 7=W of the W
3. 26=L of the A
4. 1,001=A N
5. 12=S of the Z
6. 54=C in a D (with the J)
7. 9=P in the S S
8. 50=S in the US of A
9. 88=K on a P
10. 13=S on the A F
11. 32=D F at which W F
12. S W and the 7 D
13. O=D C at which W F
14. 18=H on a G C
15. 90=D in a R A
16. 200=D for P G in M
17. 8=S on a S S
18. The P of the US L in the W H
19. 2=P in a P
20. 3=B M (SHTR)

ANSWERS:

1. Stars on the American Flag
2. Wonders of the World
3. Letters of the Alphabet
4. Arabian Nights
5. Signs of the Zodiac
6. Cards in a Deck (With the Jack)
7. Planets in the Solar System
8. States in the USA
9. Keys on a Piano
10. Stripes on the American Flag
11. Degrees Fahrenheit at which Water Freezes
12. Snow White and the Seven Dwarfs
13. Degrees Centigrade at which Water Freezes
14. Holes on a Golf Course
15. Degrees in a Right Angle
16. Dollars for Passing Go in Monopoly
17. Sides on a Stop Sign
18. The President of the United States Lives in the White House
19. Peas in a Pod
20. Three Blind Mice (See How They Run)

"Oral language development is key to effective language acquisition, whether first or second language." Dr. Clark directs teachers in an oral language drill at an ESL conference in London.

PHYSICAL MODIFICATIONS LIST
for CLASSROOM MANAGEMENT

A microphone: can greatly enhance the quality of the voice. It is recommended that the microphone be attached to the shirt so that the volume can be set very low. A microphone causes otherwise gritty voices to be rounded out and become mellow. Of course, it amplifies to give clear, audible signals for vocabulary, directions, and general instruction. Some of these features however, will depend upon the clarity of the signal and amplifier used. Using amplification keeps the voice fresh and vigorous throughout a long, grueling day of regular instruction and "raising your voice" at times to help control student behaviour. But perhaps the most exciting use for a microphone with Limited English Proficient students (or any students), is that the teacher can whisper and still be heard. Think of the possibilities for intonation and pronunciation of difficult English content words in Math and Science!

Have you ever used a microphone in class? __yes __no

Do you think it could be used effectively in your class? __yes __no __maybe

Have you ever seen a teacher use a microphone in class?__yes __no

Activities: Activities will naturally be noisy when working with either kids or adults, nevertheless, one suggestion is to use smaller groups of 2 or 3 instead of "all the boys on this side and all the girls on the other." Activities need not be too sophisticated in order to be fun and very effective. Sometimes the less props the better, but keep in mind that in the language classes, physical objects or pictures of the same objects, greatly enhance comprehension. A picture indeed, is worth a 1,000 words!

Have you used any activities other than those required in Direct Instruction this six weeks?

Internet: Use it often. When discussing the Water Cycle, pull it up on the Internet and flash the pictures using a data projector. This makes the topic much more interesting than merely seeing the pictures on a page in the textbook, plus the teacher has the added advantage of having large amounts of raw, up-to-date information at the fingertips. Of course, if computers are available, Internet is a valuable hands-on activity while asking students to locate information and data.

Have you used the Internet as a part of instruction recently? __yes __no If so, please list how you used it:_____

Windows: Use of natural sunlight has been proven to lower anxiety and foster better behaviour. If the room has none, create the illusion of windows with cardboard and curtains. Watch what happens! All the kids will want to sit by the "window."

Have you ever thought of this element of physical classroom management? __yes __no

Does it seem feasible to try to "bring in the concept" of nature & the outside into the classroom? __yes __no

Color: White walls are a classical mistake, raising anxiety levels. If not allowed to paint, simply bring wall coverings from home or ask your students to bring art work from home, or create you own. Certain colors relax while others inspire. Research this a bit and maybe you can find out which colors will work best in your classroom.

Why is color important in learning?

__Color affects the learning processes in humans

__Color radiates synchronic anomalies into the brain

Lighting: Incandescent lighting is very conducive to effective sight for tasks in general but especially for reading. Fluorescent lighting is potentially harmful to the eyes over extended periods and has been discovered to be a visual handicap for those with dyslexia since it emits a rapid flickering stream of light at a high rate of speed, but this light is not constant as one would think by first observation. Unfortunately incandescent lighting is expensive and emanates heat so therefore impractical.

Have you or your academic team ever given this any thought before now? __yes __no

Does it seem logical? __yes __no

Can you offer any ideas to remedy your classroom lighting needs?

_____

Teachers are probably the most productive people on earth! The author grins for the camera as he frantically places finishing touches on *ESL Doxography 101.* (2006)

RESEARCH PAPER GUIDESHEET for
a FIVE CHAPTER PAPER

Objective: To identify a problem in the local community, investigate it, survey 30 people about it, organize the findings and summarize, then develop possible solutions. This is a prime example of problem-solving.

No cover page allowed. No plastic covers allowed. Simply staple with MLA data top right.

5-7 pages of narrative text. Small graphs may be included but not full graph pages except in THE FINDINGS only.

MLA format. All five chapters of the paper must be centered and in all caps. No bold.

12 point font New Times Roman

CHAPTER I. First page must have the word **THE PROBLEM** as the centered heading. Student will summarize the problem. Give clear stats or a clear testimonial if needed to prove that a viable problem does indeed exist to warrant an extended research project. Use proper MLA citation. This paragraph must not exceed 100 words and must be centered in the page from top to bottom.

CHAPTER II. The second page must include the **THE NEED** as a centered heading. Student will present arguments as to why this issue is affecting people and why/how it can be helped or eradicated. Use other sources (at least five) including testimonials of people you know, quotes from books, magazines, Internet, etc. Build a case for the need for researching the topic chosen. (If no need exists, then why are you researching it anyway)? Change your topic and start again if need be. This is the longest part of the paper and contains the most pages of narrative text. This is the "meat" of the whole paper. Length and depth of your subject area must be seen in this chapter.

CHAPTER III. **THE SURVEY**. Talk about HOW you devised your survey as you answer the WHO, WHAT, WHERE, WHEN. Avoid discussing the WHY because you have addressed this already in the PROBLEM, Chapter I.

CHAPTER IV. **THE FINDINGS** heading introduces the conclusions you made about the Survey conducted with an individual chart to illustrate the outcomes of each question in the Survey. How were the results interpreted from the individual questions? Was anything significant? Why? Analyze and discuss your reasons, etc. Prepare some theories as to why your subjects answered as they did. Be sure to talk in percentages and/or raw statistics, i.e. "3 out of 4 people surveyed said..." Next, you should talk about your findings in the research in general, in other words, from the other sources, not the Survey you conducted. Was anything new found or unusual? Discuss it. Be specific. Use as many pages are necessary.

CHAPTER V. **THE SOLUTION** heading introduces your own solutions to the problem researched. Try not to rehash old, commonly-held solutions. See if you can develop novel solutions! Be specific.

The **WORKS CITED** page is next. Follow MLA guidelines.

The **APPENDIX** title should be centered and on a separate page. You should include an original of the Survey questions. Also, you might want to provide additional graphs to support your points and/or solutions, etc. The researcher may scan in photos as well and if so, they should be placed in this section. Be sure to label each for reference within the narrative, Ex. Chart 1A, Photo 2B, etc.

Teachers are ever mindful of their awesome responsibility to the State and local taxpayers. These happy teachers are attending a Clarkheller Doxography conference in exciting Las Vegas! And yes, they won big! They won great quantities of fabulous Doxographic techniques and strategies.

READABILITY STATISTICS

One of the best strategies to diagnose student writing is to conduct a simple Readability Statistics exercise. I have chosen to use Microsoft WORD only for this demonstration. Apple computers also have a similar program.

Step One: Have students type a paragraph on MSWORD.

Step Two: Make an obvious mistake in the text so that you can set up the defaults on the computer.

Step Three: Go to Tools and Spellchecker. Pause! Go immediately to Options and click on "Readability Statistics." This will set up the computer.

Step Four: Spellcheck as usual. The computer should splash a graph on the screen with large amounts of statistical information, including the grade level which is the last bit of data at the bottom.

Interpreting the Data from Readability Stats. Students are usually amazed that their writing is so low. The computer program will count every letter, word, sentence, and paragraph, resulting in a statistic composite and subsequent grade level, 1-12.

Passive voice verbs are counted as well which helps students write more aggressively, using a linear format: A-B-C-D...

Active voice verbs are usually more sought after in the business world so I recommend that teachers allow no more than 20% passive voice verbs when analyzing any non-fiction paper or non-fiction essay. Of course, if the paper is a fictional short story and such, the percentage of passive voice verbs will increase substantially which is perfectly fine.

HOW CAN WRITERS INCREASE READABILITY LEVEL?

This is the heart of the matter when analyzing language stats. Here are a few suggestions:

1. Combine shorter sentences.
2. Right click on the mouse to check for "synonyms" that are longer, but BEWARE! Students will often change to longer words that are nonsense and incorrect. Advise them to carefully weigh their choice before inserting longer words simply because they are longer!
3. Increase length of paragraphs.
4. Follow the Clarkheller Rules (page 308) or other format guidesheets.
5. Encourage students to purchase a thesaurus and quality dictionary. Beginning ESL students should purchase a Spanish-English dictionary, but beyond this level, students should rely upon strictly English-English dictionaries.

WHY TEACH WITH DOXOGRAPHY?

- ✓ AFFECTIVE LEARNING IS POWERFUL!
- ✓ SPIRITUAL NATURE IN HUMANS IS NATURAL
- ✓ ONE DIMENSION TEACHING IS NOT EFFECTIVE
- ✓ COGNITIVE LEARNING IS NOT EFFECTIVE
- ✓ RIGHT BRAIN RESEARCH
- ✓ LEARNING TO LEARN=METACOGNITION

Doxography incorporates all that is good and effective from a teacher's "bag of tricks" and places them in an Affective Learning envelope or environment for use in the language classroom. Can Doxography be used in any subject area? Of course! But the underlying principles involved in Doxography are related most directly to writing since it involves the creation process, from the original conception of an idea to the actual publishing (or turning in the paper to the teacher). This process very clearly demonstrates to the student a powerful imitation of the most creative energy imaginable—the Creator itself! And thus, the "glory" or "doxos" of writing. Enjoy the glory!

DEDICATION & EPILOGUE

DEDICATION

This book is lovingly dedicated to my mother and father. My mother, **Lillian Heller,** instilled within us the true sense of Doxography along with a gentle and loving father, **Earl Clark,** who always was faithful to country, farming, and family. Both are impressive examples of traditional values and virtues that make life worth living. I love you.

EPILOGUE

"Thus ends our brief study of Doxography. Students deserve the very best education possible. Affective principles will help in practically every classroom situation, particularly in the field of language and writing. From Canterbury Ranch on the Mexican border, we cordially bid you adieu and encourage you to press on in your quest for excellence in education. Please contact me with your success stories or questions."(clarkvonheller@yahoo.co.uk)

Dr. Clark von Heller, a teacher of English

WORKS CITED

Aguirre, A. Jr., (1995) *Ethnolinguistic Populations in California: A Focus of LEP Students and Public Education.*

Augustine, (c. 400AD) On the Teacher,

Bloomfield, Leonard, Language, (1933) New York: Henry Holt Publishers

Chomsky, Noam (1968) Language and Mind, Harcourt, Brace, Jovanovich.

Clark von Heller, (1990) Mexican American Culture, Clarkheller Institute Publications.

Clark von Heller, (1990) ESL Multilevel Handbook. Texas Adult Education ESL Project, Texas A&I University, Kingsville, Texas.

Collier, Virginia (1989) *Promoting Academic Success for ESL Students, Understanding Second Language Acquisition for School.* Jersey City, NJ NJTESOL-BE

Crystal, David OBE, The Encyclopedia of Language. Cambridge University Press.

Cummins, Jim (1979) *"Cognitive/Academic Language Proficiency, Linguistic Interdependence, the Optimum age Question and Some Other Matters."* Working Papers on Bilingualism, No. 19, 121-129.

Eoff, Audrey, Newspapers in Education consultant, formerly with the *McAllen Monitor*, McAllen, Texas.

"Every Code of the Hebrew Alphabet: An Introduction to the Language of Structure." (www.psyche.com)

Freire, Paulo (1970) Pedagogy of the Oppressed. New York: Continuum Press

Fulwiler, T. (ed) (1987) *The Journal Book,* Portsmith, NH, Boynton/cook Publishers.

Gattegno, Caleb (1963) <u>The Common Sense of Teaching Foreign Languages</u>. New York: Educational Solutions.

Goodman, Ken. http://www.u.arizona.edu (Whole Language research)

Graham, Ray. Brigham Young University.

Grumbacher, J. (1987) *How Writing Helps Physics Students Become Better Problem Solvers.* In T. Fulwiler (ed) <u>The Journal Book</u> pp 323-329. Portsmouth, NH: Boyton/Cook.

Hakuta, K. (1998) *Improving Education for All Children: Meeting the Need of Language Minority Children.* In D. Clark (Ed) Education and the Development of American Youth. Washington, DC: The Aspen Institute

Harris, Stephen L., (2002) <u>The New Testament</u>, 4th Edition, McGraw-Hill.

Holmes, Arthur Frank, (2001) <u>Building the Christian Academy</u>, ISBN 0802847447

Huttar, George (Ed) *Notes on Linguistic Special Publication. Sociolinguist Survey Conference*, 47-48. Dallas: Summer Institute of Linguistics.

Krashen, Stephen D., (1987). <u>Principles and Practice in Second Language Acquisition.</u> Prentice-Hall International,

Krashen, S. and Terrell, T.D. (1983) <u>The Natural Approach</u>. Pergammon Press.

Jenkins, Jennifer (2000) <u>Philology of English as a Foreign Language</u>. Oxford University Press.

Machado, Luis, Proceedings of 2nd International SEAL Conference, Hertfordshire, England, March 2001.

McLaughlin, B. (1987) <u>Theories of Second Language Learning</u>, London: Edward Arnold Publishers.

Montano-Harmon, M.R. "Developing English for Academic Purposes," University of California at Fullerton.

Obju, (1997) *Speech Community, Language Identity and Language Boundaries, In Language and Environment: A Cultural Approach to Education for Minority and Migrant Students,* A. Sjogren, Ed Stockholm: Botkyrka Publishers.

Peyton and Reed, Editors, Dialogue Journal Writing for Non-native English Speakers: a Handbook for Teachers, (1990) ISBN 0-030-791-37-4

Rambsel, Yacov, (2000) Genesis Factor: The Amazing Mysteries of the Bible Code, Lion's Head Publishers,

Santa-Maria, Maria L., (1984) Growth Through Meditation and Journal Writing Paulist Press. ASIN 0809125706

Saville-Troike, M. (1985) *Cultural Input in Second Language Learning. In S.M.Gass & C.G.Madden (Eds) Input in second language acquisition.* Rowley, MA: Newbury House Publishers.

Selinker, L., Swin, M., and Dumas, G. (1975) . *The Interlanguage Hypothesis Extend to Children.* Language Learning, 25, 139-191.

Skinner, B.F. (1974) About Behaviorism, New York: Alfred A. Knopf.

Vigil, N.A. & Oller, J. (1976) *"Rule Fossilization: A Tentative Model."* Language Learning, 26, 281-295.

Von Humbolt (1963) Humanist Without Portfolio: An Anthology of the writings of Wilhem von Humbolt translated by Marianne Cowan. Detroit: Wayne State University Press.

Walsh, Mark, Texas A&M Kingsville. Researcher in Adult Education literacy issues.

Watt, W.C. Editor, (1993).Writing systems and cognition: Perspectives from Psychology, Physiology, Linguistics, and Semiotics, University of California at Irvine

Wingate, Jim, (2006) How to be an Amazing Teacher! www.seal.org.uk.

INDEX

CPSIA information can be obtained at www.ICGtesting.com
Printed in the USA
BVOW02s1229010916

460349BV00011B/8/P